RAMS

FIVE DECADES OF FOOTBALL

RAMS

FIVE DECADES OF FOOTBALL

BY JOSEPH HESSION

FOGHORN PRESS
SAN FRANCISCO

Library of Congress Cataloging-in-Publication Data

Hession, Joseph

The Rams: Five Decades of Football

Includes Index.

1. Los Angeles Rams (Football team)—History.
2. Football players—United States—Biography.
3. Football—United States—Records.   I. Title.

GV956.L6H47 1986   796.332'64'0979494
86-22902.

ISBN 0-935701-40-0

Printed in the United States of America

CONTENTS

FOREWORD

I am honored to be at the helm of one of the most recognized and respected teams in all of sport. This is, after all, the team of Bob Waterfield, Norm Van Brocklin, Tom Fears, Elroy "Crazy Legs" Hirsch, Deacon Jones, Merlin Olsen and Eric Dickerson—the team that made the term "Fearsome Foursome" a household word.

This year, the Rams begin their 41st season as a Southern California sports tradition as defending NFC Western Division champions. We're seeking our fourth straight playoff berth under Coach John Robinson and will try to move one step closer to our ultimate goal of Super Bowl champions.

Certainly, one of the most important moves I've made was the hiring of John Robinson as coach on Valentine's Day of 1983. Since that time, we've gone to the playoffs three straight years and fell only one game short of the Super Bowl in 1985. John is a great motivator and has helped us create the proper environment for championship football.

The Rams organization has enjoyed many great moments, but we feel our greatest accomplishments may lie ahead. We have worked diligently on having an NFL preseason game in London and look forward to playing there. More importantly, we hope to visit military bases to spread cheer and good will among the tens of thousands of American servicemen who are stationed in Europe. We intend to do this because we believe it is important to our sport, our league, and our country. We look forward to the day when the National Football League may be an international football league . . . and football a game for all people not just all Americans. The Rams want to do everything possible to make this dream become a reality.

GEORGIA FRONTIERE
Owner and President
Los Angeles Rams

INTRODUCTION

BY HAL LEBOVITZ

The Rams were born in 1936 in exclusive Waite Hill, a suburb east of Cleveland. Homer Marshman, a long-time Cleveland attorney, is the real father of the Rams. Marshman vividly recalls his plunge into pro football.

"A friend of mine, Paul Thurlow, who owned the Boston Shamrocks, called me. He said a new football league was being formed. It was to be called the American Football League. He said a fellow named Buzz Wetzel, an All-American back from Ohio State who had played for the Chicago Bears, was trying to put together a team for Cleveland and his effort was faltering. We needed financial support.

"I never had seen a pro game and was something less than enthusiastic. But I told Wetzel and Thurlow to visit me at my home. I asked some others from Waite Hill to be there too—Dan Hanna, who was publisher of the Cleveland News, John Hadden, the attorney, Ed Bruch and Bill Otis.

"The result was our formation of a group to back the team. We invited Bill Reynolds, Dave Inglis, Bob Gries, Dean Francis, John F. Patt, Burke Paterson and a few others, all prominent Clevelanders. Each put up $1,000 and Hanna and I put up somewhat more. I can't recall the exact amount.

"Buzz was to run the show, serve as coach and player, too. One day, Buzz said, 'Now we've got to come up with a name.' Reporters from the Plain Dealer and Press were there. I asked the newspapermen for their advice. They agreed it should be a short name, 'One that would easily fit into a headline,' they said.

"Fordham was a big football school at the time and its nickname was the Rams. One of the writers suggested we use Rams, too. I said to Buzz, 'We can't get one shorter than that.' That settled it. We became the Rams."

The Rams played seven games in its birth year and won five. Not bad. But nobody cared, even if the name was a joy for the headline writers. The Rams played to empty seats. The new American Football League made no impact on the local fans, or fans elsewhere for that matter. To them, there was only one pro league—the established National Football League.

"At the end of the season," Marshman remembers, "Dan Hanna and I had lunch downtown at the Union Club. He talked about plans for the 1937 season for the Rams.

" 'Count me out,' I said. 'The American League is a failure.'

"Dan said 'Do you think we can get into the National Football League?'

"We decided to call Joe Carr, the president of the NFL. Cleveland had been in the league some years earlier. He came to Cleveland and encouraged us to apply. He said the league was going to add one team.

"So in December, 1936, I went to the NFL meeting in Chicago and made my presentation. They told me to sit down and wait. Next, a man from Houston made his presentation. They thanked him and told him to leave. I thought that was very impolite since I was allowed to remain. Next, a man from Los Angeles made a pitch for Los Angeles. They excused him, too. I couldn't understand it, because their presentations were every bit as good as mine.

"As soon as they two others had left the room, George Preston Marshall (owner of the Washington Redskins) jumped up and said, 'I move we give it to Cleveland.' Everybody agreed. It was set up. They had decided on us in advance. They wanted to keep the teams in the east and midwest.

"They asked me, 'Are you prepared to pay for the franchise? You've got to pay right now if you want it.' The amount was $10,000. This was on a Friday and I didn't have that much money. This was depression time, you know. I had $7,000 in the bank.

"But I said, 'Sure,' and wrote out a check for $10,000. I hurried back to Cleveland, got $5,000 from Hanna, took $5,000 from my savings and rushed to the bank Monday morning to cover the check."

And so, the Cleveland Rams were born again—officially in the National Football League for the first time. The Rams had a few holdover players from 1936 and 10 from the college draft. The league had made the selection for the "new team" before the franchise had been awarded. The first choice was a fullback from Purdue, Johnny Drake.

"We signed our No. 1 draft choice for $275 a game," recalls Marshman. "He turned out to be Rookie of the Year and people later said to me, 'You're a smart man, Homer. You sure know football talent.' I had nothing to do with the draft. But I smiled and looked wise."

Wetzel remained as general manager and Hugo Bezdek was hired as coach on the recommendation of Bert Bell (owner of the Philadelphia team, who later became president of the NFL). Bob Snyder, an established pro, was signed.

The squad began workouts at Lake Erie College in Painesville. The Rams had an 11-game schedule, opening with the Detroit Lions at the Stadium the night of Sept. 10. Their remaining four home games were played at League Park.

Here is how John Dietrich, the Plain Dealer sports writer, began his story of the opening game:

"From the murky depths of the Stadium (the lights were poor at the time), a drizzling rain glistening from their shiny new uniforms, the Cleveland Rams, newcomers to the National Football League, took a good, long look at what lies ahead. The outlook is somewhat fearful. Before 20,000 . . . the Rams went down before the Detroit Lions, 28-0."

The following week, Gordon Cobbledick, a writer from Philadelphia, had a brighter report:

"The doleful guessers who predicted that the Cleveland Rams would be lucky to win one game this year were thoroughly confounded tonight when the grizzled Hugo Bezdek's pupils charged to a 21-3 victory over the Philadelphia Eagles before a crowd of 11,376 in the great Philadelphia Municipal Stadium.

"Uncovering a sensational aerial battery in Bob Snyder, former Ohio University flash, and Johnny Drake, Purdue's foremost gift to Cleveland professional football, the Rams took charge of the game in the second period and never relinquished their command for a minute."

But the "doleful guessers" proved to be right. That was the only game the Rams won. The Rams' home attendance averaged 8,900 for the season. Top ticket price was $2.20, including tax.

"A local charity took over our last game of the year," Marshman recalls. "We were to play Sammy Baugh and his Redskins at League Park. There was a big snow and almost nobody showed up except the players."

For 1938 the Rams scheduled their early games at Shaw Stadium and the remaining ones at League Park. The Stadium was too big and the rent too

high. When the season started with three successive losses, Marshman and his fellow partners met at the Union Club. Something had to be done. First, Wetzel was fired. Then Bezdek. Art (Pappy) Lewis, the regular guard who also served as Bezdek's assistant, was elevated to "temporary" head coach. Under Lewis the Rams won their next game, beating the Lions at Shaw Field and finishing 4-7 for the season for a fourth-place spot in the five-team Western Division. Attendance remained low.

Despite the improvement under Pappy Lewis, it was decided a "name" coach was needed. Earl (Dutch) Clark, an experienced coach who had been a fine pro quarterback, was named to run the team in 1939. More importantly, the Rams began to acquire better players. Parker Hall was signed as Quarterback and Jim Benton as an end. Benton, although slow, had great moves and even better hands. Hall and Benton became an outstanding passing combination.

With the better players the optimistic owners moved the games to the Stadium. The team finished 5-5 and attendance improved somewhat. The owners were so delighted they made Clark a vice president and director of the club as well as coach. Next season the team dropped to 4-6.

In 1941, Dan Reeves, 29, a former athlete who had been associated with his father in a successful New York grocery chain, offered to buy the club. Marshman got his partners together. There were about 23, as he recalls. "We had been paying 'Irish dividends' each year, says Marshman. "That's an expression meaning we lost money. Not much, but a few thousand every season. We had to keep adding partners at $1,000 each and Hanna and I would loan the club $1,000 every so often, just to keep afloat. When Reeves offered us $135,000 for the franchise, everybody said 'grab it.' It meant a small profit for each of us." Now Dan Reeves had the Rams.

The youthful owner immediately made a headline move. He hired Billy Evans as his general manager. Evans had been an outstanding umpire in the American League. Then he became general manager of the Cleveland Indians. The Rams won their first two—the opener was played at the Akron Rubber Bowl—lost their next nine and finished in the cellar. Soon Evans was back in baseball.

Now it was 1942 and the world was at war. Pearl Harbor had been bombed. Dan Reeves became a lieutenant in the Army. Many of the athletes were called to service. Some had to work in war plants while they played football to stay out of the draft. The Rams, still coached by Dutch Clark, finished 5-6. At the end of the season Reeves asked the National Football League for permission to suspend operations in 1943 because of the wartime problems. It was granted. The league continued without the Cleveland Rams.

The Rams returned to business in 1944. Charles F. (Chili) Walsh was named general manager. Walsh was an old hand at pro football. He promptly named Aldo (Buff) Donelli as head coach. The problem was to find players. Some had been loaned to other clubs in 1943. Others had left the game or had been called to the service.

Walsh offered a finder's fee of $100 to anyone recommending a player who made the club. Lou Zontini, the Notre Dame star and an experienced pro, signed as a halfback. Tom Corbo was a guard. A find was Riley (Rattlesnake) Matheson, so called because he had twice been bitten by rattlesnakes.

He survived. They say the snakes died. Zontini, to this day, calls him the quickest, toughest guard he ever saw. The "pickup" team finished 4-6.

Stories began to appear that Arthur B. McBride, Cleveland's taxicab magnate, was planning to put a Cleveland team into a brand new football league, the All-America Football Conference, with Paul Brown as head coach.

And now we come to historic 1945. Tom Corbo missed it because of an injury. Zontini missed it, too. He was called into the Army. But those who were around never will forget it. It was the Year of the Ram. Walsh had put together a winner. He started by firing Donelli as coach and hiring his brother, Adam Walsh, who had been one of the "seven mules" to the famous Notre Dame Four Horsemen. Let Nate Wallack tell you about that season. Walsh hired him to handle the Rams' public relations in 1945. At the time, Nate was a social worker who moonlighted at various P.R. jobs, among other things.

"I put out the first press book the Rams ever had," said Wallack. "Here's a copy, probably the only one left." The roster revealed some of the names: Steve Nemeth, Matheson, Benton, Fred Gehrke, Ralph Ruthstrom, Jim Gillette, Albie Reisz, Milan Lazetich, Steve Pritko, Bill Rieth, Tom Colella, Floyd Konetsky, Mike Scarry, Eberle Schultz, Gil Bouley, Ray Hamilton, Pat West, Rudy Sikich, Howard (Red) Hickey, Rudy Mucha and Don Greenwood. Few of them made more than $250 a game. And there was one more name, Bob Waterfield, a rookie, the quarterback from UCLA, who had spent two years in the Army.

"We trained at Bowling Green that year," remembers Wallack. "Nobody expected the Rams to be more than ordinary. They didn't know about Waterfield. I must name him as the finest all-around player I have ever known. He was an excellent passer and a fine runner. There was nobody better than Bob on the bootleg keeper.

"In those days most of the men played both ways and he was an excellent defensive back. He also was a fine punter and an outstanding place kicker. And besides, he was married to movie star Jane Russell, his high school sweetheart. She had just made a film "The Outlaw," for Howard Hughes that was getting a lot of publicity. She and Bob lived at the St. Regis Hotel in Cleveland.

"We played our home games at League Park that year. We won our first two, beating the Chicago Cardinals, 21-0, and the Chicago Bears, 17-0.

"As soon as we beat the Bears, I got a call from Life Magazine. They wanted to do a cover story on Jane Russell and Waterfield. I called the movie studio in Hollywood. The studio did not want to publicize the fact that she was married. I went to the St. Regis Hotel to talk with Jane. That was an experience. She was gorgeous—and built. I told her my problem with the studio. I'll never forget what she said: 'I'll cooperate with you on anything that's good for Robert and Rams.' She was a living doll.

"We beat Green Bay and the Bears again and finally lost to the Eagles. It proved to be our only loss of the season. Our biggest division rivals that season were the Lions and the Packers. I remember when we beat the Giants in the Polo Grounds, right after the loss to the Eagles. We had a ticker in the press box. I waited to get the Green Bay score. As soon as I saw the Packers lost, I ran all the way to the clubhouse in center field—I was a little thinner

then—and yelled, 'The Packers have lost. The Packers have lost.' One of the New York writers made that the lead on his story. He said it typified the youthful exuberance of the Rams.

"The next week we were to play the Packers at League Park. There was a tremendous ticket demand. It was suggested we move the game to the Stadium, but Chili Walsh refused. He had a lease with League Park. Besides, he was stubborn. He got the idea to put up temporary bleachers along the right field wall. I mean temporary, strictly lumber. We built a small press box behind it. I was standing in the press box when the game started. All of a sudden it looked as though the whole ball park was moving. The temporary seats were breaking and people were falling down. Luckily there was only one serious accident, a broken leg. After the seats collapsed the fans stood on the sideline for the rest of the game. We won, 20-7.

"We still had to beat the Lions in our second to last game to be sure of the division title. It was a Thanksgiving morning game in Detroit. The team went to Detroit by train—on the Mercury. We took trains to all our games. None of this Pullman car stuff, either. The guys sat in coaches."

Konetsky recalls that Waterfield had badly bruised ribs going into that Detroit game. "Adam Walsh told us we had to protect Bob. Nobody laid a hand on him that day." The Rams won, 28-21, and had the division title. "Dan Reeves threw a nice dinner for the team at the Statler in Detroit and then we came home on the Mercury," recalls Wallack.

"Our season ticket sale was nothing those days," says Wallack. "Maybe 200 at the most. We put the championship seats on sale and immediately we sold 30,000 and we had another week to go before the game. The weather was beautiful. It looked as though we'd sell out the Stadium. Then a blizzard. I mean an awful one. It ended our sale. Now Bill Johns, our business manager, was worried about the field. He wanted to keep it from freezing. He got in his car and set out toward Sandusky, stopping at every farm to buy hay. He wanted to cover the field with it. He bought over 1,000 bales.

"The day of the game the temperature dropped to zero. I sat in the press box and the windows got so steamed we couldn't see. All the writers had to get out into the stands and freeze. Me, too. A water pipe broke in the upper deck and cascading water turned to ice immediately—a frozen waterfall. The fans burned the hay and even the wooden bleacher seats to keep warm. One fan froze his feet and didn't realize it until he started to walk home after the game. An ambulance had to be called. The game was so exciting, though, the fans stayed to the end. We sold about 35,000 tickets and 29,000 showed."

Konetsky, a defensive end, didn't think he would start. "I put on every piece of clothes I could find," he remembers. "Then when Walsh told me I was starting, I had to strip off the layers so I could move. I'll never forget that cold."

In the first quarter Sammy Baugh, back in his own end zone, tried to pull a surprise. He threw a pass. Konetsky, rushing in, managed to tip the ball. It hit the cross bar and bounced back into the end zone for a safety, giving the Rams two points. (Because of this play the rule was changed. Now a pass that hits any part of the goal posts is incomplete.) It turned out those two points made the difference. The Rams won, 15-14. They were the champions of the football world.

The next day Johns loaded what was left of the hay and put it in a truck. He tried to sell it back to the farmers without success. The Rams' players each received $1,469.74 as their share of what then was football's Super Bowl.

Meanwhile, Arthur McBride not only had hired Paul Brown to coach his entry, the Cleveland Browns, in the new All-America Conference, he also had obtained a long-term lease on the Stadium. The rival Rams, world champions, would have to play at League Park. Reeves wanted no part of that kind of competition.

On Jan. 11, 1946, Reeves asked for permission to move to Los Angeles. He threatened to disband his franchise when opposition developed. The other National Football League owners gave in. The Cleveland Rams moved west and became the Los Angeles Rams.

Hal Lebovitz is a former sports editor at the Cleveland Plain Dealer. *He is currently a columnist for The Sporting News.*

Captions for photographs on pages 2-18
Pages 2-3: Washington Redskin back Cliff Battles (20) runs through the Cleveland Rams line on a snow-blanketed field at Cleveland in 1937. **Page 4:** Rams back Cullen Bryant steps over the goal line unmolested. **Page 6:** Running back Larry Smith (38) takes the handoff from Roman Gabriel and tries to pick up yardage against the Atlanta Falcons. Linebacker Tommy Nobis (60) moves in for the tackle. **Pages 6-7:** Rams huddle. **Pages 8-9:** Detroit halfback Pat Harder is dragged down by the Rams' defensive unit in the 1952 conference playoff game. Los Angeles defensive back Jack Dwyer (29) trails the play. Detroit beat Los Angeles, 31-21. **Page 10:** Ram owner Georgia Frontiere. **Pages 10-11:** Quarterback Karl Sweetan (10) picks up five yards against the Dallas Cowboys by jumping over his own lineman, Joe Scibelli. **Page 13:** End Jim Benton started his career with the Cleveland Rams in 1938. He led the league in receiving in 1946 with 63 receptions. **Page 14:** ''Kink'' Richards (13) of the New York Giants runs through the Rams secondary on the way to a 25-yard gain at the Polo Grounds in 1938. **Page 16:** Coach Sid Gilman. **Page 17:** Earl ''Dutch'' Clark was one of the earliest coaches of the Cleveland Rams. Clark directed the club from 1939 to 1942 and posted a 16-26-2 record. Prior to joining the Rams, Clark was a quarterback for the Portsmouth Spartans from 1931-1932, and the Detroit Lions from 1934-1938. He was elected to Pro Football's Hall of Fame in 1963, its first year of existence. **This page:** Kenny Washington holds the Rams longest run from scrimmage, a 92-yard dash against the Chicago Cardinals in 1946. **Page 20:** Los Angeles Ram receiver Jim Benton hauls in a pass thrown by Bob Waterfield in a game against the Chicago Bears in 1946. Benton set an NFL single-game record in 1945 when he totaled 303 yards in receptions against the Detroit Lions.

1946–1949

CHAPTER ONE

FROM CLEVELAND TO LOS ANGELES

The year was 1946. The war was finally over. Ben Hogan was golf's leading money winner. Horse racing's triple crown was captured by "Assault," and Army's Glenn Davis was college football's Heisman Trophy winner.

Servicemen returning from overseas duty streamed into west coast ports. Housing developments began to spring up in Southern California to accommodate them.

The hit movie of the season was "Best Years of Our Lives" starring Fredric March. March received an Academy Award as the year's best actor for his outstanding performance.

The city of Los Angeles hosted several new celebrities. Local woman Marilyn Buferd was crowned Miss America in 1946, and a group of young men from Cleveland began to catch the city's attention.

The Cleveland Rams won the 1945 NFL Championship with a stunning, 15-14, victory over Sammy Baugh and the Washington Redskins. With the league championship in hand, Ram owner Dan Reeves petitioned the NFL to move his club to Los Angeles. Initially, his proposal was met with opposition by the other team owners. When Reeves pointed out that he lost over $50,000 with a championship team, they gave him permission to move. The Rams became the first NFL franchise on the west coast.

The Rams got their start in Cleveland in 1936 when attorney Homer Marshman organized a group of Cleveland businessmen to back a football team in the new American Football League. One of the investors was a Cleveland cartoonist named Damon "Buzz" Wetzel. Wetzel was appointed the team's first coach and general manager.

One of Wetzel's first acts as general manager was to decide upon a name for the Cleveland club. After consulting with investors, and reporters from the Cleveland papers, they agreed a short catchy name that easily fit into a headline was appropriate. The Fordham Rams were a well-known college team at the time, so they settled on "Rams" as a nickname.

Cleveland finished the 1936 season with a 5-2-2 record, which was good for second place in the AFL behind the Boston Shamrocks. Unfortunately, the team played to empty seats in Cleveland. Marshman's only hope of keeping the Rams alive was to leave the AFL and persuade the National Football League owners to grant him a franchise.

Marshman convinced NFL President Joe Carr and the league's other owners to absorb Cleveland into the league. For a $10,000 admittance fee, the Cleveland Rams became part of the NFL.

Wetzel remained the team's general manager in 1937 while Hugo Bezdek took over the head coaching job. That year, the NFL held its first college player draft and the Rams selected Purdue fullback Johnny Drake. Drake

Several Rams close in on Cleveland Brown return man Ken Carpenter after he fumbled a kickoff in a game at Los Angeles Memorial Coliseum in 1951.

signed with the club for $275 per game and became the league's Rookie of the Year.

In 1941, Marshman sold the Rams to 29-year-old Dan Reeves and his partner Fred Levy for $135,000. Reeves retained Earl "Dutch" Clark to coach the club. Clark led the Rams to a 2-9 record in 1941 and a 5-6 mark in 1942. Reeves then was granted permission to suspend operation for the 1943 season because of World War II.

The Rams resumed play in 1944 with Aldo "Buff" Donelli as head coach. He was relieved of his position after posting a 4-6 record and replaced with Adam Walsh for the historic 1945 season. The Rams finished with a 9-1 record in 1945, then defeated the Washington Redskins for the NFL title. A year later the Rams were playing in Los Angeles.

Among the team's players that championship season were such stars as quarterback Bob Waterfield, backs Fred Gehrke and Tom Colella,

ends Bob Shaw and Jim Benton, and linemen Gil Bouley, Riley Matheson and Milan Lazetich. In 1946, they added three gate attractions in Heisman Trophy winner Tom Harmon, ex-USC quarterback Jim Hardy and former UCLA star Kenny Washington.

The Rams were not the only game in town, however. Football fans could choose to spend their money watching several professional and college teams, including the Los Angeles Dons of the rival All-America Football Conference and college attractions like UCLA and USC. In addition, the Pacific Coast Football League had such local teams as the Los Angeles Bulldogs, the Hollywood Bears and the San Diego Bombers.

Competition for playing fields among the clubs was fierce. The Rams had to outbid the Hollywood Bears and the Los Angeles Dons to secure the use of Los Angeles Memorial Coliseum for its home games.

After gaining permission to use the Coliseum, the Rams opened the 1946 season with two exhibition games. They lost the opener in Chicago to the College All-Stars, 16-0, then returned to Los Angeles to meet the Washington Redskins and their star quarterback "Slingin'" Sammy Baugh. The game was a rematch of the 1945 NFL title

Gil Bouley 1945–1950

Gil Bouley remembers the 1945 NFL Championship Game as if it were yesterday. But then the game ranks as one of the most memorable title contests in league history, more for the bitter weather than the action on the playing field.

Bouley was a rookie tackle for the Cleveland Rams that year. He joined the Rams after his outstanding college days at Boston College under the legendary Frank Leahy. In his first year with the club, he hit paydirt. The Rams ended the season with a 9-1 record, best in the NFL, then met the Washington Redskins for the championship.

As game time approached, the temperature hovered around two degrees.

Wind whipped off Lake Erie, dropping the wind-chill factor to about 20 below zero. Grounds-keepers worked feverishly to clear the snow and ice that blanketed Cleveland's Municipal Stadium. Earlier in the week, bales of straw had been gathered from local farms and laid on the field to prevent it from freezing over. The straw had to be removed also.

Municipal Stadium held over 80,000 fans and there was a pre-game sale of 40,000 tickets, yet only 32,178 showed up for the game. The strong north wind not only discouraged fans from attending, it played an important part in the game's outcome. The Rams won it, 15-14, but the margin of victory came in the first period when Sammy Baugh attempted to throw from his own end zone. The wind-blown pass hit the goal post, giving Cleveland a two-point safety. It was just the edge the Rams needed. They held on to win and collect $1,468 each for the victory.

After winning the NFL title, owner Dan Reeves moved the club to Los Angeles. Bouley is one of a handful of Rams who played for both the Cleveland club and the Los Angeles edition. During his six years with the Rams, he helped lead them to three western division titles.

"Dan Reeves was still the Rams' owner in Los Angeles, so it was basically the same franchise," Bouley said. "We just moved. There was quite a big difference in Los Angeles.

Cleveland was an old city, while Los Angeles was just starting to grow. Obviously, the weather was different. It seems we always played in the cold back east; nothing like the 1945 championship though. In Los Angeles we had nice weather.

"We became part of the Hollywood crowd out there. In fact, they had us making movies. A bunch of us were in a movie called "Easy Living" with Victor Mature and Lucille Ball. It was a football movie. We had to get cards from the Screen Actors Guild to appear in it. Gerry Cowhig, one of our backs, doubled as Victor Mature."

That was not the only time that Hollywood came calling at the Rams' practice field. Among the other films

that Ram players performed in were "Crazy Legs, All American," about Los Angeles receiver Elroy Hirsch and "All the King's Men," starring John Derek.

"'All the King's Men' was about Huey Long, the former governor of Louisiana," Bouley said. "Long played football in college at LSU so they used several of our players for the football scenes."

Hollywood movie makers were not the only people trying to recruit Ram players. Television was a brand new medium in the late 1940s, and one crafty salesman thought the Rams could help make it popular.

"We knew this guy named Davis who tried to hire several players to sell television sets door-to-door in the off-season," he said. "This was in the 40s. Nobody even knew what television was. I remember him saying 'Pretty soon there is going to be an antenna on everybody's house.' He couldn't get anybody to work for him, though. I guess I should have listened to him."

Bouley still wonders about the string of events that made him a member of the Rams. He did not consider professional football while an undergraduate at Boston College, but when he got an offer from Ram coach Adam Walsh, he had second thoughts.

"Frank Leahy must have recommended me to Adam Walsh," Bouley said. "I knew they were friendly and

talked about the players. I really didn't want to play professional football, though. They offered me what I considered a fantastic sum, $6,000 a year. There was no bonus. I was told by a friend I better take it before they changed their minds."

As an offensive lineman, Bouley's job was to block for two of the game's greatest quarterbacks, Norm Van Brocklin and Bob Waterfield. They had contrasting personalities, he says, but their athletic skills were very similar.

"Waterfield was always the gentleman," Bouley said. "He was a good teacher who would take the time to show people their assignments. He was patient. I remember this one play where someone missed a block and Bob got creamed. We came back to the huddle and all he said was, 'Come on guys try to hold them out a little longer.' That wouldn't have happened with Van Brocklin. He would have been yelling and screaming.

"Waterfield was an amazing athlete. He was ambidextrous, and he could kick left- or right-footed equally well. He was also a good runner. I'd say he was one of the best quarterbacks ever to run the bootleg. You had to protect guys like that.

"We had a well-balanced offense though. We could run the ball as well as pass. The backfield was excellent with Tank Younger, Dick Hoerner, Fred Gehrke and the

rest."

The team's main receivers were Tom Fears and Elroy Hirsch. Both men are in Pro Football's Hall of Fame. But the Rams had some equally dangerous receivers, says Bouley.

"Jim Benton was really something," Bouley said. "You've never seen anything like him. He was 6-3 and about 225. He wasn't that fast, but boy, could he get that ball. In one game in 1945, he gained over 300 yards in receptions and he didn't even score a touchdown."

Benton's 303 yards on 10 receptions against the Detroit Lions is an NFL record.

Bouley played both offense and defense throughout most of his career. One of the greatest players he competed against was "Slingin'" Sammy Baugh of the Washington Redskins.

"It's really too bad that Sammy Baugh played on such a lousy team for most of his career," Bouley said. "He was a genuine triple threat. He could run, pass and punt. He was a great T-Formation quarterback. When he was on, he could complete them underhand, sidearm, crossarm or just about any way he wanted. In one game, we were chasing the poor guy all over the field and I started feeling sorry for him. If that was Van Brocklin, he would have been screaming at us."

Besides participating in the 1945 championship game, Bouley played in NFL title

games in both 1949 and 1950 before retiring from the NFL. Both games were disappointments. In 1949, the Philadelphia Eagles defeated the Rams 14-0 in a drenching rainstorm. In 1950, the Cleveland Browns beat Los Angeles, 30-28.

"We not only expected to win that Philadelphia game, we expected a packed house," Bouley said. "That would ensure us more money. It rained and less than 30,000 showed up at the Coliseum."

The Rams received $740 each for that game. The Eagles got $1,094.

Bouley ended his career on a heartbreaking note in the 1950 championship game against the Cleveland Browns. Cleveland's Lou Groza kicked a field goal with 28 seconds left to beat the Rams, 30-28.

"We were winning through the entire game," he said. "In fact, on the first play from scrimmage, Glenn Davis went in motion and took a swing pass from Bob Waterfield. He ran about 80 yards for the touchdown. I still can't believe we lost that.

"I have nothing but great memories of the Rams," he said. "Dan Reeves, the owner at the time, was always great to us. We even got paid for the exhibition games, which wasn't standard practice back then. I'll always remember those days."

24

game and local fans were anxious to see the outcome. A record crowd of nearly 95,000 packed into the Coliseum. The Rams beat Washington, 16-14.

Los Angeles played its first league contest at the Coliseum a week later against the Philadelphia Eagles. Attendance fell to just 30,500. Temperatures were in the mid-80s at game time. The Eagles were led by All-Pro running back Steve Van Buren and quarterbacks Leroy Zimmerman and Tommy Thompson. Earle "Greasy" Neale was the Eagle coach. Van Buren was too much for the Rams. He rushed for 80 yards to lead the Eagles to a 25-14 win.

The Rams got their first league victory a week later over the Green Bay Packers, 21-17. Sporting a 1-1 record, Los Angeles traveled to Wrigley Field to play the dangerous Chicago Bears. Nearly 44,200 fans were on hand to see the matchup between quarterbacks Sid Luckman of Chicago and Bob Waterfield of Los Angeles. They were not disappointed.

Luckman got the Bears moving early. He threw two touchdown passes in the first three minutes of the game to give Chicago a quick, 14-0, lead. He added another touchdown pass in the second period and the Rams played catch up the rest of the afternoon.

Waterfield was not to be outdone, however. He tossed scoring passes of 23 yards to receiver Jim Benton and 29 yards to Tom Harmon to bring the Rams to within a touchdown at halftime, 21-14.

Harmon came to life in the second half and dazzled the crowd at Wrigley Field. The former Michigan All-American had a spectacular day, gaining 103 yards on the ground. Late in the third quarter, he exploded through the line on an 84-yard touchdown run that put Los Angeles in front, 28-21. Chicago came back to tie the game and had a chance to win it in the final seconds, but Bear kicker Joe Stydahar missed a 40-yard field goal attempt as time ran out.

While the Rams prepared for only their second league game in Los Angeles, workers at the Coliseum went on strike. Picketers lined the stadium prior to a game with the Detroit Lions, delaying entrance to over 30,000 spectators. The strike did not affect the Rams' play. They outclassed Detroit, 35-14. The passing of Bob Waterfield and the running and receiving of Tom Harmon were the difference.

Norm Van Brocklin was the Rams' fourth-round draft choice out of Oregon in 1949. Van Brocklin and Bob Waterfield gave the Rams the best one-two quarterback punch in NFL history. Van Brocklin was traded to Philadelphia prior to the 1958 season.

On the opening drive, Waterfield directed the club 83 yards in five plays to give Los Angeles a 7-0 lead. The touchdown was set up by two long passes from Waterfield to Jim Benton. Fred Gehrke capped the drive by scoring on an 11-yard run. Harmon upped the score to 14-0 in the second quarter when he took a Waterfield screen pass and coasted 47 yards to the end zone.

Quarterback Jim Hardy replaced Waterfield on the next series and moved the club 85 yards. Bob Shaw caught a three-yard pass from Hardy to give the Rams a 21-0 halftime lead.

Detroit scored twice in the third period, but the Rams held on for a 35-14 win. Harmon gained 30 yards on six carries for a 4.8-yard average. Waterfield completed eight of 16 passes. Hardy was good on seven of 12 passes.

After losing to the Chicago Cardinals, 34-10, the Rams stayed in contention with a 41-20 win over Detroit in their second meeting of the season. Harmon gained 43 yards in eight carries for a 5.4-yard average and hauled in a 41-yard pass from Waterfield to set up a touchdown. Harmon also intercepted a pass on defense.

Waterfield completed 14 of 28 passes for 224 yards. Jim Benton was on the receiving end of six passes for 109 yards. Bob Shaw caught three passes for 60 yards. The win gave the Rams a 3-2-1 record and a tie for second place in the western division. Their next opponent, the Chicago Bears, was in first place with a 4-1-1 record.

A crowd of 68,381 packed into the Coliseum to see the two teams square off. Former Stanford star Hugh Gallarneau got Chicago on the scoreboard first when he sprinted 52 yards early in the first quarter. Chicago quarterback Sid Luckman dominated the rest of the half. He threw touchdown passes of 38 and 34 yards to receiver Ken Kavanaugh to give the Bears a 20-7 halftime lead. He added a 28-yard scoring pass to Kavanaugh in the third period.

Despite the 27-7 deficit, Los Angeles came storming back. Jack Banta intercepted a Luckman pass and returned it 40 yards to the Bears' 13. From there, Waterfield connected with Jim Benton for the touchdown. Early in the fourth period the Rams marched 56 yards and scored on a pass from Waterfield to Steve Pritko cutting the Bears' lead to 27-21.

With just over three minutes to play, the Rams regained possession of the football for the last time. Waterfield marched his club steadily downfield to Chicago's 18-yard line. A touchdown and extra point would win the game for Los Angeles. But Bear quarterback Sid Luckman, doubling as a defensive back, ended the Rams' hope for a win when he intercepted a Waterfield pass on the four-yard line.

Waterfield and Luckman put on a fantastic aerial show. Luckman completed 12 of 22 passes for 245 yards and three touchdowns. Waterfield connected on 16 of 30 tosses for 180 yards.

The Chicago Cardinals visited the Coliseum a week later. It took a miraculous series of events for the Rams to beat Chicago. The Cardinals were sitting on a 14-10 lead with time running out in the fourth quarter when Chicago running back Pat Harder lost a fumble. Los Angeles recovered on its own 38-yard line with less than four minutes to go. In seven plays the Rams moved 35 yards to the Cardinals 28. Facing a third-and-two with 1:40 to play, Waterfield

dropped back and lofted a high arching pass to Steve Pritko who was racing down the sideline. In full stride, Pritko snared the ball on his finger tips and streaked into the end zone, giving Los Angeles a 17-14 win.

The Rams won two of their last three games to finish the season with a 6-4-1 record and second place behind the Chicago Bears. Coach Adam Walsh was fired at the end of the year. He had a 15-5-1 record in his two seasons as head coach of the Rams.

The Los Angeles Dons, the Rams' intracity rival, finished with a 7-5-2 mark. The record was good enough for third place in the All-America Football Conference.

1947 Bob Snyder was appointed head coach for the 1947 season. Among the club's picks in the annual college draft were All-American running back Herman Wedemeyer from St. Mary's College, center Don Paul from UCLA, and Ohio State end Dante Lavelli. Wedemeyer signed instead with the Los Angeles Dons. Lavelli joined the Cleveland Browns of the AAFC and later was inducted into Pro Football's Hall of Fame.

The Rams appeared to be a contender in preseason, whipping the Washington Redskins, 20-7, the Boston Yanks, 24-0, and the Detroit Lions, 21-0. In the season opener, they topped the Pittsburgh Steelers, 48-7.

Coach Snyder's club then played at Milwaukee against the Green Bay Packers. Green Bay held a 17-14 lead late in the fourth period, but the Rams forced a fumble and took over with less than a minute to play. Waterfield, who played the entire game on both offense and defense, started the drive at the Packers' 30-yard line. He threw three consecutive incomplete passes. With 10 seconds remaining, Waterfield attempted a game-tying field goal from the 38. The kick sailed inches wide of the goal post as time ran out.

Despite the missed field goal, Waterfield played a magnificent game. He completed six passes, scored one touchdown, kicked two extra points, recovered one fumble, intercepted a pass and got off an 88-yard punt.

A week later Tom Harmon paced the Rams to a 27-13 win over the Detroit Lions at Briggs Stadium. Harmon had been a local hero since his

Tom Fears 1948–1956

Tom Fears is one name that constantly pops up in the Ram record book. He holds virtually every club receiving record.

Fears is the team's all-time reception leader with 400 catches. In 1950, he set a club single-season record with 84 receptions. In one game against the Green Bay Packers that year, he set an NFL mark by catching 18 passes.

The Cleveland Rams drafted Fears in 1945, a year before the team made its way to Los Angeles. The war had just ended and Fears was finishing his stint in the armed forces. Rather than join the Rams, he returned to

college at UCLA. Fears had already completed two years of under-graduate work at Santa Clara before the war. When he graduated from UCLA, the Los Angeles Rams were waiting for him.

Fears started his push toward Pro Football's Hall of Fame in 1948 when he teamed up with quarterback Bob Waterfield. He made his presence felt in that rookie season by catching 51 passes to lead the NFL.

"Bob Waterfield was one of the greatest athletes to ever step on a football field," Fears said. "Not only could he play football, he was a

good gymnast, a great swimmer and a good diver. He excelled in just about every sport he tried. On the football field he could pass and he could kick with both feet. He was a clever quarterback too. I used to watch him closely, because you could pick up little things from him.

"Off the field he was a quiet, unassuming guy. You usually would expect such a great quarterback to be kind of brash, a pop-off. He wasn't like that at all.

"Bob was married to one of the biggest stars in Hollywood at the time—Jane Russell. They lived quietly out in the (San Fernando)

Valley in a nice house with a pool. He wasn't much of a social guy. He was kind of reserved."

Fears was the NFL's leading receiver his first three seasons in the league. In 1949, he caught 77 balls to set a new NFL standard. A year later he broke his own mark by nabbing 84 passes for 1,116 yards. Nevertheless, he modestly insists his skills did not match up with some of the league's other fine receivers.

"I was a classic overachiever," he said. "I think determination played a bigger part in my success than any skill I had. I had some speed, but Elroy Hirsch and Bob Boyd were both faster than me. I was just confident that I wouldn't be outplayed. If I got my hands on a ball I was going to bring it in."

Fears also credits the Rams' offensive scheme for his productiveness. Los Angeles was the most pass-happy team in football in 1950. The offense set an NFL record that season when it averaged 309 passing yards per game. The Rams also set a league scoring mark in 1950, averaging 39 points per contest.

"We had a fairly sophisticated passing attack," Fears said. "We ran good patterns, but they were not as exact as you see today. Van Brocklin would improvise sometimes, and I would read it and adjust to what he was doing."

Fears was a tough competitor who never turned away from a challenge. In fact, it was against the class teams of the league that Fears had his best days.

"The Philadelphia Eagles were always a rough bunch," he said. "Chuck Bednarik was one of those linebackers who would try to decapitate you. The Eagles in general were like that. Pete Pihos was another one. He played both ways and was tough on both offense and defense.

"Generally I played better against the good football teams. I liked playing the Bears or the Eagles. If we had a game that was a cake-walk, sometimes I slacked off. I know that

is not the way I should have been, and I certainly did not coach people that way, but I just found it easier to prepare myself mentally for the big games. In those games, I played until my tongue was hanging out."

Fears had some of his best games when the pressure was on him. In the 1950 playoff game against the Chicago Bears, he caught three touchdown passes and paced the Rams to a 24-14 win.

A year later the Rams were matched with the Cleveland Browns in the NFL Championship Game. The score was tied, 17-17, in the fourth quarter. Fears got behind the Browns' defense and Van Brocklin fired a long spiral. Fears took it in stride to complete a 73-yard touchdown pass. It proved to be the game winner. It was the Rams' first championship in Los Angeles.

"That was probably the most satisfying win for me as a player," Fears said. "Three years in a row we finished in first place. The first two times we lost in the championship game. The third time we finally won it. It was always satisfying to beat the (Cleveland) Browns anyway, but it meant more in a championship game."

Fears retired from pro football in 1956. In 1960, he rejoined the Rams as an assistant coach under Bob Waterfield. During his two years with the Rams, they finished 4-7-1 and 4-10. At the end of the 1961 season,

Fears joined the staff of Vince Lombardi at Green Bay.

"You enjoy coaching in proportion to how you're doing," Fears said. "We weren't particularly successful either year I was with the Rams. Bob (Waterfield) was the head man at that time. He was a wonderful guy, but he was a little too nice to be a head coach. He was smart as hell. He had a great head for football, but that doesn't mean much if you can't get people to do what you want them to do."

At Green Bay, Fears had better luck. As an aide to Vince Lombardi, he watched the brilliant coach assemble one of pro football's greatest teams.

"When I got to the Packers, I could see a dynasty was in the making," Fears said. "Lombardi was very dynamic. He was a great coach, a great person. He was an actor at times. He would do what he had to do to get his players to perform. But he expected a lot from the people around him. Lombardi was a religious man too. He went to church every day. You had to have respect for a man like that."

Lombardi was one of the coaches who had an impact on Fears, but the game's most innovative coach was Clark Shaughnessy, he says. Shaughnessy was the Ram head coach in 1948 and 1949. In 1949 he led the Rams to the western division crown.

"There is no other coach I was associated

with that impressed me more than Clark Shaughnessy," Fears said. "He contributed more to football, by far, than anyone ever associated with the game. I don't think he ever got the recognition he deserved, though. He came up with the T-Formation, the man-in-motion, and he developed some defenses for the Chicago Bears. He was a phenomenal man."

Indeed, it was Shaughnessy that helped engineer the Bears' 73-0 win over the Washington Redskins in the 1940 NFL Championship Game by devising variations of the man-in-motion for George Halas. Shaughnessy is also credited with installing the T-Formation at Stanford in 1940 and taking them from a winless season in 1939 to an undefeated year in 1940.

Fears ended his coaching days in 1970 after leading the New Orleans Saints through their first four seasons. That same year he was honored for his contribution to the game, when he was elected to Pro Football's Hall of Fame.

"I'm really proud of that because there are no politics involved in the selection process," he said. "It's all based on ability. Many All-Star teams and All-America teams are based on who you know, what writers are voting for you, and all that. I'm really honored to be part of the Hall of Fame. You can't find a much better group than that."

Los Angeles end Howard ''Red'' Hickey gets behind the New York Giant defense to haul in a touchdown pass from Jim Hardy. The Rams defeated New York at the Polo Grounds, 52-37.
Pages 30-31: Los Angeles Ram end Frank Hubbell leaps high in the air to knock down a pass by Chicago Cardinal back Jim Hardy (21). Tackle Ed Champagne (86) also closes in on Hardy.

Heisman Trophy winning days at nearby Michigan. He flashed his All-American style by rushing for 58 yards on seven carries and one touchdown, catching a 32-yard pass for another touchdown, intercepting two passes on defense, and returning a kick 42 yards.

Los Angeles returned to the Coliseum for its home opener against the first place Chicago Cardinals. Over 69,000 fans were on hand to watch the Rams whip Chicago, 27-7. The win left Los Angeles in a three-way tie with Green Bay and Chicago for the western division lead.

The Rams first place standing soon vanished. They lost five of their next six games. Los Angeles' sole win during that span came at the hands of the Detroit Lions, 28-17.

In the midst of the losing streak, tempers began to flare in a lopsided loss to the Chicago Bears.

Chicago won the game handily, 41-21, but not before a free-for-all erupted on the field and continued into the locker room. Several players were ejected from the game.

The feud began in the second quarter when Ram defensive back Mel Bleeker and receiver Allen Smith of the Bears began swinging at one another. Both men were kicked out of the game. Several plays later, Chicago defensive end Ed Sprinkle sacked Waterfield. In the process, he landed a forearm that fractured Waterfield's jaw. Los Angeles halfback Dante Magnani came to the quarterback's rescue and exchanged punches with Sprinkle. When the referees finally separated the two players, they were also ejected from the game. Later, Chicago's Ed Ciefers was tossed out of the contest for unnecessary roughness.

The fisticuffs did not end there. After the game, Bear coach George Halas tried to claim the game ball from the Rams' 18-year-old club house boy, Buddy Leininger. Leininger refused to give the ball to Halas and was punched in the eye by 230-pound Chicago end Jack Matheson. Leininger suffered a black eye. Ram head coach Bob Snyder came to the boy's defense and traded blows with Matheson in the tunnel leading to

the Coliseum training quarters. Neither man was hurt.

The Rams closed out the season by winning three of their last four games, including a rematch over the Bears at Wrigley Field. They ended the season with a 6-6 record for fourth place in the western division.

Several Los Angeles stars announced their retirement at the end of the 1947 season. Tom Harmon left the Rams to pursue a career as a radio broadcaster. Guard Roger Eason and receiver Jim Benton also retired. Benton's career with the Rams began in 1938. He caught 275 passes for 4,566 yards during his playing days. Benton also gained a secure place in the NFL

Dan Reeves purchased the Cleveland Rams in 1941. After winning the NFL championship in 1945, Reeves moved the franchise to Los Angeles. **Page 35:** Cleveland Ram defensive back Ralph Ruthstrom wraps his arms around New York Giant running back Bill Paschal in a game at New York's Polo Grounds in 1945.

record book in 1945. He set an NFL single-game receiving record that year when he gained 303 yards on just 10 catches.

1948 After suffering economic losses in his first two seasons in Los Angeles, Owner Dan Reeves enlisted several other partners to help stabilize the Rams' financial situation. He originally sold 30 percent of the club to oilman Ed Pauley. Eventually, Harold Pauley, Hal Seley and entertainer Bob Hope, joined Reeves, Fred Levy and Ed Pauley as partners.

In the offseason, Clark Shaughnessy joined the Ram staff as an advisor to Coach Bob Snyder. Before the regular season got under way, Snyder was dismissed and Shaughnessy was appointed head coach. Shaughnessy brought with him impressive credentials as an offensive innovator. He spent four years as an assistant to Chicago Bear Coach George Halas before joining the Rams, and had been the head coach at the University of Chicago and Stanford University.

With the Bears he helped revolutionize the passing game by using the T-Formation and installing the man-in-motion. It was Shaughnessy who engineered the offensive plan for Halas in the 1940 NFL Championship Game between the Bears and the Washington Redskins. Chicago won that game, 73-0.

The Rams took the field in 1948 with a new look. Halfback Fred Gehrke, a graphic artist in the offseason, painted yellow horns on the side of the team's blue leather helmets. The design was an immediate sensation and inspired other teams around the league to devise their own helmet designs.

Among the new faces in training camp was a rookie end from UCLA named Tom Fears. He quickly became one of the most respected receivers in football and led the league in receptions his first year with 51 catches.

Los Angeles started the 1948 season with exhibition victories over the Hawaiian Warriors, a semi-pro team, 41-20 and 42-7. Despite those wins, the Rams were given little chance to win the division because of the retirement of star players Tom Harmon and Jim Benton. Such thinking was reflected in opening day attendance. Only 17,271 fans showed up for Los Angeles' first game against Detroit.

Tom Harmon 1946–1947

Tom Harmon joined the Rams in 1946, when professional sports were new to Los Angeles. He quickly became one of the city's first big-name sports figures.

Nearly six years earlier, Harmon was college football's most celebrated athlete. As a single-wing back at Michigan, his running skill earned him national recognition. He was awarded the Heisman Trophy in 1940, college football's highest honor, and was considered a cinch to become a professional football star.

Harmon postponed his professional career to serve with the Air Force during World War II. When the world champion Rams located to their new home in Los Angeles, Harmon was ready to join them. He became the first in a long line of Heisman Trophy winners to play for the Rams. Included in that list are Bruce Smith (Minnesota, 1941), Les Horvath (Ohio State, 1944), Glenn Davis (Army, 1946), Terry Baker (Oregon State, 1962), John Cappelletti (Penn State, 1973) and Charles White (USC, 1979). Several other Heisman winners were drafted by the Rams, but never played for them, including Billy Cannon (LSU, 1959), Mike Garrett (USC, 1966), Gary Beban (UCLA, 1967) and Doug Flutie (Boston College, 1984).

Despite Harmon's athletic prowess, he had to earn a starting spot with Los Angeles. The club already had talented backs like Fred Gehrke, Kenny Washington and Jack Banta in camp. Bob Waterfield and Jim Hardy were the signal callers.

"One of the things that impressed me on that team was the quality of the quarterbacks," Harmon said. "They were both very talented. Of course, Bob Waterfield is in the Hall of Fame. Jim Hardy was the other one. He went to school locally (USC) and was well-known around here.

"Fred Gehrke was in the backfield that year. Fred was the guy who painted the team's helmets. He was a graphic artist in the offseason. One day he took a pile full of helmets home and painted horns on the side of them."

The painted horns became the first helmet design in NFL history. Other teams around the league quickly picked up on the trend and soon every club had its own logo and helmet design.

Harmon worked his way into the starting lineup and put on a spectacular running show in just his third professional game. Los Angeles was matched with the Chicago Bears at Wrigley Field that day. Harmon gained 103 yards on the ground, including an 84-yard touchdown run. He later scored after taking a short screen pass and racing 29 yards to the end zone. It was one of the best games of Harmon's short career. He ended his rookie season with 236 yards on 47 carries and averaged five yards per rushing attempt. He gives credit for that yardage to an outstanding offensive line that included Gil Bouley, Fred Naumetz and Roger Eason.

"The Rams always had a lot of talent up front," Harmon said. "There was excellent blocking. My job was just to read the hole and hit it. Unfortunately, our record never reflected the amount of talent we had. I don't think we ever played up to our potential."

Harmon also had a difficult time adapting to the Rams style of play. Los Angeles used the T-Formation almost exclusively to take advantage of Waterfield's passing arm. At Michigan, Harmon was accustomed to running out of the single wing. He had difficulty adapting to the T-Formation.

"I enjoyed playing with the Rams, but in my particular instance, I wasn't set to play in the T-Formation," Harmon said. "In the single wing, you had blockers out in front and I was used to running behind blockers. In the T-Formation, you can't get blockers out in front of you like that."

Head Coach Adam Walsh continued using the T-Formation and never effectively utilized Harmon's running talent. But there were other skilled players that were not used properly on the 1946 club, Harmon says.

"I always felt the coaching was a little weak when I played with the Rams," he said. "They never were able to bring out the best in the players we had. The coaches were certainly nowhere near as good as those I had in college."

In his second year with the Rams, Harmon gained 306 yards on 60 carries, an average of 5.1 yards per attempt. His longest run from scrimmage was 32 yards. Los Angeles finished the season with a 6-6 record. At the end of the year, Harmon announced he was retiring from football to pursue a broadcasting career.

"Well, I had studied broadcasting in college and it was what I had planned for and trained for," Harmon said. "I never really fit in with the Rams' T-Formation. I was a single-wing back. If the Rams had been using a different formation, like the single wing, it might have been different. I don't regret it though. Everything worked out very well for me."

Harmon considers himself part of football history since he played on the original Los Angeles Rams squad. It was the first NFL franchise on the west coast. Much of that credit should go to former team owner Dan Reeves, he says.

"We were the first professional team out here on the coast," Harmon said. "Dan Reeves had to struggle to get the franchise out here, which was a real feather in his cap. The other owners didn't want him to move. They wanted him to pay all their traveling expenses. He really should be commended for putting up such a struggle to get the team out here.

"There have been a lot of changes in football since that time. There's a whole different attitude among the players and the owners. In the early days, with men like Tim Mara, George Halas and Dan Reeves, you had owners that truthfully loved the game of football and the teams they were a part of. They didn't run them as a life and death business like today's owners. Playing good football was the most important thing to them.

"The players now are concerned mostly about money. Everything revolves around the dollar. When I played, you never heard of guys breaking their contracts or wanting to hold out for more money. Everyone played because they loved football."

Two players from that era stand out in Harmon's memory as individuals who played football simply because they loved the game. He considers them the best players he competed against.

"The Philadelphia Eagles had an excellent back named Steve Van Buren," he said. "He was one of the great runners of his time. Green Bay was another good team. They had one of the NFL's best receivers in Don Hutson."

After 50 years as a player, broadcaster and observer, Harmon has also seen some significant changes in the way the game is played. Most of them can be traced back to the start of free substitution.

"There are some notable differences in the strategy teams are using," he said. "The defensives have been refined and on offense, teams have gone from primarily running the football to pass-oriented attacks. It's a lot different from the single-wing."

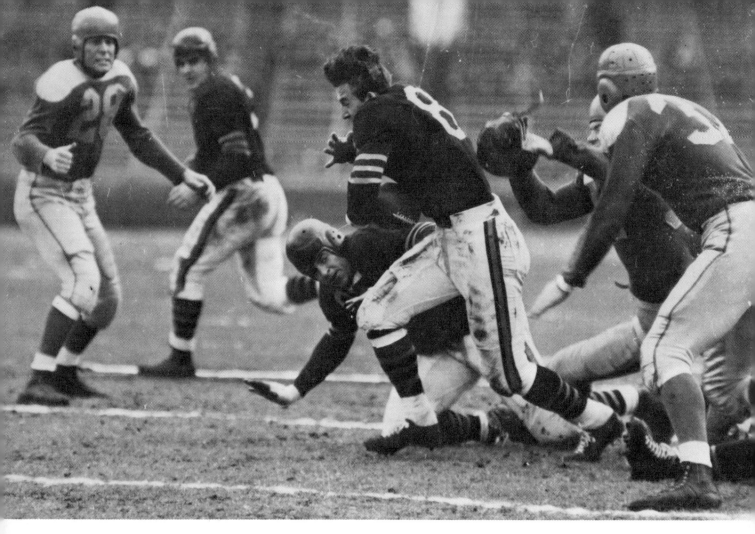

Chicago Bear fullback Hugh Gallarneau leaves his helmet behind as he sprints through the Cleveland Ram line during this 1941 game at Chicago.

The Rams surprised everyone by gaining 407 total yards in a 44-7 triumph over the Lions. Running back Fred Gehrke gained 71 yards in nine attempts for an 11.6-yard average. In his professional debut, Tom Fears caught three passes, intercepted two passes on defense and scored two touchdowns. One score came on a five-yard pass from Jim Hardy, the other on a 34-yard interception return.

The Rams' next opponent was the Philadelphia Eagles. After their impressive win over Detroit, attendance doubled as 36,884 fans made their way to the Coliseum. Los Angeles had not beaten Philadelphia since 1942, and it appeared the club would have to wait another year after spotting the Eagles a 28-0 lead late in the third period.

With three minutes to play in the third quarter, Los Angeles began to turn the game around. Waterfield recovered a fumble from his defensive back position and two plays later put the Rams on the scoreboard by hitting tight end Jack Zilly with a 27-yard pass.

Waterfield started the fourth quarter by marching the team 55 yards in six plays. He capped the drive with a five-yard pass to Bill Smyth. With eight minutes left in the game, Waterfield took over again at the Rams 45-yard line. On the first play from scrimmage, Waterfield passed 40 yards to Tom Fears. Two plays later, Bob Hoffman punched it over to make the score 28-21 with five minutes to play.

Once again the Ram defense stopped Philadelphia and the Eagles were forced to punt. Los Angeles took over at its own 27-yard line. With just under two minutes to play, the Rams were 73 yards away from paydirt.

Waterfield missed on three straight passes and faced a fourth-and-10 situation with 1:29 left. He connected with Red Hickey for a 20-yard gain, giving the Rams a first down at their 47-yard line. Time was called as the injured Hickey was taken off the field on a stretcher. When play resumed, Waterfield connected with Dante Magnani on a 15-yard pass to move to the Eagles' 42-yard line. A quick sideline pass to Fears picked up another 13 yards and the Rams were at the 29 with 35 seconds on the clock.

After throwing one incomplete pass, Water-

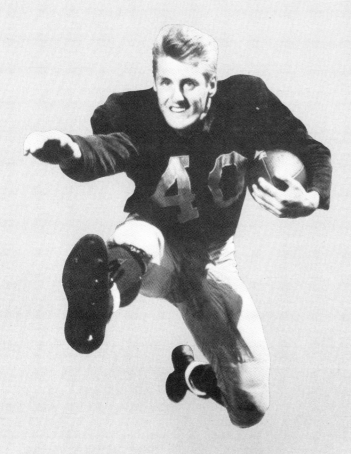

Elroy Hirsch 1949-1957

He was called "Crazy Legs" because of the way his feet wobbled behind him as he raced toward the goal line. It was Elroy Hirsch's unorthodox running style that carried him to the Hall of Fame and helped the Rams revolutionize football's passing game.

Hirsch joined the Rams in 1949 and was an immediate sensation. Although he expected to be successful in Los Angeles, many others were not so optimistic. Just a year before joining the club, Hirsch was a member of the Chicago Rockets of the All-America Football Conference. His playing days seemed finished after he was involved in a collision that severely fractured his skull. The injury left him with a temporary loss of bodily coordination. Doctors told him he would never play football again.

Hirsch refused to believe it. He worked his way back into condition and reported to the Rams in 1949. Hirsch not only made the club, he helped the passing game reach new heights.

Most NFL clubs firmly believed in a strong running attack in the late 1940s. Passing the football was an unneccessary extravagance. The Rams had a different attitude.

In 1949, Coach Clark Shaughnessy had Bob Waterfield and Norm Van Brocklin at quarterback. He was also blessed with two outstanding ends in Tom Fears and Bob Shaw. Shaughnessy wanted to work Hirsch into the passing attack, so he moved the halfback to a new position—flanker.

Hirsch became the first back to be split wide and function primarily as a receiver.

The emphasis on passing proved to be a bonanza for the Rams. They won the western division crown in 1949, 1950 and 1951, and beat the Cleveland Browns for the 1951 NFL Championship. More importantly, Hirsch perfected his new position and became a standout receiver. In 1951, he had one of the greatest seasons ever for a pass catcher. He was on the receiving end of 66 passes for 1,495 yards, setting an NFL record for yardage in a season. He averaged 22.7 yards a catch and scored 17 touchdowns to tie Don Hutson's single-season touchdown record. The 102 points Hirsch scored was tops in the league. Hirsch's miraculous comeback from the skull injuries inspired a Hollywood movie entitled, "Crazy Legs, All-American."

Not surprisingly, Don Hutson was one of Hirsch's boyhood idols. As a youth, Hirsch often made the trek from his Wisconsin home to Green Bay Packer games to watch the talented receiver. Hirsch is now alongside his idol in the Hall of Fame.

"Don Hutson was always one of my favorites," Hirsch said. "He was a great receiver. Remember, most teams didn't throw too much back then. He was way ahead of his time."

Hirsch's record-breaking statistics in 1951 helped the Rams win their first world championship in Los Angeles. After finishing the season with an 8-4 record, the Rams defeated the Cleveland Browns, 24-17, in the NFL Championship Game. The victory helped avenge a loss of a year earlier, when the Browns beat Los Angeles, 30-28, for the NFL Championship.

The Rams were much more than a passing team that year, says Hirsch. They had an excellent running game to complement their passing attack. With

backs like Tank Younger, Dan Towler, Dick Hoerner, Vitamin T. Smith and Glenn Davis, the Rams rewrote the record book in 1951, gaining 5,506 total yards in the 12-game season. In one contest against the New York Yankees, Los Angeles piled up 735 yards of total offense.

"That was the best Ram team I played on," he said. "We had a great bunch of guys in 1951. It seems like a lot of people retired in 1950 so we had a lot of younger players we counted on."

Although Hirsch was a gifted athlete, he says the quarterbacks he played with deserve much of the credit for his success.

"I don't know what skills I could really credit," he said. "I could always catch the ball and I could run fast. It helped to be surrounded by great quarterbacks, though.

"Waterfield and Van Brocklin were opposites in many ways. Both were excellent punters. Physically, Bob had a bit more speed, while Norm could throw the ball longer. On the field, Waterfield was more of a strategist. He would use three plays to set up one big play. Van Brocklin would always be looking for the big one. He would come in and immediately throw the bomb. We were always more of a finesse team, not overly physical. Our passing game was well developed for the time."

Although the Rams faced the Cleveland Browns for the league

title in 1950 and 1951, Hirsch remembers the Philadelphia Eagles as one of the teams to beat.

"The Eagles always played tough," he said. "Greasy Neale was their coach back then. I remember they had Chuck Bednarik at line-backer. He wouldn't let receivers off the line of scrimmage. The defensive back's job was a lot easier with a guy like Bednarik around. He didn't play just defense, though. He played center on offense too. He never came off the field.

"A lot of people played two ways back then. That's one of the differences I see in football today. The game's more special-ized. It's probably better for the game, because you just can't play when you're tired and have been on the field all day."

Hirsch ended his career in 1957 after nine years with the Rams. He also played three seasons with the Chicago Rockets of the AAFC before joining the Rams. During that time, he caught 387 passes for 7029 yards. He averaged over 18 yards per reception. Hirsch ranks second on the club's all-time reception list, trailing his friend and former teammate Tom Fears.

"Tom Fears was one of the greatest all-around receivers to ever play," Hirsch said. "He had great hands, just fantastic hands, and he was tough after he caught the ball. In fact, he was a pretty mean guy after he made the

catch."

Hirsch is now the athletic director at his alma mater, the Univer-sity of Wisconsin. He notes several changes in today's game that have enhanced the passing attack and made life easier for receivers.

"Now the defensive back is allowed just one chuck in a five-yard area," he said. "Back when I played there was much more contact. Pass interference wasn't called as closely as it is today. As a result, you had to be a little more physical."

Hirsch was selected to Pro Football's Hall of Fame in 1968. He was also named the best flanker of football's first 50 years by the Hall of Fame selection commit-tee. The other wide receiver picked was his childhood idol, Don Hutson.

Hirsch is honored to be mentioned alongside such outstanding play-ers, but he says the most thrilling moment in his career was a simple one. It happened before he started his pro career with the Chicago Rockets.

"I'll never forget playing in the 1946 College All-Star Game," he said. "Before the game, they darkened the stadium and announced everyone's name, one at a time. When they announced your name, you ran on the field and they put a spotlight on you. They played your college theme song as you ran out. It doesn't sound like much, but I thought it was a great experience."

Running back Don Greenwood (66) of the Cleveland Rams is stopped by a Washington Redskin player after a short gain.

field faded back and arched a long spiral to Jack Zilly. Zilly caught the ball in the end zone over the outstretched arms of two Eagle defenders to salvage a 28-28 tie.

Waterfield was the catalyst in the dramatic comeback. He completed 17 of 35 passes for 263 yards and three touchdowns, kicked four extra points, intercepted one pass and recovered a fumble.

The Rams dropped five of their next seven games, including a 16-0 shutout at the hands of the Green Bay Packers. During that stretch Waterfield injured his shoulder and was out of action for two games. He was replaced at quarterback by Jim Hardy.

In his first start, Hardy faced the defending champion Chicago Cardinals. He had a record-setting day, completing 28 of 53 passes for 406 yards and three touchdowns. The effort set team single-game records for completions, pass attempts and yardage. Despite Hardy's aerial show Chicago beat the Rams, 27-22.

Waterfield returned to action two weeks later

against the New York Giants and helped establish several new club records. He led the team to a 52-37 whipping of New York. In the process, the Rams set single-game records for most points scored (52), most touchdowns (7), most extra points (7), and most first downs (25).

Los Angeles ended the season with wins over Green Bay, 24-10, Pittsburgh, 31-14, and Washington, 41-13. Against the Redskins, Waterfield outdid his rival, Sammy Baugh, by throwing four touchdown passes to tie a club record. Baugh hit on 21 of 38 throws for 188 yards and two scores.

The Rams finished the year in third place with a 6-5-1 record. It turned out to be running back Kenny Washington's last season with the club. During his three years with the Rams, Washington gained 859 yards on 140 carries for a 6.1-yard average. He also established a club record with the longest run from scrimmage, when he dashed 92 yards to score against the Chicago Cardinals in 1946.

1949 Prior to the start of the 1949 season, the NFL took a giant step toward modernizing professional football when it adopted the free-substitution rule. Coaches were now able to platoon players and establish offensive and defensive squads, rather than have the same 11 players on the field for most of the game.

Among the team's draft choices in 1949 was a fourth-round pick from Oregon named Norm Van Brocklin. The Rams fooled everybody by selecting Van Brocklin because he was not scheduled to graduate until 1950. However, Van Brocklin had an accelerated curriculum that allowed him to graduate in time for the 1949 season. Elroy "Crazy Legs" Hirsch also joined the club after spending three years with the Chicago Rockets of the AAFC.

Although he already had two superb ends in Bob Shaw and Tom Fears, Coach Shaughnessy decided to move Hirsch from running back to flanker back. The new formation took advantage of Hirsch's speed and great hands and began a trend toward a wide-open passing game in the professional ranks.

Los Angeles opened the season with a 27-24 win over Detroit, then demolished the Green Bay Packers, 48-7. In the third game of the year, the Rams beat the Bears, 31-16, at Wrigley Field.

Waterfield was unstoppable against Chicago. He completed 16 of 33 passes for 211 yards and three touchdowns, kicked a 23-yard field goal added four extra points and averaged 46 yards on punts. Fears, Hirsch and Shaw each caught a touchdown pass.

The offensive line, anchored by team captain Fred Naumetz, tackles Dick Huffman and Gil Bouley, and guard Milan Lazetich, outplayed the Bears' tough defensive line. It limited Chicago to one quarterback sack, and helped the Los Angeles running backs gain 124 yards on the ground.

Los Angeles posted a 6-0 record to open a three-game lead in the western division before being defeated by the defending NFL Champion Philadelphia Eagles. The Eagles completely dominated the game and held a 31-7 lead in the fourth quarter before Shaughnessy replaced the ineffective Waterfield with rookie Norm Van Brocklin. In one of his first appearances with the Rams, "The Dutchman" completed three of his eight passes and led the team to one score.

Los Angeles salvaged a 7-7 tie at Pittsburgh the following week when Van Brocklin directed the club 60 yards with less than two minutes to play. Fred Gehrke scored on a one-yard dive with just 24 seconds in the game to tie it and preserve the Rams' two-game lead over Chicago.

The Rams played another thriller with the Chicago Cardinals a week later. The score was tied, 28-28, with 20 seconds left when Cardinal kicking specialist Pat Harder tried a 39-yard field goal. Fred Naumetz stormed through the Chicago line to block the kick and preserve the tie.

Los Angeles took over with 20 seconds remaining. On the first play from scrimmage halfback Tom "Cricket" Kalmanir scampered 51 yards to the Chicago 35-yard line. Waterfield then connected on a 24-yard pass to Fears, moving the ball to the 11-yard line with five seconds to play. Waterfield attempted a 19-yard field goal, but it was blocked and the game ended in a 28-28 tie.

Los Angeles went into the last game of the year against the Washington Redskins needing a victory to clinch the western division crown. The Redskins had struggled all year and brought a 4-6-1 record to the Coliseum. The Rams were atop the western division with a 7-2-2 mark.

The game was never in doubt. Los Angeles jumped out to a 20-7 first quarter lead and held

on to win, 53-27. Waterfield completed 11 of 17 passes for 235 yards. His backup, Norm Van Brocklin, was spectacular. He completed six of 10 passes for 152 yards. Four of Van Brocklin's tosses were good for touchdowns. Sammy Baugh was spectacular in a losing effort for the Redskins. He completed 29 of his 48 passes for 308 yards. The victory clinched the Rams' first western division title since moving to Los Angeles and set up an NFL Championship Game with the Philadelphia Eagles.

The game was played in a downpour at the Coliseum with only 25,245 fans in attendance. The muddy field hampered the Ram passing attack. They were able to cross the 50-yard line only twice and were unable to score.

The team's frustration mounted late in the third period with Philadelphia clinging to a 7-0 lead. Waterfield attempted a punt from his own five, but he slipped in the mud and the kick was blocked. Ed Skladany grabbed the loose ball for Philadelphia and rambled into the end zone to give the Eagles a 14-0 lead. It was the game's last score.

Eagle halfback Steve Van Buren took advantage of the soggy turf and churned out 196 yards on 31 carries to set an NFL playoff rushing record.

The 1949 season established Tom Fears as one of the league's great ends. He set an NFL single-season receiving record by catching 77 passes. The mark broke former Green Bay Packer star Don Hutson's record of 74 receptions in a season.

Despite leading the Rams to their first NFL Western Division title since moving to Los Angeles, Shaughnessy was fired at the end of the year. In two seasons with the club, he coached it to a 14-7-3 mark.

It was also Fred Gehrke's last year with the Rams. During his five seasons with the club, he gained 1,617 yards on 318 carries for a 5.1-yard average. His best season was in 1945, when he helped the Cleveland Rams win the NFL Championship by rushing for seven touchdowns in 12 games.

Page 44: Los Angeles receiver Tom Fears (55) eludes the grasp of Chicago Bear defender George McAfee to score in this 1950 playoff game. Los Angeles held on to win, 24-14, as Fears caught three touchdown passes.

Fred Naumetz 1946–1950

Fred Naumetz was selected by the Cleveland Rams in the 1942 college draft after starring as a linebacker and offensive lineman at Boston College. Rather than join the Rams, Naumetz served in the armed forces. When World War II was over, he found the club had moved to Los Angeles.

Naumetz immediately worked his way into the Rams' starting lineup in 1946. Within two years he was the team captain. The free substitution rule had not been adopted yet, so Naumetz found himself playing both offense and defense.

"My skills were mostly as a linebacker," Naumetz said. "That's where I had the most fun, although I enjoyed playing center too. I was kind of small for a center though. I only weighed 215 or 220 when I was playing, which was small for those days. Playing both ways, I generally averaged 58 to 60 minutes per game."

Naumetz played just five seasons with the Rams, but two of those teams were western conference champions. Both years the Rams lost heartbreakers in the NFL Championship Game. They lost the 1949 title contest to the Philadelphia Eagles, 14-0. A year later they faced the Cleveland Browns for the NFL crown. They were leading Cleveland, 28-27, with less than a minute to play when the roofed caved in.

"It seemed like we had everything under control," Naumetz said. "Then Otto Graham did his thing. He kept hitting those short passes to his receivers and they moved the ball right down the field. Lou Groza kicked a field goal with 28 seconds left to win it. Needless to say we were heartbroken."

The 16-yard field goal gave Cleveland a 30-28 win and the league title. It was Cleveland's first season as a member of the National Football League.

"That Browns' team was super," Naumetz recalled. "Besides the great passing attack, they had Marion Motley at fullback. He had to be the biggest back in the league. And he was fast. They had him listed at 235 pounds, but they must have weighed only one side of him.''

When Los Angeles played the Philadelphia Eagles for the NFL crown in 1949, they also faced one of the game's premier backs, according to Naumetz. In that game, Steve Van Buren rushed for 196 yards against the Rams.

''Van Buren was a tough one to bring down,'' he said. ''He ran all over us. You have to give that guy a lot of credit. He led the Eagles to the championship. Jim Brown reminded me a lot of Van Buren.''

As the club's center, Naumetz was quite familiar with the idio-syncracies of two of football's greatest signal callers—Norm Van Brocklin and Bob Waterfield. The two men alternated at quarterback in 1950, Naumetz' final season with the Rams.

''Well, they were both super people,'' he said. ''I used to say it was like having two Cadillacs in your garage. If one of them was sluggish then you could always start the other one. They were both magnificent athletes. They could kick, punt, pass, whatever needed to be done on the field they could do. And they were great field leaders. They had different person-alities, but they had complete command during a football game.''

In 1950, Naumetz anchored the line for one of the finest offensive teams in league history. The Rams set an NFL record by scoring 466

points in 12 games, an average of 39 points per contest. They accumu-lated 3,709 yards through the air, an average of 309 yards per game. They shattered the previous NFL single-season passing mark by four hundred yards. On the ground, Naumetz led the way for the ''Bull Elephant Backfield'' of Tank Younger, Dan Towler and Dick Hoerner. The backs averaged nearly 4.5 yards per carry.

''To tell you the truth, they didn't need much blocking,'' Naumetz said. ''They were like three fullbacks. All of them weighed about 230, but they were quick. They were fantastic on the goal line. One would carry the ball and the other two would block. They were the original thundering herd.''

Naumetz claims the Los Angeles offense really began to open up in 1948 when Clark Shaughnessy took over as head coach. Shaughnessy had a reputation as an innovative offensive leader. He helped develop the man- in-motion play and the T-Formation.

''Actually a lot of the things you see today, we were doing back then,'' Naumetz said. ''We were one of the first teams to use a spread formation and split out the ends. Shaughnessy used Elroy Hirsch as a flanker back. That was the first time it was used.''

Before taking over the Los Angeles coaching duties, Shaughnessy

was an assistant coach under George Halas at Chicago. Naumetz regards those early Bear teams among the toughest to ever play in the NFL.

''That's when they were the real 'Monsters of the Midway','' Naumetz said. ''On the defensive line, there was two tough ones in George Connor and Ed Sprinkle. They liked to beat on you. Another good team back then was the Chicago Cardinals. They had an outstanding backfield with Charlie Trippi, Pat Harder and their quarterback Paul Christman. That was one of the best backfields around.''

Naumetz claims he was a better linebacker than lineman. But his fondest memories are of the offensive line.

''We had lots of fun on the line,'' he said. ''There was generally some kind of conver-sation going on across the line of scrimmage. I was a little overmatched against guys like Les Bingaman (Detroit Lions). He weighed over 300 pounds. There was no way I could move him out alone. Another big guy was Ed Neal. He played for the Packers and I'm sure he was around 300 pounds too.''

When not playing football, many Ram players were distracted by the glamour of Hollywood during its golden age. Naumetz was one of the Rams that occasionally appeared as an extra in films. Former Rams Glenn Davis and Elroy

Hirsch were the subject of movies.

''One movie I can remember was a foot-ball story starring Victor Mature and Lucille Ball,'' Naumetz said. ''It couldn't have been too good because I'm not even sure of its name. I'm not sure if it was ever released.''

Naumetz made an interesting career change in 1950. He left the Rams to join forces with J. Edgar Hoover and the FBI. But it's his days with the Rams that he'll always cherish.

''I'll never forget those days,'' he said nostalgically. ''The Rams treated us real well. Dan Reeves was a good man to play for. There was a lot of camaraderie on those teams. I'll never forget the fans, either. They were always good to us in Los Angeles.

''I do have one regret, though. My biggest moment with the team came in a game against the Detroit Lions. I intercepted a pass and ran 70 yards for a touchdown. It was the only touchdown I ever scored. I felt like a real halfback out there. But the play was called back because of a clip. I was so mad.

''I still feel some pains from those days when I get up in the morning. I have two artificial hips and a rebuilt knee. But that was just part of the game. There is a positive side to that though. The new joints have helped me straighten out my slice.''

1950–1959

CHAPTER TWO

LOS ANGELES HAS A CHAMPION

I n 1950, Jake LaMotta was the middleweight champion of the world. Sugar Ray Robinson dominated the welterweight ranks. The two met a year later when Robinson moved up to the middleweight division. He then took LaMotta's title in a brutal 15-round bout.

The Brooklyn Dodgers made another run for the pennant in 1950, but ended the season two games behind the Philadelphia Phillies. Preacher Roe and Don Newcombe both won 19 games for the Dodgers.

J.D. Salinger continued to plug away at his new novel that year and in 1951 he finally released "The Catcher in the Rye."

The All-America Football Conference was abandoned prior to the 1950 season after four years of play. Three clubs from the AAFC—the Cleveland Browns, the San Francisco 49ers and the Baltimore Colts—were absorbed into the National Football League. The Rams' intracity rivals, the Los Angeles Dons, folded.

Joe Stydahar was appointed head coach of the Rams. Stydahar had been a star tackle with the Chicago Bears from 1936 to 1946. He joined the Ram staff as an assistant in 1947 before being elevated to the head coaching job. In his first season at the helm, he put together one of the most potent offensive machines in league history. The Rams shattered the NFL record for points scored in a season. They produced 466 points in 12 games, an average of 39-points per contest.

In the college draft, the Rams skipped over All-American lineman Leo Nomellini to choose Villanova fullback Ralph Pasquariello. Pasquariello lasted just one season with the Rams, while Nomellini played in 10 Pro Bowls with the San Francisco 49ers and was selected to Pro Football's Hall of Fame. Among the other new faces on the Rams' squad were guard Stan West from Oklahoma and former Heisman Trophy winner Glenn Davis of West Point. Davis gained fame at Army, along with Doc Blanchard, as one of the "Touchdown Twins."

The Rams made history in 1950 by becoming one of the first teams to have their games regularly televised. Both home and away games were seen locally. The network sponsor then reimbursed the Rams for vacant seats at the Coliseum when the gate fell below a predetermined figure. Thousands of fans stayed at home to watch the games and the average attendance at the Coliseum was only 25,000. At the end of the year, the sponsors found themselves with an enormous bill for the empty seats. The Ram front office was pleased, however, because the added revenue helped them show a profit and the television exposure converted thousands of viewers into Ram fans.

In preseason play, the western division champs chalked up a 3-2 record, including a 70-21 shelling of the Baltimore Colts. Los Angeles scored 10

Fullback Dan Towler bursts over right tackle for a sizable gain against the Chicago Bears. Towler attended USC Theology School while a member of the Rams and later became a minister.

touchdowns against the Colts and gained 641 total yards to set team records in both categories. It was just a sample of the offensive fireworks the Rams would display throughout the year.

The team opened the season at the Coliseum against the Chicago Bears. A disappointing crowd of only 18,219 fans was in attendance to see the Bears prevail, 24-20.

Rookie Glenn Davis was the team's leading ground gainer against the Bears with 33 yards in 10 carries. Waterfield and Van Brocklin continued to alternate at the quarterback position. Waterfield completed nine of 14 passes for 149 yards. Van Brocklin was good on seven of 15 tosses for 114 yards.

The Rams bounced back a week later to beat the New York Yankees, 45-28, before traveling to San Francisco's Kezar Stadium for their first meeting ever with the 49ers. Waterfield opened at quarterback but was knocked out of the game in the second period after a vicious tackle by 49er linebacker Pete Wismann. A 97-yard kickoff return by Verda "Vitamin" T. Smith helped

the Rams build a 21-14 halftime lead.

In the third quarter, the Rams broke the game open when Tank Younger scored on a three-yard run. Deacon Dan Towler followed that by scoring on a 34-yard scamper to give Los Angeles a 35-10 victory. Once again, Glenn Davis was the leading ground gainer, picking up 70 yards on 12 carries and scoring one touchdown.

With a 2-1 record to its credit, Los Angeles traveled to Philadelphia for a rematch with the defending champion Eagles. Philadelphia completely outplayed the Rams, scoring two touchdowns in each quarter to win, 56-20. It was the worst defeat suffered by the Rams since 1942.

Coach Stydahar got his club back on track the next week with a 30-28 win over Bobby Layne and the Detroit Lions. Waterfield was the hero, booting a 10-yard field goal with one minute to play.

Los Angeles then went on the biggest scoring binge in club history, putting 135 points on the scoreboard in two games. The club demolished Baltimore, 70-27, and Detroit, 65-24.

Only 16,025 were on hand at the Coliseum to see the Rams annihilate the Colts for the second time in 1950. Los Angeles had beaten the Colts,

Glenn Davis 1950–1951

Glenn Davis was a household name in the 1940s. While a cadet at West Point, he teamed up with fullback Doc Blanchard. The two were virtually unstoppable. Blanchard was dubbed "Mr. Inside" because of his pile-driving runs through the middle. Davis was called "Mr. Outside" because of his speed and deceptive moves.

Both men won the Heisman Trophy— Blanchard in 1945, and Davis in 1946. Never before or since have two men from the same backfield won consecutive Heisman

Trophies. They led Army to three straight undefeated seasons and National Championships in 1944 and 1945.

In 1947, San Francisco 49er Owner Tony Morabito tried to persuade the two to sign with the 49ers and play during their 90-day furloughs. Army brass quickly prohibited its men from playing pro football while on active duty.

The achievements of Davis and Blanchard were chronicled in a movie entitled "Spirit of West Point." Both men were used in the film. During one scene, Davis

twisted a knee. The injury never completely healed and it eventually cut short his promising professional career.

"Blanchard and I were both in this scene where I caught a punt and ran it about 60 yards," Davis said. "While I was running with the punt, I made a cut and twisted my knee. I had to have it operated on and then laid off the game for three years while I was in the Army. For a person that relies on speed and moves, laying off that long can make it difficult to come back. When I finally started playing with the Rams,

my knee and achilles gave me an awful time. I was kind of handi-capped as a running back."

Davis made his debut with the Rams in 1950 after being released from the Army. In his first year with the club, he gained 416 yards on 88 carries. Davis also caught 42 passes for 593 yards and scored seven touchdowns. Los Angeles went on to win the western conference title that year and advanced to the NFL Championship Game against the Cleveland Browns.

In the championship

game, Davis got things started early. On the first play from scrimmage, he caught a screen pass from Bob Waterfield and ran 82 yards to score. The Rams couldn't capitalize on the touchdown, however. The Browns came back to win the game, 30-28, on Lou Groza's field goal with less than 30 seconds remaining. But Davis' outstanding play that season earned him a spot in the Pro Bowl.

"I really thought we had Cleveland beat in that championship game," he said. "We were ahead most of the game. I'm still not sure Groza made that field goal. It was awfully close. If he did make it, it wasn't by much."

A year later the situation was different. Davis helped the Rams beat Cleveland, 24-17, to capture their first NFL title in Los Angeles.

Moving from the college ranks to the professional game was quite a change for Davis. Army was predominately a running team that rarely threw more than six or seven passes a game. At Los Angeles, Davis was surrounded by two of football's finest quarterbacks in Bob Waterfield and Norm Van Brocklin. Their main targets were Tom Fears and Elroy "Crazy Legs" Hirsch. All four men are in Pro Football's Hall of Fame.

"There was quite a difference in the style of play I was involved in at the professional level," Davis said. "I was used to carrying the ball quite a bit in college. The

Rams were a little different. They liked to throw. It wasn't unusual for them to pass 40-45 times a game. And the passing game was much more precise. The receivers ran patterns that were very exact."

Prior to Davis' arrival, Coach Clark Shaughnessy helped develop the Ram passing game by using the T-Formation almost exclusively. He also became the first coach to use a back as a third receiver when he spread Hirsch wide and created the flanker position.

"I remember those teams because of the amount of talent I was surrounded by," Davis said. "The two quarterbacks, Waterfield and Van Brocklin, were outstanding. That goes without saying because they're already in the Hall of Fame. There was also a lot of camaraderie on those teams."

"Both quarterbacks were great competitors," recalls Davis. "They hated to lose. Their temperaments were a little different, though. Van Brocklin could get hot-headed out there when things went wrong. Waterfield was a little more even-tempered."

Davis remembers the Chicago Bears as one of the most intense rivals the Rams faced. In 1950, the Rams beat Chicago in a playoff before going onto the NFL Championship Game against Cleveland.

"That's when the Bears were really the 'Monsters of the Midway,'" he said. "They had some rough

customers back then. Bulldog Turner was one of those guys you had to watch out for. He would take you apart."

Davis retired from professional football in 1951 after just two seasons with the Rams. He gained 616 yards on 152 carries to maintain a 3.9-yard rushing average during his professional career. He also caught 50 passes for 683 yards. Davis finds it ironic that his playing days were shortened by an injury suffered while filming a movie.

"I was always a pretty durable back in college," he said. "I never got hurt in a game. Even though the injury shortened my career, things worked out for the best. I have no regrets about anything. I'm proud of what I accomplished."

Not many people can list accomplishments that rival those of Glenn Davis. But each of those achievements was the result of a team effort, he says. And playing alongside a Heisman Trophy winner like Doc Blanchard took much of the pressure off of him. Opposing teams could not key on one back.

"Blanchard was a bruising fullback," Davis recalled. "He had the size and speed to go up the middle. He was a pretty good receiver, too. I was used more on off-tackle plays and just tried to outsprint people. I'd also throw an occasional pass.

"We were lucky to play under a good coach at Army. Red Blaik was a West Point grad, so he understood cadets. He

got a lot of respect from the players. Probably his best quality was that he surrounded himself with great assistants. Vince Lombardi was an assistant for a while.

"Winning the Heisman Trophy was the single biggest thrill of my career, but I have to qualify things when I say that. I played on a great team and I couldn't have won it single-handedly. Any guy that wins that award must be on a winning team and be surrounded by outstanding teammates. We went undefeated for three years. We beat Notre Dame by scores of 48-0 and 59-0. That tells you something about the team I was on.

"Besides the NFL championships, the biggest games I played in were all college games. Playing Navy was always a big game for us. At West Point, you could lose every game of the season and beat Navy, and you would consider the season a success.

"In my last game against Navy we were favored by about seven touchdowns. In the first half we jumped out to a 21-0 lead. We went into the locker room thinking we'd beat them about 100-0. They made a great comeback and in the fourth quarter Navy was trailing, 21-17. They were driving and had the ball on the four-yard line when the clock ran out. That's one game I'll always remember because it was my last one for Army."

Dick Hoerner hurdles over the Chicago Bears line to score for Los Angeles. Hoerner played with the Rams from 1947 to 1951 and was selected to the Pro Bowl team in 1950.

70-21, in preseason play. The Rams scored on the first play from scrimmage when Glenn Davis hit ''Crazy Legs'' Hirsch with a 58-yard scoring pass. The Colts never recovered.

Vitamin T. Smith scored two touchdowns, including a 95-yard kickoff return. Bob Boyd, a rookie receiver from Loyola, also scored two touchdowns against the Colts. Hirsch, Waterfield, Fears, Towler, Pasquariello and Dick Hoerner each added a touchdown. Waterfield set a team record by kicking nine extra points. Van Brocklin was the game's leading passer, completing 11 of 14 tosses for 204 yards.

The Rams put on another scoring show against the Lions a week later. They built a 24-10 halftime lead, then exploded for 41 points in the third quarter to win, 65-24. Van Brocklin had the hot hand connecting on 13 of 17 passes including five for touchdowns. Waterfield completed six of nine passes for 136 yards.

Vitamin T. Smith returned another kickoff for a touchdown, his third in three games. This one was returned 93 yards. Smith also scored on a 66-yard pass from Waterfield to give him five touchdowns in three games. Fears added two touchdowns against the Lions, while Van Brocklin, Hirsch, Davis, Towler and Boyd scored once.

After two spectacular victories, the Rams were 20-point favorites against the 49ers at the Coliseum. San Francisco prepared well for the Rams and held a 14-7 lead midway through the third quarter. Then Waterfield sparked the club on a 60-yard march in nine plays. Dick Hoerner scored the touchdown on a two-yard dive. Less than five minutes later, the Rams scored again when Paul Barry plowed over from one yard out. Barry's touchdown gave the Rams a 21-14 lead. They added one final touchdown on an intercepted pass, returned 25 yards by defensive back Tom Keane.

With one game left on the schedule, the Rams were tied for first place with the Chicago Bears. Both teams had 8-3 records. Los Angeles' opponent in the season's final was the Green Bay Packers. Chicago faced the Detroit Lions. Los Angeles took no chances as it rolled over the Packers, 51-14. But Chicago squeaked by Detroit, 6-3, to set up a conference playoff between the Rams and the Bears.

Quarterback Bob Waterfield picks up some tough yardage against the Cleveland Browns. Tony Adamle (74) makes the tackle.

Several days before the game Waterfield was stricken with the flu and was unable to practice. His temperature soared to 103 degrees by game time. Although Waterfield suited up, Van Brocklin got the starting call at quarterback. A shirt-sleeve crowd of nearly 84,000 packed the Coliseum as Waterfield watched from the sidelines. Early in the game, Van Brocklin was hit hard and suffered a broken rib. The injury affected Van Brocklin's throwing ability and he missed on eight straight passing attempts. With Van Brocklin obviously in pain, Waterfield began to loosen his arm on the sideline.

In the second quarter, Chicago held a 7-3 lead when Waterfield took over for the injured Van Brocklin. Before the half ended, Waterfield threw touchdown passes of 68 and 28 yards to Tom Fears to give Los Angeles a 17-7 lead.

Waterfield continued to have a hot hand in the second half, throwing another touchdown pass of 22 yards to Fears. In a remarkable display of courage and stamina, Waterfield finished the day with 14 completions for 280 yards. He also han-

dled all the punting and. kicking chores. He booted three extra points and a 43-yard field goal in the 24-14 Los Angeles win. Fears was the leading receiver in the game with seven receptions for 199 yards.

The victory gave the Rams their second consecutive western division crown and enabled them to advance to the NFL Championship Game against the Cleveland Browns. The Browns were in their first season of NFL play after winning four consecutive titles in the AAFC. Cleveland defeated the New York Giants in a playoff to advance to the championship game.

Ironically, the Rams returned to Cleveland, the site of the team's beginning, to play for the championship. A disappointing crowd of just 29,751 was on hand at Municipal Stadium to watch the Christmas Eve clash. One reason for the dismal turnout was the brutal weather. The temperature hovered near 25 degrees at game time with occasional snow flurries.

The Rams raced to a 7-0 lead on the very first play from scrimmage when Waterfield passed 82 yards to Glenn Davis. But Cleveland came back to tie the game at 7-7. On its next possession, Los Angeles drove 67 yards and scored again on Dick Hoerner's four-yard run. The Rams added

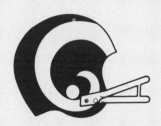

Woodley Lewis 1950–1955

Woodley Lewis was a rookie when the Rams faced the Cleveland Browns in the 1950 NFL Championship Game. In the waning seconds of the game, Los Angeles was clinging to a 28-27 lead. Otto Graham was at quarterback for the Browns. Lewis was in Los Angeles' defensive backfield. His objective was to cover either Dante Lavelli or Dub Jones, depending on which one lined up on his side of the field. Both of them were All-Pros.

"That was a tough assignment," Lewis said. "Jones and Lavelli were pretty good receivers, but the Browns also had Mac Speedie. He was good too. It wasn't the receivers that beat us though. Otto Graham outsmarted us. He was good at picking up what was happening on the field. On one play, we had the receivers covered and Graham took off running. That's what got them in position for the field goal."

With just 28 seconds to play, Lou Groza came on to kick a 16-yard field goal. It gave Cleveland a 30-28 victory.

"Cleveland was always one of the top teams in the league," Lewis said. "Marion Motley was a heck of a back for them. He was one of the first big backs. He weighed in at about 235."

Despite the loss to Cleveland, Lewis' rookie season was a resounding success. He intercepted 12 passes that year and returned them 275 yards. He led the league in both categories and was selected to play in the Pro Bowl game.

Lewis roamed the Los Angeles secondary until 1955, when he was traded to the Chicago

Cardinals. During his six seasons with the Rams, Lewis was not only a standout defensive back, he was an exciting kick returner. He is second on the club's all-time kickoff return list with 2,603 yards. He was also one of the league's most effective punt returners. Between 1950 and 1960 he gained 1,026 yards on returns. Only one man had more return yardage during that time—Hall of Famer Emlen Tunnell.

In one game against the Detroit Lions in 1953, Lewis returned three kickoffs a total of 174 yards. He gained another 120 yards on punt returns that day.

"That was probably the best all-around day I ever had in football," Lewis said. "I also got two interceptions."

Like most kick returners, Lewis recalls one runback above all the others. It happened against the San Francisco 49ers before 90,000 people in the Los Angeles Coliseum. He returned the kick 94 yards for a touchdown.

"It was muddy and wet on the field," he said. "As soon as I caught the punt, Charlie Powell from the 49ers went right past me. He couldn't slow down in the mud. I started up field and could see two guys had the angle on me near the sideline. I quickly stopped and they went sliding past me too. I had clear sailing the rest of the way, but just as I was about to cross the goal line, here comes Charlie Powell again. He missed me twice on that one kick."

Lewis was not strictly a defensive player. He also doubled as an offensive threat. He was comfortable at either wide receiver or running back, but it was as a receiver that he really made his mark. Lewis nabbed 123 passes for 1,885 yards and 12 touchdowns in his career and averaged 15.3 yards per catch.

"I liked the offensive side, but defensive back was a challenging position to play," Lewis said. "I was fortunate to have good coaches at Oregon and gained a lot of knowledge and skills there. I think the most important quality for a secondary man, after knowledge of the game, is speed. You have to keep up with those big, fast receivers.

"I kept myself in pretty good shape. You have to be in tip-top condition to play football. When you start having those two-a-day drills in camp, you get awfully stiff and sore if you're not ready."

Lewis played with two of pro football's best receivers in Elroy Hirsch and Tom Fears. Since he practiced against the best, he had high standards from which to judge the rest of the league's pass catchers. He is unequivocal about the best receiver he faced in his 11 years of pro ball.

"Cloyce Box (Detroit Lions) was quite a competitor," he said. "He had all the tools. He was a fast, big guy, and he had excellent hands. There were a couple of other ends who were very good. Gordy Soltau up in San Francisco and

Bill Howton of Green Bay deserve credit. Of course, we had some pretty good receivers in Tom Fears and Elroy Hirsch."

In 1952, Lewis was joined in the Ram secondary by Dick "Night Train" Lane. Lane was an immediate star with Los Angeles. As a rookie, he intercepted 14 passes, an NFL record. After just two seasons with the Rams, he was traded to the Chicago Cardinals. Lane was later enshrined in Pro Football's Hall of Fame.

"Now, he was a hell of a player," Lewis said. "I worked with 'Night Train' quite a bit. He was a very aggressive tackler. On pass coverage he was able to recover well if he got in trouble. He was rarely off-balance."

Lewis rates Lane the best defensive back that ever played. Among the other good defensive backs he's seen are Emlen Tunnell, who played most of his career with the New York Giants, Abe Woodson of the San Francisco 49ers and St. Louis Cardinals, and Jim David from the Detroit Lions.

"It's hard to compare these guys with the present-day players," Lewis said. "Tunnell and Woodson did everything. They handled punts and kicks, played defense and could play offense too. Most of today's guys are specialists. But back then we only had 34-35 players on the roster, so you had to be versatile."

Lewis looks back with respect on former team

owner Dan Reeves and head coaches Joe Stydahar, Hampton Pool and Sid Gillman. He even finds humor in the circumstances surrounding his trade to the Cardinals.

"The Rams sponsored a team party at the Beverly Hills Hotel and Sid Gillman was introducing all the players," Lewis said. "He introduced me and said, 'Now, here's a guy that's going to be with the club a long time.' The next day they told me they traded me. I couldn't believe it. I was a little mad at first, but now I find it kind of funny."

Lewis continues to follow football closely, although his allegiance has switched to the Los Angeles Raiders. Lewis, who still lives in the Los Angeles area, says Anaheim is too far to go to watch the Rams. He now buys season tickets to the Raider games.

"The name of the game is still the same," he said. "Blocking and tackling is what you have to do. The biggest change I have seen is in the equipment. We didn't have face masks for a while. I remember a game against Detroit. Leon Hart hit me square in the face with his head gear. It broke my nose. My whole face was black and blue.

"I was lucky though. One of the things I am most happy about is getting out of the game alive. I'm in good shape. I had no severe injuries. Many of the people I played with start to feel those injuries when they get older. I don't have any of those problems."

two more touchdowns in the third quarter on a two-yard run by Hoerner and an eight-yard fumble return by Larry Brink. However, Cleveland kept pace with the Rams and at the end of three quarters, Los Angeles led just 28-20.

It was the skillful passing of Otto Graham and the running of Marion Motley that kept Cleveland in the game. Early in the fourth quarter, the Browns cut the margin to 28-27 on a 14-yard pass from Graham to Rex Baumgardner. The Rams were unable to score in the final period, and with just two minutes to play, Cleveland took over at its own 32-yard line.

Graham ran for 17 yards on the first play from scrimmage, giving the Browns a first down on the 49-yard line. He then moved the ball steadily downfield with passes to Baumgardner and Dub Jones. With 20 seconds left, 240-pound tackle Lou Groza was called on to attempt a 22-yard field goal. Groza booted the ball through the uprights to give Cleveland a 30-28 win and its first NFL title. The winners received $1,113. The loser's share was $686.

Eight Rams were selected to play in the Pro Bowl at season's end, including quarterbacks Bob Waterfield and Norm Van Brocklin, receiver Tom Fears, running backs Glenn Davis and Dick Hoerner, tackle Dick Huffman, defensive back Woodley Lewis and defensive end Larry Brink.

Tom Fears had another outstanding year. He broke his own NFL mark of 77 catches in a season by grabbing 84 passes. In one game against the Packers, he caught 18 passes to set a single-game reception record.

1951 Stydahar's goal in the 1951 college draft was to strengthen the offensive and defensive lines. Among his choices were first-round pick Bud McFadin, a guard from Texas, tackle Charley Toogood from Nebraska and defensive end Andy Robustelli from Arnold College. Robustelli eventually was selected to Pro Football's Hall of Fame.

Los Angeles got off to a great start by winning its first four exhibition games. Excitement was high and local reporters were predicting another western division title for the Rams. The forecasts looked accurate after the Rams beat the New York Yanks in the league opener, 54-14. Van Brocklin was unstoppable in that game. He set an

Elroy Hirsch gets behind Green Bay Packer defender to haul in a 73-yard touchdown pass.

NFL record by throwing for 554 yards. The Dutchman completed 27 of 41 passes, including five for touchdowns. The Rams had 735 yards of total offense to shatter the old NFL record of 682 yards, set by the New York Giants in 1943.

Los Angeles met its match in the second game of the season against the Cleveland Browns. In their first rematch since the 1950 championship game, Cleveland reaffirmed its superiority with a 38-23 win.

The Browns ran right at the Rams, gaining 307 yards on the ground and another 219 yards passing. Marion Motley, the Browns 235-pound fullback, gained 106 yards in 13 carries. Dub Jones added 110 yards on 15 carries.

The Rams regrouped and beat the Detroit Lions a week later, 27-21, then shut out Green Bay, 28-0, to land in a first-place tie with the Chicago Bears. After a loss at San Francisco, Los Angeles won four of its next six games to post a 7-4 record. With one game left in the season, Los Angeles was 1/2 game behind the Detroit Lions. Detroit was scheduled to play the San Francisco

49ers on the last day of the season, while the Rams faced the Green Bay Packers. A 49er victory, coupled with a Los Angeles win, would give the Rams their third consecutive western division title. Everything went according to plan. The 49ers squeaked by Detroit, while Los Angeles blitzed the Packers, 42-14.

For the second year in a row, the Rams faced the Cleveland Browns in the NFL title game. Nearly 60,000 fans made their way into the Coliseum to see the rematch. After a scoreless first half, Waterfield got the Rams moving and drove them 55 yards to the two-yard line. Fullback Dick Hoerner scored from there to give Los Angeles a 7-0 edge.

The two teams battled back and forth, and midway through the fourth quarter, the game was tied at 17-17. Van Brocklin was at quarterback for the Rams. With eight minutes to play, he unleashed a 73-yard touchdown pass to Tom Fears to put Los Angeles on top, 24-17. The Rams held Cleveland the rest of the way to win the world championship. The victory allowed each Ram to collect $2,108. Each Cleveland player received $1,483.

Waterfield and Van Brocklin both were selected to play in the Pro Bowl at the conclusion of the season. Defensive end Larry Brink made the team for the second time. Elroy Hirsch, Don Paul, Dan Towler, Stan West and Tank Younger all were selected to play in their first Pro Bowl.

It was Dick Hoerner's last year with Los Angeles. During his five season's with the club, he gained 2020 yards in 457 carries. He was the team's leading rusher in 1948, when he gained 354 yards, and in 1949, with 592 yards. He scored 27 rushing touchdowns for the Rams, including a team high of 10 in 1950.

1952 In the 1952 college draft, the Rams won the coveted bonus pick which gave them the league's first draft choice. They selected Vanderbilt quarterback Bill Wade. Wade did not challenge Van Brocklin and Waterfield for the starting quarterback spot that season because he was committed to two years of military duty before he could join the Rams.

Los Angeles started the year by winning its first four preseason games, including a 10-7 win over the College All-Stars. Then things began to sour.

The Rams lost their last three exhibition games and were demolished by the Cleveland Browns in the league opener, 37-7. A 15-yard run by Dan Towler in the fourth quarter averted a shutout at Cleveland. Towler was the only offensive weapon for the Rams. He gained 65 yards on 11 carries. Waterfield and Van Brocklin completed just three passes apiece.

After the game, Coach Joe Stydahar resigned and his assistant, Hampton Pool, was named head coach. Stydahar had a 17-7 record in two seasons with the Rams, including two straight

Page 54: Elroy "Crazy Legs" Hirsch hangs on to a Bob Waterfield pass as New York Yankee defensive back Pete Layden attempts to knock the ball away. **This page:** Tackle Gene Lipscomb (78), who is 6-7, hoists 6-4 Don Burroughs on his shoulders in an effort to block a field goal by Chicago Bear George Blanda. The 48-yard kick was good.

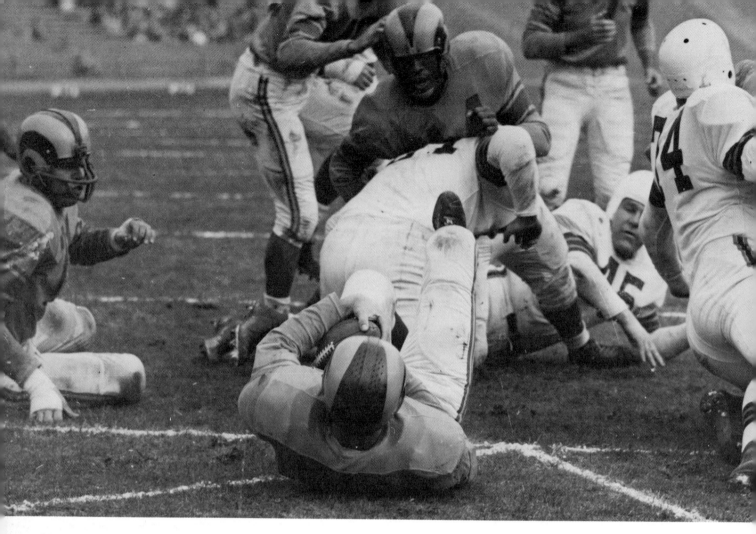

Fullback Dick Hoerner dives into the end zone to score against the Cleveland Browns. Los Angeles beat the Browns, 24-17, to win the NFL title. **Page 59:** Jim Winkler, a 250-pound Los Angeles tackle, stops the 49ers' Verl Lillywhite from gaining any yardage as the Rams beat San Francisco at the Coliseum in 1951.

appearances in the NFL Championship Game.

The Rams' rocky start continued under Pool as they lost two of their next three games. Pool finally got the club back on track with a 31-7 win over the Chicago Bears. Towler paced the Rams' offense with 124 yards rushing in 16 carries.

The win turned the season around for Los Angeles. They went on to win eight straight games. Going into the last game of the season, Los Angeles was tied with the Detroit Lions for first place at 8-3. They needed a win over the Pittsburgh Steelers to force a playoff with the Lions.

Nearly 73,000 fans braved 101 degree temperatures at the Coliseum to watch the contest. But it wasn't the sun that scorched the Steelers, it was quarterback Norm Van Brocklin. He com-

pleted 17 of 28 passes for 289 yards and three touchdowns to lead the Rams to a 28-14 win. Tom Fears hauled in two scoring passes, while Hirsch caught a 63-yard touchdown pass. Dan Towler added 74 yards in 12 carries. He finished the year as the NFL's leading rusher with 894 yards.

Dick "Night Train" Lane was the defensive hero of the game. He nabbed three interceptions and returned one 42 yards for a touchdown. Lane set an NFL record in 1952 by intercepting 14 passes.

The Rams traveled to Briggs Stadium in Detroit for the conference playoff with the Lions. Detroit was led by backs Bobby Layne, Doak Walker and Pat Harder, and receivers Leon Hart and Cloyce Box. In contrast with the 100-degree weather at the Coliseum a week earlier, Detroit was experiencing temperatures in the low 30s.

Detroit held a 21-7 lead in the third quarter when Van Brocklin marched the Rams 80 yards to the five-yard line. Four cracks from the five gained only four yards and the Rams came away empty-handed. Los Angeles posted two touchdowns in the fourth quarter to close the score to 24-21, but that was the closest they got. Detroit held on to win 31-21 and take the league title.

Dan Towler 1950–1955

It seemed unlikely that a 25th-round draft pick from tiny Washington and Jefferson College would make it to the NFL in 1950. But Deacon Dan Towler was not an ordinary running back.

After a mediocre rookie season, Towler came on like gang busters. In his second year with the Rams, he led the NFL in rushing and was a star in the Pro Bowl. He gained 894 yards that season

as Los Angeles went on to win the 1951 NFL Championship Game over the Cleveland Browns. In the Pro Bowl, he gained over 100 yards and was named the most valuable player. It was the first of Towler's four straight appearances in the post-season all-star classic.

"I remember that Pro Bowl Game because it was played in the rain and mud," he said. "I had a good day and

ended up gaining more yardage than the other club's entire backfield. I was excited to be playing with the best players in football. The thing that really thrilled me though, was leading the team in a prayer before the game. Here were these huge hunks down on their knees on the floor of the Coliseum, praying. I was really excited to be a part of that."

As good as Towler was with a football

tucked under his arm, he considered it nothing more than an extra-curricular activity. While playing for the Rams, he was also a full-time theology student. When he wasn't running over linebackers, he was attending USC, where he earned a master's degree in theology.

"It wasn't easy studying while I played, but I liked going to school," said Towler. "When we were on the road, I would fly back home immediately after a game so I could get to class on Monday. Sometimes the team was on the road for two or three weeks at a time, so then I would have to fly back to meet them again for games. The Rams were very understanding about it. I had to miss quite a bit of practice because of school, but they never complained about it."

Towler anchored one of the most punishing running trios in league history. The Rams' "Bull Elephant Backfield" of the early 1950s consisted of Towler, Paul "Tank" Younger and Dick Hoerner.

"We all weighed over 220 pounds," Towler said. "We had plays designed so that two of us would block for the ball carrier. That's about 450 pounds coming at the exposed linebacker. He would generally get out of the way or get crunched. We were all interchangeable. All of us could play any of the three running back positions."

The team's overwhelming running game made it easier for the team's passing attack to click. If opposing teams concentrated on the Rams' running backs, quarterbacks Bob Waterfield and Norm Van Brocklin would open up the aerial game.

"Linebackers couldn't move into pass coverage against us," Towler said. "They were frozen. They had to watch for the running game and that opened things up for the quarterbacks."

Van Brocklin and Waterfield often alternated between quarters. The man with the hot hand on Sunday generally got the most playing time. Towler claims it was a rare day when one of them did not have the hot hand.

"Waterfield was a fantastic all-around player," he said. "He could punt, run, kick extra points and field goals, play defense and he was an excellent passer. He was like a big brother to me. He made me feel like I belonged. Van Brocklin was an outstanding passer. He couldn't run, but he had a stronger arm. He was a pure passer.

"They had different personalities. Waterfield was more personable. You played your best for him because you loved him. Van Brocklin was ruthless. You played just as hard for him, but it was out of fear. If you made a mistake he would cuss you out or get you out of the game.

"We had some outstanding coaches at that time too," Towler said. "Joe Stydahar was the head man and Hampton Pool was the backfield coach. I considered Hampton Pool an offensive genius. Red Hickey was also good with the receivers."

When Towler joined the club in 1950, there were very few black players in the league. But the Los Angeles organization went out of its way to make him feel welcome, Towler says. Even in other NFL cities there were rarely signs of racial discrimination.

"There were small incidents here and there, nothing big,"

Towler said. "That was mostly in the south. I found that when you do something well, people appreciate that, regardless. Anyway, people couldn't tell Tank (Younger) and I apart. People would yell at me thinking it was him and vica versa."

Since Towler's retirement in 1955, religious work has been the major focus of his life. Still, football played a big part in his development as a person and influenced his religious thinking.

"Football was one of the greatest things in my life," he said. "I was fortunate to be able to play the game. I hurt my knee as a senior in college and had to have it operated on. Having a knee opeartion at that time (1949) was a lot different than today. The Rams still picked me, although it was on the 25th round. They coddled me along and watched out for me. Bob Waterfield was one of the guys who watched out for me. He was a magnificent human being. He was like a big brother to me.

"I feel very fortunate to have played for the Rams. They were always a class organization. I didn't really expect to stay with the club since I was a low draft pick, but they took care of me. I was able to get my master's degree and still play football. I'll always be thankful for that.

"Dan Reeves was the owner when I got started. He liked football and he liked the players. Later on, some other people were involved in

the Rams' ownership, like Bob Hope, but they always went out of their way for the players."

In his six seasons of pro ball, Towler set several Los Angeles rushing records. Many have since been broken. Nevertheless, he is fourth on the team's all-time rushing list with 3,493 yards in 672 carries. His rushing average of 5.2 yards per carry is the highest in team history. Eric Dickerson is second with a 5.1-yard average. Towler is also the team's all-time leader in rushing touchdowns with 44. That record will soon be broken by Eric Dickerson.

"You have to remember that we didn't carry the ball a lot back then," Towler said. "Not like you see Dickerson carrying today. If you carried 15 times a game that was a lot. The team wasn't built around one guy. We had people like Tom Fears, Bob Boyd and Elroy Hirsch catching a lot of passes and there were about four running backs that carried the ball regularly."

During his football career Towler strived to be the best player on the field. It's an attitude he retains to this day and often preaches to the young people he encounters in his daily work.

"Whatever you do in life, do it with all your might," Towler said. "Do it good, do it clean and do it the best you can. That's all you can ask of yourself."

Fullback Dick Hoerner plows through the Detroit Lions for a 22-yard gain. Clearing the way for Hoerner is tackle Charlie Toogood. Detroit halfback Don Doll (44) tries to make the tackle.

Despite the loss, Van Brocklin continued his hot passing. He completed 15 of 19 passes for 166 yards and a touchdown.

The Detroit game marked the end of Bob Waterfield's professional football career after eight seasons with the Rams. During that time, Los Angeles competed in four NFL championship games and won two league crowns. In his career, Waterfield completed 814 of 1618 passes for 11,849 yards. He threw 99 touchdown passes and rushed for 13 scores.

Waterfield was also one of the league's most accurate kickers. He made 315 of 336 extra point attempts and connected on 60 of 110 field goal tries. He set a club record in 1951 by kicking five field goals in a game against Detroit. As a punter, he averaged 42.4 yards per kick, including an 88-yard punt that is the longest in club history. Only Sammy Baugh, with a 44.9-yard average, had a higher punting average during the 1940s. Waterfield is the Rams' all-time leading scorer with 573 points.

1953 The Rams made a blockbuster trade before the 1953 season when they dealt 11 players to the Dallas Texans for rookie linebacker Les Richter. Unfortunately, Richter entered the Army and was unable to play in 1953. In the draft, Los Angeles selected quarterback Rudy Bukich of USC in the second round and tackle Bob Fry of Kentucky in the third round.

The Rams opened the regular season as a nine-point favorite over the New York Giants. Los Angeles won convincingly, 21-7, on the arm and leg of Van Brocklin. "The Dutchman" completed 13 of 26 passes for 203 yards and threw touchdown passes of 15 yards to Tom Fears and 16 yards to Elroy Hirsch. He also averaged 49 yards on six punts.

After a heartbreaking, 31-30, loss to the San Francisco 49ers, the Rams reeled off wins over Green Bay and Chicago and twice beat the World Champion Detroit Lions. In one win over the Lions at the Coliseum, a league record 93,757 fans were in attendance. The Rams were beginning to look like contenders.

But a midseason slump knocked the Rams out of the playoff picture. They lost close games to San Francisco, 31-27, and the Chicago Bears, 24-21, and tied the Chicago Cardinals. The Rams closed the season with decisive wins over the Baltimore Colts, 45-2, and the Green Bay Packers, 33-17. Los Angeles finished in third place with an 8-3-1 record.

Six Rams were selected to play in the Pro Bowl. Norm Van Brocklin made the team for the fourth straight year. Elroy Hirsch, Dan Towler, Tank Younger and Don Paul all played in their third Pro Bowl. Future Hall of Fame defensive end Andy Robustelli was selected for the first time. Center Leon McLaughlin was named the team's Most Valuable Player.

1954 Quarterback Bill Wade and linebacker Les Richter joined the Rams in 1954 after finishing their military duty. They were the only prizes in the club's rookie crop that year.

Los Angeles looked strong in preseason play. The club won its first five exhibition matches before opening the season at Baltimore. The Rams continued their strong play as they demolished the hapless Colts, 48-0. Van Brocklin completed 15 of 19 passes for 293 yards and two touchdowns. Wade saw action in his first league game and completed three of six passes for 79 yards. He also scored on a five-yard run.

The Rams struggled through the rest of the year, playing .500 football. The high point of the season was a 42-38 win over Chicago. Against the powerful Bear defense, Tank Younger rushed 27 times for 188 yards and Dan Towler carried 15 times for 123 yards. Van Brocklin passed for 253 yards to help the Rams pile up 557 yards of total offense.

Before the final game of the year against the Green Bay Packers, the Rams presented new Oldsmobiles to Elroy Hirsch and team captain Don Paul as retirement gifts. The gesture proved to be premature. Paul came back to play one more season and Hirsch played three more years with the Rams.

Los Angeles went on to defeat Green Bay, 35-27. Wade played three quarters and hit on 18 of 28 passes for 290 yards. The win gave Los Angeles a 6-5-1 record, but it was the club's poorest showing since 1947.

Halfback Jon Arnett displays his running ability in this photo. He takes a screen pass from quarterback Bill Wade and runs 72 yards through the Chicago Bears defense to the three-yard line.

Hampton Pool and his staff resigned at the end of the 1954 season and Sid Gillman, the head football coach at the University of Cincinnati, was hired to replace him.

1955 In the 1955 college draft, Los Angeles used its first two picks to select linebacker Larry Morris of Georgia Tech and running back Cecil Taylor of Kansas State. With its 30th choice, USF basketball star K.C. Jones was selected as an end. Jones went on to become a great basketball player and coach with the Boston Celtics.

After winning five games in the exhibition season, the Rams opened the regular season with wins over San Francisco, Pittsburgh and Detroit. Against the Steelers, they needed the clutch kicking of Les Richter to pull out a win. Richter booted a 30-yard field goal with one second on the clock to beat Pittsburgh, 27-26.

Five weeks into the season, the Rams gained undisputed possession of first place by beating the western division champion Detroit Lions.

Trailing 13-10 in the fourth quarter, Van Brocklin rallied his team to two touchdowns. Hirsch scored one touchdown on a 46-yard pass from Van Brocklin. Four minutes later, Ron Waller ran one in from the 21-yard line to give Los Angeles a 24-13 win. Waller, a rookie running back from Maryland, was the game's star. He gained 132 yards on 16 rushing attempts.

On the final day of the season, Los Angeles was still on top of the division with a 7-3-1 record. The Chicago Bears were in second place at 7-4. A win over the Green Bay Packers would give Los Angeles the western conference title. The Rams whipped the Packers, 31-17.

Los Angeles hosted the Cleveland Browns in the 1955 NFL Championship Game at Memorial Coliseum. Cleveland won the eastern conference with a 9-2-1 mark and was making its sixth straight appearance in the championship game. The Cleveland roster consisted of many of the same players who participated in the 1951 title contest against the Rams. Otto Graham, Dante Lavelli, Dub Jones and Lou Groza were just a handful of the Brown stars.

Nearly 88,000 fans packed the Coliseum for the matchup. The Browns took a 17-7 lead at halftime. Los Angeles' sole touchdown came on a

Bill Wade 1954–1960

When Bill Wade was drafted by the Rams in 1952 he received the highest compliment a rookie could possibly receive.

As the team's bonus choice, he was the first player selected in the college draft. Despite having two of the greatest quarterbacks in the game in Bob Waterfield and Norm Van Brocklin, the Rams picked Wade over some of the most talented collegians to come along in years. Among the graduating seniors that year were Hugh McElhenny, Babe Parilli, Ollie Matson and Frank Gifford. Wade was selected before all of them.

Wade did not join the club immediately. After graduating from Vanderbilt, he spent two years in the Navy before reporting to the Rams in 1954. By that time Bob Waterfield had retired, but the Rams still had two accomplished quarterbacks in camp. Wade found himself competing with future Hall of Famer Norm Van Brocklin, and Rudy Bukich, a second-round draft choice in 1953.

One of the first things Wade noticed was the different lifestyle enjoyed in Southern California. It was quite a change from his hometown of Nashville, Tennessee.

"I'd never been west of the Rockies until I went in the Navy," Wade said. "When I reported to the Rams, it was a whole different thing. I was thrilled to meet movie stars like Jane Russell, who was married to Bob Waterfield, and Bob Hope, who was part owner of the team. In fact, I'll never forget Bob Hope sending me a Christmas Card one year. He probably doesn't remember it, but it's something I'll never forget. It was a lot different from anything I experienced in Nashville.''

Van Brocklin had a lock on the starting quarterback position in Wade's rookie season. He saw limited action during that year, but when Van Brocklin was traded to the Philadelphia Eagles after the 1957 season, Wade stepped into the starter's role. He immediately got the offense rolling.

In 1958, his first year as the starter, Wade broke virtually every club passing record and was selected to play in the Pro Bowl. He completed 181 of his 341 passes for 2,875 yards, setting records in all three categories. His 2,875 yards passing was just 63 yards short of the NFL single-season record set by Sammy Baugh in 1943.

''I did things a lot different from Van Brocklin,'' Wade said. ''He had his methods, which I didn't always agree with, and I had mine. He got most of the playing time when he was around, but I won the starting position fair and square in 1958.''

Since joining the NFL in 1945, Los Angeles has consistently had one of the best passing attacks in football. With Wade at the controls, the Rams continued to throw the ball. Wade claims he was always an accurate passer, but he also was lucky to work with some of the best receivers in football.

''The Rams always had reliable receivers,'' Wade said. ''But my favorite was whoever ran the proper pass pattern. I didn't like sloppy patterns. I liked to throw to Tom Fears and Elroy Hirsch. Both were outstanding receivers. Del Shofner was another good one. In fact, it was Shofner and I that developed the comeback pass.''

Surprisingly, one of Wade's favorite receivers played just one season with the Rams. He left the club to pursue business interests.

''I'll tell you who was one of the best receivers the Rams had,'' he said. ''Ron Miller. He came from Southern Cal. He was pretty good size, about 6-4. He got married to one of the Disney's, Diane Disney I believe, and only played one year. He would have been fantastic.''

While calling the signals, Wade often found himself peering over the line of scrimmage into the eyes of football's most feared defensive players. Without hesitation he names the most intimidating players he's faced.

''Dick Butkus was probably the greatest linebacker I ever played against or with,'' he said. ''He would definitely try to put a little fear into you. Luckily, I was on his side in my later years at Chicago.

'' 'Big Daddy' Lipscomb was a phenomenal athlete. I remember the first time I saw him he was playing for the Marine Corps football team. He was about 6-8 and 285 and he was lean. I was awestruck. I'd never seen anyone that big. And he was quick too.

''Herb Adderly was one of the best cornerbacks I ever played against. He was big enough to knock fullbacks down and he was fast enough to keep up with receivers that were sprinters.''

Wade continues to have a love affair with football's passing attack. He still follows the game closely and constantly watches for new quarterbacks that are coming along or new developments in the aerial game.

''I love to watch passing teams,'' Wade said. ''I think it is the most delicate and beautiful aspect of football. That's why I enjoy watching teams like the San Diego Chargers, and Brigham Young at the college level. Coryell does a good job at San Diego. Those teams like to throw. Of course, they have the talent to make it work.

''One of my favorite quarterbacks right now is Jim McMahon,'' Wade said. ''I admire McMahon. I like the way he plays the game. If I was starting a football franchise, I'd have to take McMahon at quarterback. He's a clutch player. We saw that in the playoffs last year. He's got the desire. And another good quality he has is he avoids throwing into crowds. Those are the things I like in a quarterback.''

Wade finished his playing days with the Chicago Bears in 1966. During his career, he completed 1,379 of his 2,523 passing attempts. He also threw for 18,530 yards and 124 touchdowns. He is now a banker in Nashville and fondly recalls his days as a professional quarterback. One of the things he misses is the camaraderie he shared with his former teammates.

''In the banking business I have some good friends,'' he said. ''But in football there was so much more camaraderie. The friendships you make in football are deeper. I think when there is a possibility of violent injury like in war, or to a lesser extent football, the friendships you establish are much deeper. You count on each other so much more. You have to watch out for the well being of your teammate.

''I always worked hard as the devil when I was playing. I never missed practice. I think I might have missed one practice in 14 years and that was because I was making a commercial for George Halas. I loved football. I love to watch it today. I still keep myself in shape doing leglifts and stuff. If I wanted to, I could still go out and throw a football 70 yards.

''Ability can only take you so far though. In my case, God played a big role both on and off the field. I have a strong belief in God and always wanted to use my God-given talent. I think that helped make me a successful quarterback.''

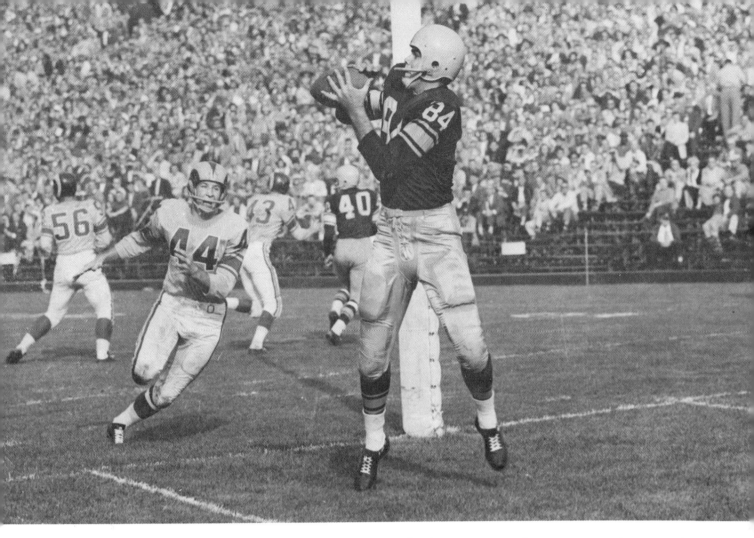

Green Bay Packer end Gary Knafelc (84) grabs a 15-yard scoring pass over Los Angeles defensive back Jesse Whittenton. **Pages 66-67:** The Ram defense closes in on Detroit Lion fullback Bill Bowman. Harland Svare grabs Bowman around the waist, while tackle Lewis ''Bud'' McFadin prepares to hit Bowman at the knees. Gene ''Big Daddy'' Lipscomb (78) and Andy Robustelli (84) are in close pursuit. **Page 68:** Ram halfback Paul Barry runs into the goal post as he crosses the goal line in a game against the San Francisco 49ers in 1950. Dan Towler (32), Bob Waterfield (7) look on as Barry scores.

67-yard pass from Van Brocklin to running back Skeet Quinlan.

In the third quarter, the Browns erupted for 21 unanswered points to build a 38-7 lead. Graham, who was playing in his last NFL game, ran for two Cleveland scores and threw a touchdown pass. Meanwhile, the Rams were stymied by Cleveland's defense. Van Brocklin was pressured all afternoon as the Browns intercepted seven passes.

Los Angeles scored one last touchdown in the fourth quarter on a four-yard run by Ron Waller to make the final score 38-14. Each Los Angeles player received $2,316 for participating in the championship game. The winner's received $3,508 apiece.

The Rams set a single-season attendance mark in 1955 by drawing 397,997 fans to their home games, an increase of 71,000 from their 1954 attendance figure.

1956 The Rams returned to camp in 1956 eager to repeat as western division champions. They won their league opener over Philadelphia, 27-7, then dropped eight of their next nine games. Wade and Van Brocklin alternated at quarterback during that stretch. Included in the losses were a 42-17 blowout at Green Bay and a 56-21 loss at Baltimore.

On the final day of the 1956 season, Tom Fears was honored for his contributions to the franchise. It was declared Tom Fears Day at the Coliseum and the future Hall of Famer was presented with a 1957 station wagon as a retirement gift.

In his last game as a Los Angeles Ram, Fears failed to catch a pass. Instead, the game belonged to Van Brocklin and rookie running back Tom Wilson. Van Brocklin completed 17 of 22 passes for 289 yards and three touchdowns. The 23-year-old Wilson never played college football but against the Packers no one noticed. He established a pro football rushing record by gaining

223 yards on 23 carries.

Los Angeles' 4-8 record was its worst showing in 15 years. It left the Rams stranded in the western conference cellar with the Green Bay Packers.

1957 After several years of poor college picks, the Rams finally got some blue-chip players in the 1957 draft. They chose running back Jon Arnett from USC in the first round, Texas A&M linebacker Jack Pardee in the second round and Arkansas tackle Billy Ray Smith in the third round.

Changes were made in the front office also. Publicity director Pete Rozelle was named the club's general manager during the offseason.

Van Brocklin looked sharp in preseason play as the Rams whipped the California All-Stars, a group of semi-pro players, 84-0. The offense continued to roll up big scores in wins over the Washington Redskins 45-14, the Chicago Cardinals, 63-21, and the San Francisco 49ers, 58-27.

The regular season turned out to be a different story, however. The club lost four of its first six games and found itself in last place midway through the schedule.

The Rams rebounded to win four games before the season ended and finished with a 6-6 record. Despite their lackluster performance, the Rams were an attraction at the box office. They became the first team in football history to draw over one million spectators in a single season. Included in that figure was a league-record crowd of 102,368 who watched the Rams battle the San Francisco 49ers at Memorial Coliseum.

1958 The Rams traded Norm Van Brocklin to the Philadelphia Eagles prior to the 1958 season, paving the way for Bill Wade at quarterback. Then they strengthened their receiving corps by selecting Auburn end Jim Phillips in the first round of the college draft.

In the home opener against Cleveland, Wade was brilliant at quarterback. He hit on 17 of 22 passes for 209 yards. Del Shofner was the team's leading receiver. He nabbed six passes for 149 yards. Tom Wilson gained 109 yards to lead Los Angeles rushers, while Jon Arnett racked up 70 yards. Unfortunately, Cleveland kicker Lou Groza ruined things for the Rams. He kicked a 10-yard field goal with 23 seconds on the clock

Ram Tom Keane (10) tries to outjump Detroit's Leon Hart (82) to grab this pass, but it fell incomplete.

to give the Browns a 30-27 win.

Midway through the season, Jon Arnett had one of his best days as a football player. In front of 101,000 fans at the Coliseum, the second largest crowd in league history, the former USC great put on a running exhibition. He gained 98 yards rushing against the Chicago Bears, including runs of 52 and 38 yards, and returned three punts for a total of 118 yards. In addition, Arnett caught a screen pass from Bill Wade that he turned into a 72-yard gain. Arnett failed to score, but he set up five Ram touchdowns in their 41-35 win. The victory gave the Rams a 3-3 record. They finished the season by winning five of their final six games to post an 8-4 mark.

In his first season as the starting quarterback, Bill Wade rewrote the Ram record book. He broke Van Brocklin's marks for passes attempted in a season with 341, passes completed with 181, and total yardage in a season with 2,875. Wade missed breaking the NFL's single-season yardage mark, set by Sammy Baugh in 1947, by just 63 yards.

1959 The Rams made a bid to strengthen their running game in the 1959 college draft. They selected Dick Bass from College of Pacific on the first round although he was only a junior. Bass continued his education at COP and joined the Rams a year later.

Also selected in the draft were Arkansas Tech defensive back Eddie Meador in the seventh round, and UCLA track star Rafer Johnson on the 28th round. Rather than join the Rams, Johnson went to the 1960 Olympics and captured a gold medal in the decathalon.

After the draft, the Rams made the trade of the season by exchanging nine players for Chicago Cardinal running back Ollie Matson. Los Angeles gave up four starters in the trade, defensive tackles Frank Fuller and Art Hauser, defensive end Glenn Holtzman and tackle Ken Panfil. In addition, they yielded two future draft choices and newly selected rookies Don Brown, Larry Hickman and John Tracey.

The season was a disaster for the Rams. They opened with consecutive loses to New York, 23-21, and San Francisco, 34-0, then bounced back to win their next two games. That was the high point of the season. After posting a 2-2 record, Los Angeles ended the year with eight straight losses.

The Rams tried to change their luck at midseason against the Chicago Bears with a new offensive look. Jon Arnett and Jim Phillips were used as wide receivers on one side, and Leon Clarke and Del Shofner were spread wide to the other side. Ollie Matson was the lone set back.

Initially, the four receiver offense made little difference against the Bears. Chicago held a 21-7 lead in the third quarter when the Rams replaced starting quarterback Bill Wade with Frank Ryan. Ryan immediately directed the Rams on a 55-yard drive that was capped by Ollie Matson's 19-yard touchdown run.

In the fourth quarter, with Chicago holding a 26-14 advantage, Ryan began to move the Rams again. He took them 98 yards on two big plays to narrow the score to 26-21. Halfback Tom Wilson started that drive with a 60-yard run. After two incomplete passes, Ryan connected on a 38-yard touchdown pass to Jon Arnett. Los Angeles was unable to score again, but the new formation proved instrumental in Ryan's ability to move the offense. Ollie Matson gained 85 yards in 12 car-

ries against the Bears, giving him 582 yards in just six games.

Norm Van Brocklin and Paige Cothren, a pair of Ram castoffs, came back to haunt their old teammates in a game at Philadelphia late in the season. The game was tied, 20-20, with 1:30 left to play when old pro Norm Van Brocklin took over. Van Brocklin had experienced limited success against the Ram defense earlier, but with the game on the line, he was revitalized.

Knowing Van Brocklin had limited mobility, Los Angeles dropped eight defensive backs into the secondary to guard against his passes. The Dutchman was still able to move the Eagles downfield with short passes to his backs. Starting from his own 11, he drove Philadelphia the length of the field to the Los Angeles seven-yard line. With 16 seconds on the clock, kicker Paige Cothren came on to boot a field goal and give Philadelphia a 23-20 win. It was Cothren's third field goal of the day. Jon Arnett gained 108 yards on six carries in the losing effort, including an 80-yard touchdown run.

The Rams ended the season with a 2-10 record, their worst finish since moving to Los Angeles in 1946. After the final game, Coach Sid Gillman was fired. Gillman's four year record with the Rams was 28-31-1.

During the offseason, General Manager Pete Rozelle began his search for a new head coach. Among those he considered for the job were New York Giant assistant Tom Landry, Notre Dame's Joe Kuharich, Otto Graham of the Coast Guard Academy, and former Ram great Bob Waterfield. Waterfield was made the new head coach. It was one of Rozelle's last deals on behalf of the Rams.

Midway through the 1959 season, NFL Commissioner Bert Bell died of a heart attack. With the season finally behind them, the NFL team owners voted on a new commissioner. Pete Rozelle was a compromise choice for the post.

Rozelle's initial duty as commissioner was to contend with the NFL's new rival, the American Football League, which was scheduled to begin operation in 1960. The Rams had a new intracity rival in the AFL, the Los Angeles Chargers.

Page 72: Frank Ryan (15) saw limited action as a quarterback for Los Angeles between 1958 and 1961. On this play he is brought down hard by Pittsburgh's George Tarasovic.

1960–1969

CHAPTER THREE

FROM THE CELLAR TO THE PLAYOFFS

While the AFL and NFL were engaged in a bidding war for players in 1960, the Democratic Party was celebrating the election of John F. Kennedy as the 35th president of the United States.

Bobby Darin was still at the top of the hit parade that year with "Mack the Knife," and Ray Charles won a Grammy for "Georgia on my Mind."

In Hollywood, Burt Lancaster was an Academy Award winner for his part in "Elmer Gantry," while Elizabeth Taylor's performance in "Butterfield 8" also won an Oscar.

The Los Angeles Dodgers found a new slugger in young Frank Howard. He hit 23 homers in 1960 and became National League Rookie of the Year.

The Rams had the first choice in the 1960 college draft and they did not hesitate to choose Louisiana State's Heisman Trophy winning halfback Billy Cannon. But Cannon signed instead with the Houston Oilers of the AFL for $110,000.

In preseason play, quarterback Buddy Humphrey, a former Baylor ace, appeared to have the inside track on a starting job. He completed 16 of 28 passes against the Washington Redskins and Coach Waterfield announced his pleasure with Humphrey's play.

Veteran quarterback Bill Wade ruined Humphrey's try for the starting slot a week later. Humphrey opened at quarterback against the league's newest entry, the Dallas Cowboys, and led the Rams to two touchdowns in the first half. But Wade took over in the second half and guided them to five touchdowns. He threw three scoring passes, then marched the Rams to two other scores in the 49-14 victory. Wade ended the day with 10 completions in 18 attempts for 204 yards.

The Rams opened the 1960 season at the Coliseum with high hopes. Over 47,000 fans were on hand to see them square off with the St. Louis Cardinals. The Cardinals were starting a new era. It was their first season in St. Louis after relocating from Chicago. Wade got the starting call at quarterback and promptly put the Rams in front, 7-0, on a 13-yard pass to Clendon Thomas. He added a 57-yard touchdown pass to Jim Phillips to give the Rams a 14-10 halftime lead.

The Cardinals opened the second half with John Roach at quarterback. Roach threw four second-half touchdown passes and led the Cardinals to a 43-21 win.

The Rams continued their losing streak against San Francisco, Chicago and Baltimore. They ran their string of consecutive defeats to 12 league games dating back to 1959.

After the loss at Chicago, Waterfield filed a complaint with NFL Commissioner Pete Rozelle claiming that Bear Coach George Halas ordered his

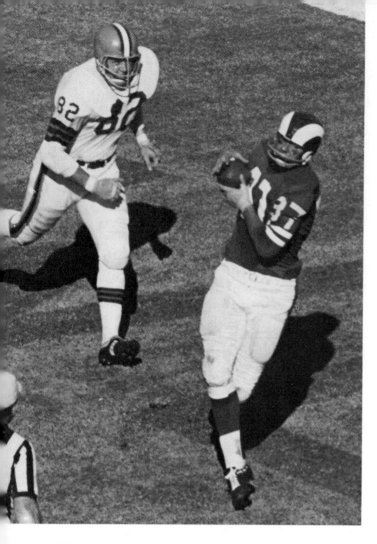

Tight end Billy Truax hauls in a two-yard scoring pass from Roman Gabriel during the 1967 Playoff Bowl with Cleveland. Los Angeles ran away with the game, 30-6. **Page 77:** Defensive back Lindon Crow (41) intercepts a pass intended for Detroit's Gail Cogdill (89). Elbert Kimbrough (83) is about to land on Cogdill's back.

defensive players to disrupt the Rams' signals. Waterfield claimed that Chicago linebacker Bill George had mimicked the signals of quarterback Bill Wade, causing the Rams to jump offside. In all, the Rams were penalized five times for being offside.

"Either the commissioner has guts and does something about it, or Halas makes a travesty of the league," said Waterfield.

The Rams finally ended the losing streak in a rematch with the Chicago Bears in the fifth week of the season. Still, they were not in the win column. They tied Chicago, 24-24, but the tie knocked the Bears out of first place in the NFL's Western Conference.

Los Angeles erupted in its next game against the Detroit Lions, racking up six touchdowns in a 48-35 win. The Rams made it two victories in a row the following week when they demolished

the Dallas Cowboys, 38-13. Former SMU quarterback Don Meredith got his first start as a pro in that game and completed just nine of 28 passes for 75 yards. He also had three tosses intercepted. Fortunately for Meredith, only 15,600 fans were on hand. It was the smallest crowd ever to see the Cowboys play at the Cotton Bowl.

Despite the disappointing year, the Rams gained some respect near the end of the season by beating the World Champion Baltimore Colts, 10-3. The win knocked the Colts out of contention for the championship. Baltimore quarterback John Unitas was harassed by a tough Rams defensive unit led by Les Richter, Lou Michaels, George Strughar, Lamar Lundy and Ed Meador. It was the first time the Colts had failed to score a touchdown in 54 games. The Rams ended the season in sixth place with a 4-7-1 record.

The Rams' intracity rivals, the Los Angeles Chargers, won the AFL Western Division crown with a 12-2 record. Led by former Ram Coach Sid Gillman and quarterback Jack Kemp, the Chargers faced the Houston Oilers in the first AFL Championship Game. Houston defeated Los Angeles, 24-16. At the conclusion of the season the Chargers relocated to San Diego.

1961 Prior to the 1961 season, the Rams dealt quarterback Bill Wade to Chicago for quarterback Zeke Bratkowski and a first-round draft pick in 1962. In the 1961 player draft, the Rams selected USC linebacker Marlin McKeever on the first round, Notre Dame tackle Joe Scibelli on the tenth round, South Carolina State end Deacon Jones on the 14th round and tackle Charles Cowan, from New Mexico Highlands, on the 21st round.

Bratkowski won the Rams' starting quarterback job from Frank Ryan after leading the club to a 2-2-1 record in preseason. In the league opener at Baltimore, Los Angeles rallied to a 24-17 lead in the fourth period behind the slick passing of Bratkowski. Early in the last quarter Bratkowski was buried under a ferocious Baltimore rush and was forced to leave the game. With Bratkowski gone, the Ram offense vanished.

In the second half, Johnny Unitas showed why he was an All-Pro. He scored one touchdown on an eight-yard run and set up two field goals with his accurate passes as Baltimore defeated Los An-

Dick Bass 1960–1969

It takes rare talent to become a first-round choice in pro football's annual college draft. It takes exceptional ability to be chosen on the first round while still a junior in college.

Dick Bass had such extraordinary skill. In 1959, while still a junior at College of Pacific in Stockton, California, Bass impressed Los Angeles Ram scouts enough to become their first-round pick. Rather than turn pro, he decided to continue his education. After breaking virtually every school rushing record at Pacific, Bass joined the Rams in 1960.

When he reported to training camp, the Rams already had a full complement of out-standing backs. Jon Arnett, Ollie Matson, Joe Marconi and Tom Wilson all shared time in the backfield. Bass wondered how he would break into the lineup.

"When I got to camp,

hazing was still in effect," Bass said. "The rookies weren't supposed to start and the vets let you know it. I was used mostly to return punts and kicks that first year. Occasion-ally I was used on a reverse, but I didn't carry the ball much from scrimmage. They thought I was mostly a blocking back, so that's how I was used."

Bass was not used as a blocking back for long. In 1962 he gained 1,033 yards to become the first Ram to go over the 1,000 yard mark in a season. He did it again in 1966, gaining 1,090 yards and scoring eight touchdowns. When he retired in 1969 after 10 years with the Rams, he was the club's all-time leading rusher with 5,417 yards. He carried a 4.5-yard rushing average.

Lawrence McCutcheon later gained 6,186 yards with the Rams to break Bass'

club rushing mark. Eric Dickerson is rapidly gaining on both of them.

During Bass' early years with the Rams, the team had little success on the field. Between 1960 and 1965 the club's highest finish was fifth place. That all changed when George Allen took over the head coaching job. Under Allen, the Rams won at least eight games every season and finished in first place in 1967 and 1969. Los Angeles also had second place finishes in 1968 and 1970.

"Allen was a very thorough coach," Bass said. "He worked harder than anybody, and as a result, he was successful on the field. The man lived for football. For example, he would find old rules in the rule book, dust them off and use them to his advantage.

"One of the things he always said was, 'If we're going to be

champs, we have to look like champs.' So when he took over the Rams job, one of the first things he did was have the locker room carpeted and fixed up. The floors were just concrete before that.

"George did everything first class. He was definitely a player's coach. If you played for him, he took care of you."

In addition to Allen's coaching and manage-rial talents, the Rams were fortunate to have a great field leader in Roman Gabriel, Bass says.

"Gabriel was a winner," he said. "He was big, about 6-4 and 230 pounds. If he was blitzed, he could withstand a beating and still get the pass off. And he wasn't afraid to run. He liked to roll out and if there was someone in the way, he'd run over them."

As the team's fullback during those years, Bass

went head-to-head with some of football's greatest defensive players. His most memorable duels were with the Detroit Lions.

"Joe Schmidt was just a great linebacker," he said. "Everyone talked about Sam Huff back then, but I think Schmidt could do it all. He was quick, had great lateral movement and he liked to get after people.

"Detroit also had great defensive linemen in Alex Karras and Roger Brown. Roger weighed about 300 pounds and had 18-inch calves. Karras was very quick for his size. He could get off the line fast, so we used sucker plays on him. That was the best way to play Karras. You had to use traps on him.

"I remember one time I was supposed to block Roger Brown. I would talk to Roger while we were playing and I guess he wasn't used to that. On this one play, rather than hit him, I just fell down in front of him. I guess that really mixed him up, because he just stood there and looked at me."

The Baltimore Colts were another team that was particularly tough during the 1960s, according to Bass. Baltimore defensive end Eugene "Big Daddy" Lipscomb was one of the terrors of the league at that time. Bass was never overjoyed to see Lipscomb coming his way.

"Big Daddy was about 6-6 and 315, but he was exceptionally quick," he said. "He had great lateral movement and could cover the field

sideline to sideline. One time when I was carrying the ball, I caught him on his heels and knocked him straight on his butt. Then I kept going. I ran right over his chest with my cleats. That made him mad. Coming back to the huddle, I told him we were going to come right at him again. I could see him getting madder. You could tell when he was mad because he would get so worked up sometimes he would cry.

"Of the other linebackers, of course, Dick Butkus was one of the greats. I'm sure I have number 51 tattooed on me somewhere. Tommy Nobis was excellent on pass coverage. He was fast enought to cover the backs. Ray Nitschke was good but he had tiny legs for a linebacker and a fullback could sometimes run over him."

As a youngster growing up in Vallejo, California, Bass often watched the San Francisco 49ers play at Kezar Stadium. One of the players he kept his eyes on was 49er tackle Leo Nomellini. Nomellini played in 10 Pro Bowls and was voted the best defensive tackle during pro football's first 50 years.

"I watched Leo Nomellini play and I knew he was good, but I didn't think much of it," Bass said. "When I got on the field and played against him, I quickly realized it was easier to watch him from the stands than to try running at him."

Although Bass is

known mostly for his ability as a ball carrier, he was also an excellent receiver. He ranks sixth on the club's all-time reception list with 214 catches for 1,846 yards.

Bass kept himself in shape during the off-season with his own workout schedule. By his own admission, it was a strange routine.

"I don't know why, but I never liked people watching me workout," he said. "I would get up early, maybe three in the morning, and run wind sprints on the beach. I liked to be alone. Maybe I didn't want to give away any training secrets."

It takes more than natural ability to be successful in professional sports, Bass says. He has seen hundreds of college athletes with the proper physical tools, who failed in the professional ranks. He believes the one ingredient they were missing was mental toughness.

"When I came out of college, I had a good grasp of the game as far as fundamentals were concerned, but I think my attitude is what really mattered," he said. "I had a good mental approach to the game. I never made a mental mistake. I think I was just as effective in the fourth quarter as in the first quarter, mostly because I concentrated."

Bass is now a color commentator on the Los Angeles Rams' radio broadcasts. In that capacity he can take a close look at modern day football. He notices quite a difference between the players of

his era and those of today.

"We were more together as a team," he said. "Today's player tends to go off on his own. I ran around with the linemen quite a bit when I played. These were the guys that protected me when I had the ball and I remembered them for it."

As a former running back, Bass knows a great runner when he sees one. Eric Dickerson is already in that category, he says.

"When Dickerson walks into a room, he just lights it up," Bass said. "He's got that star quality. On the field he's got all the tools. He's got great size, outstanding speed and is tough physically. I was allowed to vote for the team's MVP in 1985, and I voted for him. Every team the Rams play against keys on Dickerson. That shows how much he means to the club.

"It's hard to compare running backs, because they all have something different that makes them great. With Gale Sayers it was his great moves and elusiveness. O.J. played 'cat and mouse' with you. He wouldn't do much for a couple of quarters, then all of a sudden he would explode on a 60-yard run. Dickerson is kind of a cross between Willie Galimore and Lenny Moore. He's able to get through the hole on nearly every play, then he can take off with those long strides. A player like him doesn't come along that often."

Page 78: Linebacker Maxie Baughn (55) grabs the jersey of Cleveland Brown quarterback Frank Ryan, causing an incomplete pass. Baughn starred with the Rams from 1966 to 1970 and played in four Pro Bowls while a member of the club. **Above:** Ram linebacker Tony Guillory (88) blocks a punt by Donny Anderson of the Green Bay Packers. Deacon Jones (75) and Willie Daniel (46) assist.

geles, 27-24. Bratkowski completed 10 of 17 passes for 140 yards before leaving the game. Running back Tom Wilson paced the Los Angeles ball carriers with 118 yards.

After an 0-2 start, Los Angeles finally got in the win column against the Pittsburgh Steelers. The game was tied, 14-14, late in the fourth quarter when Frank Ryan connected on a dramatic 96-yard touchdown pass to Ollie Matson. Danny Villanueva added a field goal with 12 seconds to play to give the Rams a 24-14 win. Then as time was winding down, a fight broke out on the field. Steeler fullback John Henry Johnson picked up a plywood goal-line marker and took a swing at

linebacker Bill Jobko. Johnson missed Jobko but connected with tackle Urban Henry. Both benches emptied, but the referees quickly stepped in to restore order.

In the fourth week of the season the Rams were humiliated by the San Francisco 49ers, 35-0. Former UCLA star Billy Kilmer led the 49ers and their new Shotgun Formation against Los Angeles. Kilmer gained 131 yards on the ground and scored two touchdowns.

At midseason, the Rams had a 1-6 record when they put together consecutive wins over the Minnesota Vikings and the San Francisco 49ers. They closed out the season by dropping four of their last five games to finish in sixth place with a 4-10 record.

The Rams displayed a lot of offensive talent for a sixth-place team. End Jim Phillips was the league's leading receiver with 78 catches. He edged Baltimore's Raymond Berry, who caught 75 passes, for the reception title. Jon Arnett and Dick Bass were an effective combination in the

Defensive back Claude Crabb (49) is escorted to the end zone by the rest of the defensive unit after picking up a Green Bay Packer fumble.

backfield. They combined to gain over 1,200 yards rushing. Phillips and Arnett were chosen the team's Most Valuable Players. Les Richter, Arnett and Phillips also appeared in the Pro Bowl.

1962 The Rams had two first-round picks in the 1962 college draft and they used them wisely. They selected Roman Gabriel, a quarterback from North Carolina State, and tackle Merlin Olsen from Utah State. In the second round they chose Notre Dame tackle Joe Carollo. All three eventually became All-Pros for Los Angeles.

Zeke Bratkowski opened the year at quarterback for the Rams. In the first two preseason games, Bratkowski led them to convincing wins over Washington, 37-7, and Minnesota, 33-24. Then reality set in. The club lost three consecutive preseason contests. In their first regular season game, the Rams blew an 11-point lead in the fourth quarter.

Los Angeles started the fourth period of its opener against Baltimore with a 27-16 advantage. But Johnny Unitas began to move the Colts in the final period, connecting on a 21-yard touchdown pass to Ray Berry with less than five minutes to play. The Rams fumbled away the ensuing kickoff. Two minutes later, Unitas hooked up with Jimmy Orr on a 14-yard pass to provide the Colts with a 30-27 win.

The Rams lost more than the game, however. Halfback Jon Arnett was forced to leave the field on a stretcher after suffering a severely sprained ankle. He would be out of action for four weeks.

Los Angeles went on to lose its next five contests to Chicago, Dallas, Washington, Detroit and Minnesota. It was all alone in the western division cellar before getting its only win of the season against the San Francisco 49ers.

The Rams were 14½ point underdogs against the 49ers at San Francisco's Kezar Stadium. They fooled the oddsmakers by jumping out to a 21-0 lead and then holding on for a 28-14 victory. Jon Arnett returned to duty against San Francisco and gained 60 yards on the ground including a three-yard touchdown run. Dick Bass picked up 95 rushing yards.

The winning streak lasted only one week, as

Roman Gabriel 1962-1972

When Roman Gabriel was a senior at North Carolina State, he was a wanted man. It wasn't the law that was after him, but the Los Angeles Rams and the Oakland Raiders.

Gabriel was the nation's premier college quarterback in 1962. He was drafted on the first round that year by both the Raiders and the Rams. The Raiders dangled a $36,000 three-year contract in front of him, while the Rams offered him $45,000 for three seasons. Both teams were willing to toss in a $5,000 signing bonus.

The financial figures offered by the Rams appealed to Gabriel, but he also wanted to prove himself in the NFL. The AFL was still considered an inferior league at that time. Gabriel chose to sign with the Rams.

He reported to Los Angeles and found veteran quarterback Zeke Bratkowski was the man to beat for a starting role. Bob Waterfield was the head coach. Gabriel looked forward to receiving instruction from Waterfield, one of the game's legendary quarterbacks. It never happened.

"Waterfield was a very quiet guy," Gabriel said. "He figured we were professionals by the time we got to the Rams and that we didn't need that much help. At one point, he even told the press he thought I was clumsy and not smart enough to play quarterback. That offended me a little, but I think it inspired me to play better."

Waterfield was replaced by Harland Svare midway through the 1962 season, but the Rams languished in mediocrity. It wasn't until George Allen was appointed head coach of the Rams in 1966 that the club's fortune began to change. In his first season at the helm, the Rams finished 8-6. More importantly he instilled a winning spirit in the club.

"When George came in he gave people a lot of confidence in themselves," Gabriel said. "He was a good communicator, that was one of his best traits. A lot of coaches are good at the blackboard, but they are not really good communicators. George was also a good role model. He was a leader and coach in the same mold as people like Bud Grant, Don Shula and Chuck Noll."

Allen may have been popular with his players, but he ran into problems with management because of his insistence on trading draft picks for veteran players. At the end of the 1970 season he was fired.

"Everybody believed George ran into problems with management because he shopped off the rookies in favor of veterans," Gabriel said. "That may have been one reason he got fired, but I think another reason was that he didn't drink and mingle with management. He was more dedicated to the players and winning ball games.

"Although George did bring in a lot of veterans, he didn't bring in many offensive players. He was always shopping for defensive players. His philosophy was that if you had a good defense you could stay in any game. On offense he just wanted to keep from turning over the ball."

Gabriel and Allen helped guide the Rams to first place finishes in 1967 and 1969. Both years they were defeated in the western conference playoffs. In 1969, Gabriel was voted the league's most valuable player. He completed 217 of 399 passes for 2549 yards and 24 touchdowns. He also scored five rushing touchdowns to lead the team.

"That was an outstanding season for me, but what I always strived for was consistency," Gabriel said. "I wanted everybody to know they could count on me being there. More than any physical ability, I think desire was the single quality that made me a respectable player. I always worked hard.

Many people work hard when they're in a group. I always tried to go one better and work out on my own as well. I always had my weights and a film projector with me. Whenever my wife and I moved anywhere we had the weights, the projector and our horses."

During his 11 years with the Rams, a string of competitors challenged Gabriel for the quarterback position. A quarterback controversy developed nearly every season. Among the challengers for Gabriel's job were Heisman Trophy winners Terry Baker and Gary Beban. Veterans Milt Plum, Bill Munson, Karl Sweetan and Jerry Rhome also took a shot at the quarterback spot. Gabriel outlasted them all.

"I didn't mind being challenged," Gabriel said. "What bothered me was when they brought in a guy and said, 'This guy is going to be the new quarterback.'"

Besides being an accurate passer, Gabriel was known as a bruising runner. At 6-4 and 225 pounds, he wasn't afraid of linebackers. He has vivid memories of those defensive gladiators.

"There was a lot of good linebackers back then," Gabriel said. "If I was still playing I wouldn't pick out just one. That would make the rest of them mad. I don't think there is much doubt that Dick Butkus was probably the best I faced. There was some other good ones around, like Bill

George, Joe Schmidt, Ray Nitschke, Tommy Nobis and Bill Bergey. I think Butkus stood out because he was so quick to analyze plays. He might as well have been in the huddle because he reacted so fast. He had great lateral speed and you have to remember he played at about 245 or 250."

It's not surprising that a native of Wilmington, North Carolina would be interested in basketball. Wilmington is not only Gabriel's hometown, but that of basketball great Michael Jordan. North Carolina State, Gabriel's alma mater, is an annual powerhouse as are two other teams from the state, North Carolina and Duke. What is surprising is that a man who played 15 years in the NFL would consider basketball his favorite sport. Gabriel says his biggest thrill as an athlete was not winning the NFL's Most Valuable Player award in 1969, or the Comeback Player of the Year award in 1973. Nor was it being offered a baseball contract by the New York Yankees as a senior in high school. Gabriel's biggest thrill was leading his high school basketball team to three straight championships.

Gabriel has such an obsession with basketball, he is leading a committee to bring the professional game to North Carolina. He hopes to win an National Basketball Association franchise for Charlotte, N.C.

Basketball may be Gabriel's favorite sport,

but it was football that he excelled in. He owns virtually every Ram passing record. In 11 seasons with the club, Gabriel completed 1,705 of his 3,313 passes for 22,223 yards. He also threw 154 touchdown passes. He is the club's all-time leader in every category. When he retired in 1977, after spending four years with the Philadelphia Eagles, he was ranked seventh on the NFL's all-time completion list.

"I guess the most unique thing about playing in Los Angeles was the adjustment I had to make," Gabriel said. "It was such a big city compared to Wilmington. Some people helped me along and made it easy for me. Merlin Olsen was my roommate for 11 years and he was always a good friend. Dick Bass and Ken Iman were some others. There was just so many of them."

Like many former Rams, Gabriel appeared in television and movie spots. He worked as a sportscaster and had some movie roles.

"I was into Hollywood for a while, but then I decided to get back to my upbringing," Gabriel said. "I was raised a little different in North Carolina and I wanted to get back to that. The Hollywood lifestyle just wasn't for me. I had some good years out there with the Rams and I have some good friends from those days. That's what is important to me."

Ram kicker Danny Villanueva has a field goal attempt blocked by New York Giant Erich Barnes (49). Frank Ryan (15) holds for Villanueva. Villanueva handled the team's punting and placekicking chores from 1960 to 1964.

the Rams lost their next game at home against Detroit. Coach Bob Waterfield resigned after the game and was replaced by his 31-year-old assistant, Harland Svare.

Svare had little luck turning the Rams around, but then Vince Lombardi would have had difficulty making a winner out of the 1962 club. The Rams lost five of their remaining six games and tied the other contest to close out the worst season in their history at 1-12-1.

Despite the lackluster year, Svare was successful in putting together an accomplished defensive unit led by Merlin Olsen, Deacon Jones and Lamar Lundy. Roman Gabriel also added hope for the future with his fine quarterback performance near the end of the season. He completed 56 percent of his 101 passes for 670 yards and three touchdowns. Dick Bass showed promise in the backfield. He set a team single-season rushing record with 1,033 yards and became the first Ram running back to gain over 1,000 yards in a season.

Les Richter, one of the team's all-time great linebackers, retired at the end of the season. Richter played in eight Pro Bowls during his nine years with the Rams.

In the offseason, Dan Reeves reacquired a majority interest in the club by purchasing the shares of Bob Hope, Fred Levy, Hal Seley and Harold Pauley. He later sold 49-percent interest in the Rams to Gene Autrey, Leonard Firestone, Paul O'Bryan, Robert Lehman, Joseph Thomas, Bob Reynolds and J.D. Stetson Coleman.

1963 Heisman Trophy winner Terry Baker, from Oregon State, was the Rams' first selection in the 1963 draft. Coach Svare decided to use Baker strictly as a quarterback and the rookie battled Gabriel for the starting job during the exhibition season.

Before the opening league game with the Detroit Lions, Svare kept the identity of his starting quarterback a secret. He decided to open with lefthanded Terry Baker. It made little difference. The offense was unable to put any points on the board with either Baker or Gabriel at quarterback.

Baker played the first half and completed six of

Willie Ellison (33) takes off behind the blocking of guards Tom Mack (65) and Joe Scibelli. Mack played in 11 Pro Bowls while a member of the Rams.

his 12 passes. Three of his tosses were intercepted. He was replaced at the half by Roman Gabriel. Detroit was firmly in command at the time, 20-0. Gabriel could not get any offense generated either and the Lions held on for a 23-2 win. The Rams' only points came when Lindon Crow tripped Detroit halfback Larry Ferguson in the end zone for a safety.

The season opener provided a taste of things to come for the Rams. They went on to lose to Washington, 37-14, Cleveland, 20-6, Green Bay, 42-10 and were demolished by Chicago, 52-14. The 38-point loss to the Bears was the team's worst defeat since moving to Los Angeles in 1946.

During the losing streak Coach Svare tried to ignite the offensive unit by alternating quarterbacks Gabriel, Baker and Bratkowski. The strategy allowed Svare to send in every play with his quarterback. It failed to work. In their first five contests, the Rams averaged just one touchdown per game. Svare then settled on Gabriel as his sole quarterback.

Los Angeles' first win came in its sixth game of the season against the Minnesota Vikings. Only 30,000 fans were on hand at the Coliseum to witness it. Los Angeles got on the scoreboard in the first half on a pair of 80-yard touchdown drives commandeered by Roman Gabriel. Carroll Dale caught a 13-yard pass from Gabriel for the first score while running back Art Perkins capped the second drive with a two-yard plunge.

Gabriel went all the way at quarterback. He connected on 12 of 26 passes for 202 yards, but it was the defense that set up the victory. With the score tied 24-24 and nine minutes left in the game, safety Nat Whitmyer intercepted a Fran Tarkenton pass and returned it 27 yards. The return set up Danny Villanaueva's game-winning 27-yard field goal.

Tarkenton had two more chances in the fourth quarter to put the Vikings in front, but the Rams front line of Rosey Grier, Merlin Olsen, Lamar Lundy and Deacon Jones put tremendous pressure on him. The Minnesota quarterback was sacked six times for 102 yards in losses and was forced into throwing two interceptions.

The following week, Los Angeles came from behind to beat the San Francisco 49ers, 28-21. The win gave the Rams their first two-game winning streak in over two years. Roman Gabriel had an excellent day at quarterback against San Francisco. He completed 15 of 25 passes for 251 yards and engineered scoring drives of 76, 74, 80 and 56 yards. Most importantly, he came up with the big plays when needed.

In the fourth quarter, with the Rams trailing San Francisco, 21-14, Gabriel connected on a 51-yard touchdown pass to Carroll Dale to tie the game. With less than nine minutes to go, Gabriel guided his team to the San Francisco 12-yard line and scored himself on a quarterback draw to give the Rams the winning margin.

The winning streak ended at Minnesota a week later as the Vikings got revenge for their earlier loss at Los Angeles with a 21-13 victory. Running backs Jon Arnett and Dick Bass were both sidelined with ankle and knee injuries and the Rams were limited to just 70 yards rushing. Their only touchdown came on a 99-yard kickoff return by Carver Shannon.

The Rams' lack of offensive punch lasted another week as they lost a heartbreaker to Chicago, 6-0. The Bears harassed and battered Gabriel all day, but with 40 seconds remaining he had one last chance to win it.

Los Angeles linebacker Jack Pardee blocked a 13-yard field goal effort which the Rams recovered on their own 39-yard line. Gabriel went to work from there. He completed a 15-yard pass to Carroll Dale at the sideline that moved the Rams into Chicago territory at the 45. His next pass, to the usually reliable Jim Phillips, was dropped at the 30. Two consecutive passes fell incomplete. On fourth down with eight seconds left to play, Gabriel dropped back to pass and was buried by Chicago linebacker Bill George. The tackle not only ended the game, it broke Gabriel's nose.

The Rams got back on track with a 28-21 win over the Detroit Lions the following week. Despite the injury, Gabriel threw three touchdown passes to Carroll Dale covering 65, 42 and 51 yards. In all, Gabriel connected on 17 of 31 passes for 289 yards. Dale was on the receiving end of seven passes for 207 yards.

Once again, Gabriel endured a terrific pounding. In the fourth quarter, he was knocked cold by 300-pound defensive tackle Roger Brown when the Detroit lineman flattened Gabriel with a forearm. The Ram quarterback sat out most of the fourth period after the blow.

Just four days after the Rams' victory, President John F. Kennedy was assassinated. While the country was in mourning, Commissioner Pete Rozelle and the NFL management debated whether the league should play its scheduled weekend games. They elected to play the games despite the protest of many fans around the league. That Sunday, over 48,000 fans were at the Coliseum to see the Rams beat the Baltimore Colts. It was the team's third straight win.

Dick Bass was the club's workhorse, gaining 120 yards on 19 carries for a 6.3-yard average. His 51-yard scamper in the first period set up Art Perkins' one-yard plunge. Perkins added another touchdown before the half ended to give the Rams a 14-13 lead. Los Angeles held on to win, 17-16.

Chicago's Roosevelt Taylor eludes Ram tacklers on his way to a 60-yard touchdown run. Taylor recovered Bruce Gossett's blocked field goal attempt.

Willie Ellison (33) takes off behind the blocking of guards Tom Mack (65) and Joe Scibelli. Mack played in 11 Pro Bowls while a member of the Rams. Scibelli played in 202 games for Los Angeles. **Page 89:** Rookie running back Henry Dyer of Grambling dashes through the Minnesota line enroute to a big pickup during a game in 1966.

The Rams dropped their final two games of the season to the defending champion Green Bay Packers and the Baltimore Colts. They finished with a 5-9 record for sixth place in the western division.

1964 Coach Harland Svare selected another quarterback in the 1964 college draft. With his first-round choice he picked Utah State star Bill Munson. Munson was then handed the starting job in preseason over Terry Baker and Roman Gabriel. He made the most of the opportunity and led the Rams to a respectable 3-2 exhibition record. In the league opener, Svare decided to start Munson at quarterback. The experiment didn't last long. By midseason, Gabriel was the team's signal caller.

Munson wasn't the only first-year man to help the Rams in 1964. Other newcomers who contributed were running back Les Josephson, a 215-pounder from Augustana College, and kicker Bruce Gossett from Richmond.

The Rams opened the league schedule as 6½ point underdogs at Pittsburgh. Behind a ferocious defensive effort, Los Angeles jumped out to a 26-7 lead and held on to beat the Steelers, 26-14. It was the first opening day win for the Rams since 1957.

The Rams' "Fearsome Foursome" lived up to its reputation by forcing Pittsburgh quarterback Ed Brown to hurry his passes most of the game. He compiled just 63 yards passing and was intercepted four times. The defense also forced five Steeler fumbles. Defensive end Lamar Lundy even got into the scoring act when he picked off a pass and ran 14 yards for a touchdown.

The first Ram touchdown was set up by Ed Meador. Meador hit Ed Brown on a safety blitz, forcing the Steeler quarterback to fumble. Linebacker Cliff Livingston recovered at the three-yard line. Running back Ben Wilson took the ball in for the score.

Munson completed just eight of 23 passes against Pittsburgh for 55 yards, but it was enough to get rookie kicker Bruce Gossett in range to boot field goals of nine and 39 yards.

Ollie Matson 1959–1962

Ollie Matson joined the Los Angeles Rams in 1959 after a monumental trade. The former Olympic medal winner and world-class sprinter was obtained from the Chicago Cardinals for nine players.

Matson knew it would be difficult to fill the shoes of four starters and five top draft choices, but in his first season with the club he did just that. He gained 863 yards and was the league's second leading rusher behind Cleveland's Jim Brown.

"Basically I wanted to get back to the west coast," said Matson. "I always wanted to be a Ram. In fact, I thought they would pick me in the draft in 1952 when I got out of college."

Matson starred at the University of San Francisco in the early 1950s, on a team that sent eight players to the pro ranks. Three men associated with that team are in Pro Football's Hall of Fame. Matson and Gino Marchetti were selected in 1972. The third man to enter the Hall of Fame was the team's publicity director—NFL Commissioner Pete Rozelle.

Before joining the Cardinals as a rookie, Matson went to the 1952 Olympics at Helsinki. He captured a bronze medal in the 400-meter run and a silver medal in the 1600-meter relay.

"I was supposed to go to the Olympics in 1948, but I just didn't have the experience," he said. "I was too young and I just wasn't ready. During the next four years, I got a little more track experience and was better prepared for the 1952 Olympics. Let me tell you, experience makes all the difference. The most valuable thing a person can have is experience.''

Playing for the Rams was a unique opportunity, according to Matson. He was pleased to leave the icy football weather in Chicago for the warmth of Southern California. Once in Los Angeles, he discovered that many teams were gunning for the Rams because of their ''Hollywood'' image.

''In those days everybody wanted to beat the Rams,'' Matson said. ''Los Angeles was a big city with movie stars and all that. We were classified as the Hollywood team.''

The image was not far off. Bob Waterfield, the Rams' coach in 1959, was married to actress Jane Russell. Comedian Bob Hope was a co-owner of the club until 1962. And members of the team were frequently invited to the movie studios and Hollywood parties.

One of the teams that apparently disliked the Rams and their Hollywood image was the Chicago Bears, Matson says. Their ferocious defense was always tough on Los Angeles.

''The Bears had players like Bill George and Richie Petitbone who could really make it rough on a back,'' he said with a laugh. ''Playing them in Chicago was almost impossible. It was tough to beat them at Wrigley Field. You had to beat

them by two touchdowns to be sure you really beat them.''

Although Matson was a great natural athlete, he says it takes more than natural ability to make it in the pro ranks. Desire is one of the qualities that helped him throughout his career.

''A lot of people have the ability to do something, but you have to use that ability,'' he said. ''I was very determined to use my athletic skill. If I was to say what qualities made me successful, it would be more than physical ability. I would say I was disciplined, I was cooperative, I was receptive to ideas, and I had confidence in myself. Those qualities helped me not only in athletics, but in life.''

''Whenever I went out on the field, I always made sure to give it my best. I knew that people were paying to see me perform. I didn't want to let them down. I wanted to give them their money's worth. I always tried to do something so that when fans left they would say, 'That Ollie Matson put on a great show.' After all, they were paying the freight.

''I've been pretty successful as an athlete, but there are so many people around me that contributed to that success. In sports and in life you get help from many people. My mom, and later my wife, were always supportive. It's the people around you that really help you and make you succeed. There are always people that are going to tell you what you can't do. I had people around me that

told me what I could do. That makes a big difference.''

Matson was one of football's greatest all-around performers. Not only was he an outstanding running back and an effective receiver, he also was one of the league's best kick returners. When he retired in 1966 after 14 seasons, he had gained 5,173 yards from scrimmage and averaged 4.4 yards per carry. He returned kickoffs another 3,746 yards for a 26.5 yard average. Six kickoffs and four punts were returned for touchdowns. Matson scored 73 touchdowns during his career. He modestly credits his former teammates and coaches for many of his achievements.

''I couldn't have accomplished what I did on my own,'' he said. ''I had great players around me who helped me out. I couldn't have gained all those yards by myself.

''All the way back through high school my coaches have been supportive. Joe Kuharich was one coach. He helped a lot. Before I got out of USF, he said he might get a job with the Chicago Cardinals, and if he did, he would pick me on the first round. I told him I couldn't play in cold weather. He said, 'Well I guess you'll just have to learn to play when it's cold.' Sure enough, the Cardinals picked me.''

Matson has earned numerous awards during his outstanding career. It's impossible for him to pick one honor

over the others.

''There are three things that have happened in my life that I've always held high,'' he said. ''The first is making All-America in college. The next would be representing the United States in the Olympics and winning two medals. I was told I couldn't do it because I was a football player, so winning those medals was important to me. The third thing would be going into football's Hall of Fame. I mean, after those three things what more could I ask?''

Matson still follows professional football closely and has seen numerous changes in the game. The biggest difference, he says, is in the players themselves.

''The fellows you see today are bigger, faster and stronger,'' he said. ''There are better coaches that can teach fundamental skills. There are better training routines to build up the players. Facilities and equipment are better. In our day, we didn't wear a lot of pads because they would weigh you down. Now the pads can be worn because they are made of different materials and very light.''

''Another thing is the superstars change every year,'' he said. ''Every season you see a new star emerge. In our day, the superstars stayed the same from year to year. I think it has something to do with television. The game is much more commercialized now. We played for the love of the game. I think money is more of an incentive now.''

Los Angeles played tough defensive football the next two weeks. The team tied the Detroit Lions, 17-17, and beat Minnesota, 22-13. After dropping games to Baltimore and Chicago, the Rams returned to the Coliseum to meet their northern rivals, the San Francisco 49ers.

A crowd of 54,350 settled in at the Coliseum to watch one of the finest defensive displays in Ram history. For the record, Roman Gabriel threw four touchdown passes, including three to rookie wide receiver Bucky Pope, but it was the sterling play of the defensive unit, particularly the secondary, that set up the scoring.

The defense intercepted seven 49er passes and returned them for an NFL record 314 yards. Rookie defensive back Jerry Richardson was the team's leading bandit. He picked off three passes. Bobby Smith intercepted one toss and returned it 97 yards to score. Rookie Aaron Martin also returned an intercepted pass 71 yards for a touchdown.

Smith's interception turned the tide early in the fourth quarter. The Rams were ahead, 28-14, at the time, but they had clearly lost momentum. The 49ers were driving and had possession at the Los Angeles six-yard line. A touchdown would put the 49ers back in the game with over seven minutes to play. But Smith stepped in front of a George Mira pass at the three-yard line and rambled 97 yards. Less than a minute later, Martin picked off a Brodie pass to ice the game.

Rookie Les Josephson helped lead the offensive charge. He gained 56 yards on 14 carries. Ben Wilson ran for 75 yards on 20 rushes.

The Rams seemed to be heading in the right direction after wins over Green Bay and Philadelphia gave them a 5-3-1 record and a tie for second place in the western division. Then the club went into a tailspin. It lost four straight games and tied Green Bay on the last day of the season to finish in fifth place with a 5-7-2 record.

Against the Packers, Bill Munson directed the Rams to a 24-10 lead with less than 13 minutes to play. The Ram defensive line had been superb all day, sacking quarterback Bart Starr six times for 65 yards in losses and forcing the All-Pro quarterback to fumble three times. But with the game on the line, Starr and fullback Jim Taylor were suddenly revitalized. Starr led the team on successive touchdown drives of 62 and 58 yards with Taylor grinding out large chunks of yardage.

In all, Taylor gained 167 yards on the ground and 56 yards in receptions. He scored the tying touchdown with less than two minutes to play.

One of the bright spots in 1964 was kicker Bruce Gossett who set a team record by kicking 18 field goals. It broke Paige Cothren's previous single-season record of 14 field goals set in 1958. The club's defensive unit also began to solidify. Three members of the defense—Deacon Jones, Ed Meador and Merlin Olsen—were all selected to play in the Pro Bowl.

1965 The Ram defense began to show signs of maturing during the 1965 exhibition season. It shut out the Dallas Cowboys, 9-0, and the Philadelphia Eagles, 10-0, before opening the season at Detroit.

The Lions turned the tide on the Rams and stopped them, 20-0. Bill Munson started at quarterback for Los Angeles, but completed only eight of his 19 passes and had three intercepted. The running game never got moving either. The Rams totaled 65 yards on the ground. Dick Bass led Los Angeles rushers with 39 yards.

In the second week of the season, Bill Munson hooked up with a forgotten halfback to give the Rams a dramatic come-from-behind win over the Chicago Bears. Los Angeles got on the scoreboard first when defensive back Aaron Martin intercepted a pass from former Ram quarterback Bill Wade and returned it 36 yards for a touchdown. But the Bears came back to open a 28-9 lead in the fourth quarter.

With only 12 minutes left to play, Munson began to work his magic. He led the Rams on a 79-yard drive and scored on a one-yard run. He closed the gap to 28-23, when he took his club on a 49-yard scoring drive. He capped that march with a five-yard pass to receiver Tommy McDonald.

The Rams got the ball back one more time with five minutes to play. Working from his own 20, Munson hit former Heisman Trophy winner Terry Baker on a 19-yard pass. Baker then picked up eight yards on a draw play to move the ball to the Chicago 47-yard line. Munson then completed a 12-yard pass to Tommy McDonald. Several running plays moved the ball to the 10-yard line, where the Rams faced a fourth-and-eight with 30 seconds to play. From there, Munson dropped back and lobbed a pass to Baker in the end zone for the winning score.

It was Munson's best day as a pro. He hit on 27 of 45 passes for 295 yards and two touchdowns. He also scored on a one-yard run. Baker, who was used solely as a running back, gained 33 yards on seven carries and caught eight passes for 82 yards.

The Chicago game was the highlight of the Rams' season. After beating the Bears, they went into a tailspin and lost eight games in a row. During that span they gave up an average of 30 points per game.

Just as suddenly, the Rams reversed directions again and won three of their last four games. In those three victories they gave up an average of only 6.6 points a game.

During its late season winning streak, Los Angeles beat the defending champion Cleveland Browns, 42-7. Roman Gabriel accounted for six touchdowns in that game. He threw five scoring passes and ran for one touchdown. Gabriel completed 15 of 31 passes for 323 yards and had scoring tosses of five, 22, 43, 46 and 43 yards. Receiver Tommy McDonald was on the receiving end of three of those passes. The defense was equally proficient against Cleveland, limiting All-Pro running back Jim Brown to just 20 yards in 13 carries.

Los Angeles ended the year in seventh place with a 4-10 record. Harland Svare was relieved of his coaching duties and George Allen was hired as the Rams new head coach. Allen did not come to the Rams without a court fight, however. Chicago Bear Owner George Halas refused to allow Allen out of his contract as an assistant coach with the Bears. After a bitter court battle, Halas finally released Allen.

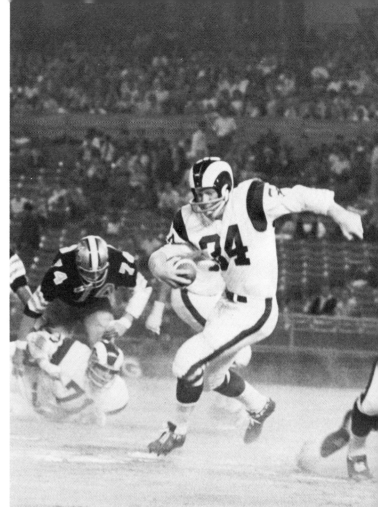

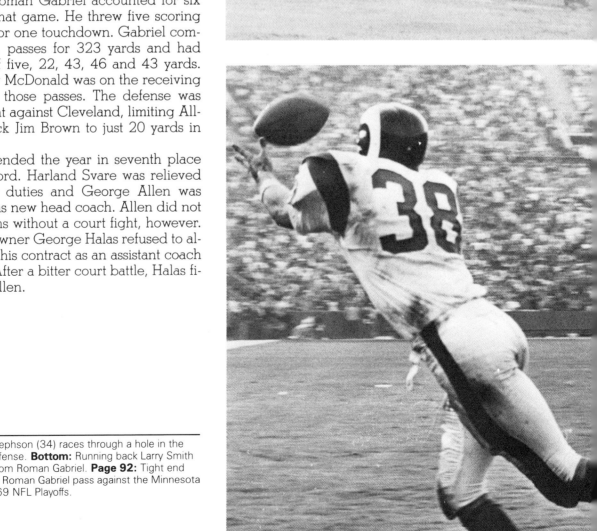

Top: Fullback Les Josephson (34) races through a hole in the New Orleans Saint defense. **Bottom:** Running back Larry Smith (38) hauls in a pass from Roman Gabriel. **Page 92:** Tight end Billy Truax scores on a Roman Gabriel pass against the Minnesota Vikings during the 1969 NFL Playoffs.

Ed Meador 1959–1970

Ed Meador admits that he never expected to become a member of the Los Angeles Rams. He was a seventh-round draft choice from Arkansas Tech in 1959. He thought he'd have a brief tryout with Los Angeles, then be on the next plane home.

"When I first reported to camp they already had some good ball-players in the secondary," he said. "I wasn't sure where I would fit in. Will Sherman was playing real well. Don Burroughs and Jack Morris were some of the other defensive backs still with the Rams at that time. I knew it would take hard work just to make the team."

Meador was equal to the task. He won a cornerback position in his rookie season with the Rams. The next year he played well enough to be selected for the Pro Bowl. Meador continued to star at cornerback for four more years, then he was switched to safety. He manned one of the Ram safety spots until his retirement in 1970.

There were subtle differences between the cornerback and safety positions, Meador says. Most significant were the one-on-one match-ups he faced as a cornerback. It gave him the opportunity to become familiar with the league's finest receivers.

"The passing game wasn't as well developed as it is today, but there were some very good receivers around," Meador said. "I think Johnny Morris from the Chicago Bears probably gave me the most trouble. He was fast and had very good moves. After Morris, I'd say Raymond Berry was probably one of the toughest to defend. Of course, he had Johnny Unitas throwing to him. That helps a lot. The Colts always seemed to have a good passing game."

At the safety position, Meador had a different role to play. Instead of going head-to-head with swift receivers, he became more of a field general, observing the entire field and reacting to the opposing offense.

"The corner was mostly one-on-one type of play," he said. "You had a little help here and there, but for the most part you were always on your own. It could get pretty lonely out there sometimes. At safety your main function was to cover backs out of the backfield and help out the corners. There wasn't as much man-to-man responsibility."

Playing in the secondary obviously agreed with Meador. He holds the Rams' all-time interception record with 46. He returned the interceptions 547 yards, another team record.

The Rams' defensive

unit was mediocre at best when George Allen was appointed head coach in 1966. Between Meador's rookie season and 1966, the Rams best finish was in 1964 when they won five games and finished in fifth place. Allen's first priority with the Rams was to revamp the defense.

Allen put together one of the best defensive units in football. He already had a strong nucleus in the defensive line which consisted of Merlin Olsen, Deacon Jones, Rosey Grier and Lamar Lundy. They earned the nickname, the "Fearsome Foursome," and became one of the most heralded defensive fronts in football history. Their ability to pressure the quarterback added to Meador's proficiency as a defensive back.

"The front four was a lot more responsible for those good defensive units than you think," Meador said. "They made everything work. Opposing teams spent a week before a game preparing to deal with them. We would have been nothing without that line."

From his secondary position, Meador found himself confronting some of the game's top running backs. He is unequivocal about the best one he's faced.

"Jim Brown was the greatest back I ever played against," he said. "I don't think many people could top his ability. Jim Taylor from Green Bay was a hard man to bring down, but so was Brown. Brown had more speed than Taylor so that gave him an edge. Gale Sayers was another good running back I saw. He was probably the most elusive running back I faced. Lenny Moore was a standout because he was a great receiver and runner."

Richter was selected to play in five Pro Bowls during his 12 seasons with the Rams. But the highlight of his career, he says, was participating in the playoffs during the late 1960s. The Rams won the western division title in 1967 and 1969. Both years they were defeated in the playoffs and failed to make the Super Bowl.

"George Allen really seemed to turn the team around," Meador said. "I learned more under him than any other coach I played for. He was a great student of the game and he was able to pass that knowledge on to his players. He was a good teacher. He really cared about his players. I don't think he had the same affection for management though.

"I guess George's mistake was bringing in too many veterans. He got results, but sooner or later that catches up to you because eventually you have no draft picks left. I think the front office resented the fact that he traded away so many draft picks."

When Meador retired in 1970, he had played in 159 straight games for the Rams. Only four men have played in more consecutive contests with Los Angeles. Jack Youngblood tops the list with 201 straight games, Merlin Olsen is next with 198 games, Tom Mack played in 184 games and Rich Saul appeared in 176.

"I had 12 tremendous years with the Rams and have nothing but good memories of people like Dick Bass and Deacon Jones and my old roommates, Les Richter and Jack Pardee," Meador said. "I wish I was still young enough to get out there and play."

Since his retirement, Meador's interest in the game has dwindled. But he still watches enough football to notice some major changes in the game.

"I don't follow the Rams or pro football as closely as I should, but I have seen some obvious changes," Meador said. "It's easy to see that people are bigger and faster now. I watch the receivers a lot and notice little things they do differently. It used to be that a guy like Raymond Berry was the best around. He had great moves and relied on that to get open. Then it started to change so that you had speed burners like Bob Hayes at receiver who blew right past you. The emphasis seems to have changed from precision patterns and technique to speed.

"Another thing that is different is the defenses are a lot more sophisticated. Everything was man-to-man before. You knew who you would be playing against. There is a lot more substitution and specialization now."

1966 The NFL and AFL agreed to an historic merger in the spring of 1966. However, the merger did not keep AFL clubs from outbidding NFL teams for collegiate talent, as the Rams quickly discovered.

The Rams' main objective in 1966 was to bolster their offensive production after averaging just 19 points a game in 1965. They chose Tom Mack, an All-American tackle from Michigan on the first round of the college draft, and Mike Garrett, a halfback from USC, on the second round. Garrett was lured away from the Rams by the Kansas City Chiefs of the AFL. Mack signed with the Rams and went on to play in 11 Pro Bowls.

The Rams opened the season against the league's newest entry, the Atlanta Falcons. They sneaked by the Falcons, 19-14, to give new Coach George Allen his first win. Gabriel, who won the starting quarterback role during the preseason, hit on 21 of 35 passes for 294 yards and a touchdown. Tommy McDonald hauled in nine of Gabriel's passes for 114 yards. Dick Bass was the team's leading ground gainer with 81 yards on 14 carries.

The Rams extended their record to 2-0 with a 31-17 victory over Chicago before dropping a game to the Green Bay Packers, 24-13. Wins over Detroit and San Francisco ran the Rams record to 4-1 and gave them their best start since 1955. Against San Francisco, Dick Bass became the club's all-time leading rusher. He gained 3,493 yards in his first six years with the club to break Dan Towler's previous team record.

The unpredictable Rams went into a slump after their encouraging start and lost four straight games. During that span they managed just 33 points, an average of eight points per game.

Then the Rams reversed form again and exploded against the New York Giants. They set an NFL single-game record with 38 first downs in compiling a 55-14 win. Los Angeles rolled up 572 total yards in the game. The 55 points were the most scored by any Ram team in nearly eight years.

Gabriel completed 24 of 35 passes against the Giants for 298 yards and two touchdowns. He also scored twice on a pair of one-yard runs. Munson entered the game with eight minutes to play and also threw two touchdown passes. Dick Bass led the Rams' ground attack. He gained 106 yards on 19 carries.

The defense also got into the scoring show against New York. Defensive back Irv Cross returned an intercepted pass 60 yards for a touchdown.

The strong defense that Coach Allen was trying to establish finally began to jell near the end of the 1966 season. In wins over Minnesota, Baltimore and Detroit, the defense gave up a total of one touchdown. Over the last five games of the season, the Rams allowed an average of just 11 points per game.

With one game left in the season, the Rams had an 8-5 mark. A win over Green Bay in the final game of the season would give Los Angeles a berth in the Playoff Bowl held annually between the second place teams in the NFL's Eastern and Western Divisions.

The largest crowd of the season, over 72,400, packed into the Coliseum assured that Los Angeles would end the year with its first winning record since 1958. Green Bay had already clinched the western division title and had nothing at stake. Nevertheless, Vince Lombardi's Packers did not roll over. They took the lead when defensive back Bob Jeter intercepted a Gabriel pass and returned it 76 yards to score.

With All-Pro quarterback Bart Starr on the bench resting for the playoffs, ex-Ram Zeke Bratkowski took over the Packer offense. He drove the team 78 yards for one score. Later, he hooked up with another former Ram, Carroll Dale, on a 23-yard touchdown pass. In the fourth quarter, Green Bay held a 27-9 lead.

The Rams continued to play hard-nosed football. Facing a fourth-and-nine with five minutes to play, Ram punter Jon Kilgore fooled the Packers by throwing a 47-yard pass to back Claude Crabb. Two plays later Gabriel scored on an 11-yard run to make the score 27-16.

Green Bay was stopped on its next series and the Rams took over on their own 45-yard line. Gabriel immediately connected on a 50-yard pass to receiver Steve Heckard, moving the Rams to the five-yard line. On the next play, Gabriel's pass was completed in the end zone to Marlin McKeever making, the score 27-23. Only 34 seconds remained and a desperate onside kick was recovered by Green Bay to end the game.

The Rams closed out the season with an 8-6 record for third place in the western division. Dick Bass, who finished the year with 1,090 yards

Rams Irv Cross, left, and Chuck Lamson dive for the ball fumbled by Cleveland's Leroy Kelly during the 1968 NFL Playoff Game.

rushing, was voted the team MVP.

1967 The NFL added another franchise in 1967. The admittance of the New Orleans Saints as an expansion team brought league membership to 16 clubs. The eastern and western conferences were then realigned into four divisions. Los Angeles found itself in the coastal division with the Baltimore Colts, San Francisco 49ers and Atlanta Falcons.

The Rams had only two picks in the first eight rounds of the 1967 college draft. Most of the draft choices had been dealt away in George Allen's effort to obtain veteran players. Among the established stars he brought into camp was Roger Brown. He started on the defensive line for the injured Rosey Grier. Halfback Willie Ellison, a second-round choice from Texas Southern, was the Rams' only noteworthy draft pick.

The Rams had their best preseason ever, finish-ing 6-0 and allowing an average of just 11 points per game. They opened the regular season against the New Orleans Saints. The Saints were coached by former Ram great Tom Fears.

Over 80,000 New Orleans fans packed into the Sugar Bowl to see their new team. They were quickly on their feet when Saint rookie John Gilliam returned the opening kickoff 94 yards for a touchdown.

The Rams took control of the game in the second half to beat New Orleans, 27-13. Dick Bass churned out 98 yards rushing, including a 13-yard touchdown run. Les Josephson added 41 yards on the ground and 78 yards on five catches. Josephson also scored the Rams' final touchdown on a 14-yard pass from Gabriel.

Los Angeles demolished Minnesota, 39-3, and Dallas, 35-13, before meeting the San Francisco 49ers at the Coliseum. The 49ers jumped out to a 20-0 halftime lead behind John Brodie's two long touchdown passes.

In the second half, the Rams came storming back. They scored 24 unanswered points on a field goal, an interception returned by Jack Pardee for a touchdown, a nine-yard run by Roman Gabriel and Gabriel's 12-yard pass to Les Josephson. With nine minutes left in the game, the

Page 97: Linebaker Carl Eckern brings down Bears running back Walter Payton.

Pages 98-99: Running back John Cappelletti picks up good yardage on a sweep around right end.

Left, above: Quarterback Vince Ferragamo (5) returned from the Canadian Football League in 1982 and battled Bert Jones for the starting position. **Left, below:** Jack Reynolds (64) leads a strategy session on the Ram bench. Isiah Robertson (58), Merlin Olsen (74), Mike Fanning (79) and Rod Perry look on.

Right, above: The Ram reserves watch as Los Angeles battles San Francisco at Candlestick Park during a game in 1974. **Right, below, from top left to bottom right, 1:** Joe Namath during the 1977 season, his last in pro football. He passed for 27,663 yards during his 13-year career. **2:** Merlin Olsen. **3:**John Robinson was named NFC Coach of the Year in 1983, his first season with the club. He directed the Rams to the playoffs every year from 1983 to 1986. **4:** Coach Chuck Knox guided the Rams to a 12-2 record in 1973, his first year at the helm. **5:** Kicker David Ray is third on the Rams all-time scoring list with 497 points. His 130 points in 1973 led the NFL. **6:** Since joining the Rams staff in 1983, Coach Gil Haskell has molded the Rams' special teams into a model for the rest of the NFL. Haskell previously coached at USC under John Robinson. **7:** Defensive end Fred Dryer was a leader on the Ram defensive line until his retirement in 1981. **8:** Running back Barry Redden is tripped up. Redden was a first-round draft choice out of Richmond in 1982.

1

2

3

4

5

6

7

8

Right, from left to right, 1: Johnnie Johnson drops back into pass coverage. The former Texas star was the Rams' first-round pick in 1980. **2:** Lawrence McCutcheon is ranked third on the Rams all-time list for total yardage (rushing; receiving; punt, kickoff and interception returns). His 7,869 total yards is topped by Dick Bass with 9,213 and Jon Arnett with 8,076. **3:** Linebacker Jack Reynolds. **4:** Quarterback John Hadl was named NFC Player of the Year in 1973 after leading the Rams to the western division title. Hadl threw 22 touchdown passes that season. **5:** Tackle Charlie Cowan played 15 seasons with the Rams until his retirement in 1975. **6:** Former defensive end and team captain Jack Youngblood. **Below:** Eric Dickerson (29) takes a handoff from Vince Ferragamo. **Page 104:** Dickerson breaks upfield.

1

2

3   4   5   6

Rams held a 24-20 lead.

San Francisco refused to let the game slip away. Midway through the fourth period, Brodie threw a 28-yard touchdown pass over Ram cornerback Irv Cross to put the 49ers back on top, 27-24. The 49er defense preserved the win. It turned out to be Los Angeles' only loss in the regular season.

The Rams tied their next two games against Baltimore and Washington. In the final eight games of the season, the Rams finally played the kind of defense that Allen had envisioned. They won all eight contests and gave up an average of just 11 points. Five of their opponents were held to under 10 points.

On the final day of the season, Los Angeles faced the unbeaten Baltimore Colts and the NFL Player of the Year, Johnny Unitas. Baltimore entered the game with an 11-0-2 record. The Rams were 10-1-2. A victory by the Rams would give them the NFL Coastal Division championship over Baltimore under the league tie-breaker rules.

Gabriel was hot all afternoon. In the second quarter, he hit Jack Snow with an 80-yard touchdown pass. Minutes later he connected with Bernie Casey on a 23-yard scoring toss to put Los Angeles ahead at the half, 17-7. It was a lead the Rams never relinquished. They scored 17 second-half points to destroy Baltimore, 34-10.

Gabriel was on target with 18 of his 22 passes for 257 yards and three touchdowns. Bernie Casey caught four passes for 78 yards, while Billy Truax caught five passes for 51 yards.

The Ram defense pressured Unitas throughout the day. He had been sacked only 13 times coming into the game, but the Ram defensive line got to Unitas seven times and forced him to hurry several other throws. He completed 19 of 31 passes, but was intercepted twice.

Los Angeles' opponent in the western conference title game was the Green Bay Packers. The game matched Green Bay's All-Pro offensive line, featuring Jerry Kramer, Forrest Gregg and Gale Gillingham, against the Rams' great defensive front of Deacon Jones, Merlin Olsen, Roger Brown and Lamar Lundy.

The Rams got on the board first on a 29-yard pass from Gabriel to Bernie Casey, but that was the highlight of the game for Los Angeles. The Packer offensive line dominated the Rams.

Green Bay rolled up 163 yards on the ground and scored three rushing touchdowns in the 28-7 win. Rookie running back Travis Williams was the leading ball carrier for Green Bay. He picked up 88 yards in 18 carries, while Donny Anderson netted 53 yards in 12 carries. Bart Starr completed 17 of 22 passes for 222 yards.

Green Bay's defense got to Gabriel five times and limited him to just 11 completions in 31 passes. On the ground the Rams gained a lowly 75 yards. Dick Bass was the club's leading rusher with 40 yards in 14 carries.

The Packers went on to defeat the Dallas Cowboys in the NFL Championship Game, then beat the Oakland Raiders in Super Bowl II. Los Angeles won a trip to the Playoff Bowl which matched the second place teams in the eastern and western conferences. The Rams outmuscled Cleveland in that game, 30-6.

Ten Rams were selected for the Pro Bowl, including Roman Gabriel, Bernie Casey, Les Josephson, Jack Snow, Maxie Baughn, Roger Brown, Deacon Jones, Merlin Olsen, Tom Mack and Ed Meador.

1968 The Rams took another Heisman Trophy winner in the 1968 draft, UCLA quarterback Gary Beban. They also acquired veteran signal-caller Milt Plum from the Detroit Lions. Beban competed with Plum and Gabriel for the quarterback spot, but failed to make the club. He later caught on with the Washington Redskins as a receiver and back. Wide receiver Harold Jackson, a 12th-round pick from Jackson State, was one of the few rookies to stick with the team.

The Rams finished the preseason with a 4-2 record, then got off to a fantastic start in league play, winning their first six games. The defense was overwhelming, giving up an average of just 11.5 points per game during that time.

In the opener against St. Louis, the front four of Lamar Lundy, Roger Brown, Merlin Olsen and Deacon Jones chased Cardinal quarterback Jim Hart all over the field. They blocked five of Hart's

Pages 106-107: Art Perkins, a 240-pound Los Angeles Ram fullback, tries to score from the two-yard line against the San Francisco 49ers. Perkins is met head on by linebacker Mike Dowdle, who keeps Perkins out of the end zone.

passing attempts, sacked him six times and forced him to throw three interceptions.

The offensive spark was supplied by Ron Smith. He returned the second-half kickoff 94 yards for a touchdown, giving Los Angeles a 17-3 advantage. Running back Tommy Mason gained 82 yards on 16 carries, and Dick Bass added 56 yards on 13 carries. The Rams scored their final touchdown on a six-yard pass from Gabriel to Jack Snow to cap the 24-13 win.

The defense came to the rescue again in the fourth game of the season against San Francisco. Near the end of the third quarter, the 49ers had a first-and-goal at the two-yard line. Three consecutive running plays produced one yard and the 49ers elected to kick a field goal on fourth down. The Rams took the ensuing kickoff and marched 80 yards. They scored on Henry Dyer's one-yard run then went on to beat San Francisco, 24-10.

Victories over the Green Bay Packers and the Atlanta Falcons gave the Rams a 6-0 record and a tie with Baltimore for first place in the coastal division. The six-game winning streak in 1968, coupled with the Rams eight wins at the end of the 1967 regular season, gave them a club record 14 consecutive wins in league play.

With two games left on the schedule, Los Angeles had a 10-1-1 record. Baltimore was in first place with a 11-1 mark. The two teams were slated to play on the final day of the season with the winner going to the western conference playoff.

Before meeting Baltimore, however, the Rams had to get by the Chicago Bears, who had a 5-7 record. In one of the most bizarre games in Ram history, Chicago beat Los Angeles, 17-16. The Bears took advantage of several Los Angeles mistakes in the fourth period to come out on top. Ram running back Tommy Mason lost a crucial fumble when the team was in scoring position, kicker Bruce Gossett missed a 35-yard field goal late in the game and then a holding call in the closing seconds moved the Rams out of field goal range. The holding call was made even more bizarre because the referees mistakely gave the Rams only three plays on that series rather than four.

The controversial call came with less than a minute to play. Roman Gabriel had returned to action in the fourth quarter after being knocked unconscious in the first half. He completed a 32-yard pass to Jack Snow, giving Los Angeles a first down on the Chicago 32-yard line. With just 30 seconds to play, the Rams could have tried a field goal from that point. Instead, they tried to move within comfortable kicking range for Bruce Gossett.

On the next play, tackle Charlie Cowan was detected holding. The 15-yard penalty moved the Rams back to the Bears' 47-yard line and out of field goal range. They should have had a first-and-25 from that position, but the down marker was inexplicably changed to second down. Gabriel missed on his next three passes, then, on what should have been fourth down, the ball was turned over to the Bears.

Commissioner Pete Rozelle later admitted the game officials goofed. All six officials were suspended from handling NFL games for the remainder of the season.

The Rams' loss gave Baltimore the division title. The Colts went on to defeat Cleveland in the NFL Championship Game, 34-0, but lost Super Bowl III to Joe Namath and the New York Jets, 16-7.

Just four days after the Rams completed their season, George Allen was fired. In his three years with the club, he posted a 29-10-3 record and led the team from the division cellar to a third, first and second place finish. Owner Dan Reeves cited Allen's propensity for dealing away draft picks for veteran players as one reason for the decision. However, two weeks later the team's management reversed itself and rehired Allen.

1969 Allen made several shrewd picks in the 1969 draft including first-round choices Larry Smith, a running back from Florida and Bob Klein, a tight end from USC. Linebacker Pat Curran, of tiny Lakeland College in Wisconsin, was picked on the seventh round.

Roman Gabriel (18) is flipped in the air by Cleveland tackle Walter Johnson (71) after a quarterback sneak. Brown linebacker Dale Lindsey (51) prepares to lend a hand. **Page 110:** Willie Ellison (33) eludes the grasp of Cleveland's Bob Matheson to score. Ellison set a team single-game record in 1971 when he gained 247 yards against the New Orleans Saints.

Myron Pottios 1966–1970

George Allen took over the Ram head coaching job in 1966 and immediately began to rebuild the defense. His first chore was to obtain veteran linebackers to anchor his defensive unit. One of the men he chose was Myron Pottios.

Allen obtained Pottios from the Pittsburgh Steelers for a second-round draft choice, then acquired veterans Maxie

Baughn, Bill George and Jack Pardee to round out the linebacking corps. The defensive line already consisted of Merlin Olsen, Deacon Jones, Lamar Lundy and Rosey Grier. The resulting defense led the Rams to their first winning season since 1958.

"The Rams weren't doing too good during the early 1960s, so George (Allen) began

trading for veterans, which is what he liked to do," said Pottios. "It worked for him because we were in the playoffs within two years.

"George liked to have a field general out there, so he brought in Bill George to run the defense. All our defenses were called on the field, either in the huddle or as an automatic. When Bill left, Maxie Baughn

became the field general."

When Allen took over in 1966, the Rams were coming off a 4-10 season. In his first year at the helm, Los Angeles finished in third place with an 8-6 record. A year later the Rams were 11-1-2 and playing for the NFC Western Conference Championship.

"We had a fantastic defensive line at that

111

time with the 'Fearsome Foursome,''' Pottios said. ''The acquisition of several veteran linebackers helped solidify the defense. What made it most effective was getting into the right defenses, though. And that was because we were calling them on the field and could switch into the right defense before the snap. We watched a lot of movies to pick up the other team's tendencies. George was always big on game films.''

Although the Rams were well prepared on game day, certain teams were still difficult to defend. Pottios remembers those that gave the Rams trouble.

''San Francisco was always a big rival, of course,'' he said. '' But Baltimore was the team we had to watch for. They were in our division at that time and they always seemed to be breathing down our neck. If we lost two or three games in a season, we had to chase the Colts the rest of the year.

''There were certain guys that gave you fits, too. The Packers' Jim Ringo was a tough one. He wasn't that big so he didn't beat you up physically, but he was very quick. He gave me problems because he moved so well. Bruce Bosley from the 49ers was just the opposite. He was strong and physical.

''Among the running backs, Jim Brown was in his own league. When you tackled him it was like hitting a rock. You'd put your shoulder into

him and it would go numb. Jim Taylor was another punishing runner. He wouldn't try to avoid you. In fact, he'd run right at you. Let's put it this way, when you played the Packers you knew you played a football game. They were a physical team all the way around.''

Pottios considers the 1969 Rams club one of the best he ever played on. The team started the season by winning its first 11 games and clinching the league title with an 11-0 record. They lost their final three games that year and blew the western conference playoff game to Minnesota.

''We went to Minnesota for the playoffs and had a 17-7 lead at halftime,'' Pottios said. ''They came out in the second half all fired up and took it to us. One of the things I remember about that game was Carl Eller tackling Gabriel for a safety near the end of the game. It happened just when we were trying to get something going. That ended our chances.'' The Vikings won it, 23-20.

Pottios was drafted by the Pittsburgh Steelers in 1961 after starring at Notre Dame. At Pittsburgh, Coach Buddy Parker tried to mold a solid defense around Pottios. Unfortunately, the Steelers had trouble climbing out of the second divison. At Los Angeles, Pottios met George Allen. He considers Allen one of the game's great defensive coordinators.

''Buddy was a good

defensive coach, but I learned more about football from George Allen than anybody I ever played under,'' Pottios said. ''George stressed the mental aspect of the game. He wanted everybody to be prepared mentally for the opponent. That's why we watched a lot of films. One of the other things George liked to do was surround himself with bodies. He'd have 35-40 players on the taxi squad. When we went out to practice there would be 100 guys on the field.''

In 1968, his third season as head coach, Allen led the Rams to a 10-3-1 mark. He was promptly fired at the end of the year by former owner Dan Reeves. Several veteran players protested the firing and Allen was rehired two weeks later.

''George was always popular with the players,'' Pottios said. ''He was easy going. As long as you got your job done on the field, there was no problem. When he was fired, the team rallied to his defense. There were other people in the community that had petitions passed around to get him back.''

Allen served two more seasons with the Rams before moving on to the Washington Redskins. Pottios was reunited with his old coach when he was traded to the Washington Redskins in 1971. But his former association with the Rams is something he can't easily forget.

''I can't help thinking about my years with the Rams almost every

day,'' he said. ''I drive by Chapman College on the way to work, which is where we used to practice. Whenever I drive by I wonder how in the heck we ever practiced there. The place is so tiny. People used to get dressed for practice under the stands. We had 100 guys on the field and I don't see now where we put them all.

''The facilities we used then don't compare to what they have now. For example, players rarely worked out with weights back then because the club didn't have any weights. They finally got a Universal weight machine around 1969 and that's when I started lifting.''

Although Pottios played with some top-notch teams in Los Angeles, he insists his biggest thrill as a player came as a member of the Washington Redskins in 1972. It gave him a chance to play in the Super Bowl. The Redskins were defeated in Super Bowl VII by the Miami Dolphins, 14-7. Miami posted a perfect 17-0 record that season.

''There were many great, great situations I was a part of in football,'' he said. ''I had some great times with the Rams, but nothing can compare to playing in a Super Bowl. I played in a couple of Pro Bowls and I got a lot of satisfaction out of that, but the Super Bowl is the ultimate. That's my favorite memory.''

The strength of the Rams remained its veterans, however, and Roman Gabriel continued to operate an efficient offense behind an outstanding line. The Rams' ball-control style of attack featured Bob Brown, Charlie Cowan, Tom Mack, Joe Scibelli and Ken Iman on the line. They paved the way for backs Willie Ellison, Tommy Mason, Les Josephson and 220-pound rookie Larry Smith. They were effective enough to lead the Rams to wins in their first 11 games.

Los Angeles opened the regular season at Baltimore. The Colts were still reeling from their Super Bowl loss to the New York Jets. Baltimore was the first NFL team to lose to an AFL team in the Super Bowl.

Baltimore held a 17-10 lead in the third quarter when Gabriel ignited a 17-point outburst in just seven minutes of play. First, Gabriel marched the club 82 yards to tie the score at 17-17. The big play was a 46-yard run by Larry Smith. The touchdown came on a 12-yard pass from Gabriel to Willie Ellison.

Ed Meador then intercepted a Unitas pass to set up a Bruce Gossett field goal. Less than two minutes later, Klein recovered a Baltimore fumble on the Colts' 13-yard line. Gabriel quickly completed a 13-yard touchdown pass to Wendell Tucker to give the Rams a 27-20 lead. The defense held Baltimore the rest of the way.

Smith was the Los Angeles workhorse. He gained 73 yards on 10 carries. Gabriel completed 20 of 33 tosses for 268 yards. The team's leading receiver was Tucker with six receptions.

The win over the defending NFL champions was an indication of things to come for the Rams. They dominated the rest of the league, winning their first 11 games and clinching the conference title with three games left to play. During that span, the Rams routed Green Bay, 34-21, and

Top: Tight end Billy Truax snags a touchdown pass against Baltimore in 1967. Los Angeles went on to win the game and clinch the coastal division championship. **Bottom:** Coach George Allen gets a ride off the field after his Los Angeles Rams beat the Baltimore Colts, 34-10, to clinch the NFL's Coastal Division Championship in 1967.

Washington, 24-13, won twice over San Francisco and gained a dramatic, 24-23, victory over Dallas.

While leading his team to 11 straight wins, quarterback Roman Gabriel was nearly unstoppable. He threw 23 touchdown passes and was intercepted only six times during the winning streak.

After clinching the division crown, the Rams went into a slump. They dropped a game to Minnesota, 20-13, were shut out by Detroit, 28-0, and ended the regular season with a 13-7 loss to Baltimore. Riding a three-game losing streak, the Rams prepared to play the Minnesota Vikings for the western conference title. Minnesota had also dropped its final game of the season. They ended the year with a 12-2 record. The Rams were 11-3.

The temperature hovered near 21 degrees in Minnesota at game time. Ignoring the weather, Gabriel directed the Rams to a 17-7 halftime lead. He marched the club 45 and 56 yards to touchdowns, and 65 yards to set up a field goal.

In the second half, the momentum began to change. Ram linebacker Maxie Baughn was forced to the bench after suffering a knee injury, then Minnesota scored to come within a field goal at 17-14. The Rams responded with their own three-pointer, and with 12 minutes to play, Los Angeles had a 20-14 advantage.

In the fourth period, Viking quarterback Joe Kapp chipped away at the Ram defense with running plays and short passes. Midway through the final period, he put the Vikings ahead for the first time when he ran one in from the three-yard line.

After taking a 21-20 lead, the Vikings held the Rams the rest of the way. Minnesota defensive end Carl Eller added two points for the Vikings when he sacked Gabriel in the end zone for a safety.

Gabriel completed 22 of 32 passes, but had several of his throws dropped. He ended his finest season as the NFL's Most Valuable Player.

Once again Los Angeles appeared in the Play-off Bowl in Miami. They proved they were the best second-place team in the NFL by rolling over the Dallas Cowboys, 31-0.

Merlin Olsen was selected to play in his eighth straight Pro Bowl game in 1969. Among the other Rams participating in the post-season game were Deacon Jones, Maxie Baughn, Roman Gabriel, Tom Mack, Charlie Cowan and Bob Brown.

Page 116: Jack Snow takes a pass from Roman Gabriel as San Francisco's Bruce Taylor prepares to flatten the receiver.

1970–1979

CHAPTER FOUR

THE ROAD TO SUPER BOWL XIV

In 1970, Milwaukee Bucks center Lew Alcindor was selected NBA Rookie of the Year. Jim Plunkett guided Stanford to the Rose Bowl and was awarded the Heisman Trophy. And John Newcombe defeated Ken Rosewall to capture his second Wimbledon Championship.

It took Joe Frazier just five rounds to knock out Jimmy Ellis that year and win boxing's heavyweight title. And Larry Mahan continued to dominate the rodeo scene by winning his fifth straight World Rodeo Championship.

The NFL saw some changes in 1970 as it completed its merger with the AFL. The leagues were realigned, with the Rams joining San Francisco, Atlanta and New Orleans in the National Football Conference's Western Division.

The Rams' first-round draft choice that year was Jack "Hacksaw" Reynolds, a linebacker from Tennessee. The team's eighth-round choice was Michigan State linebacker Rich Saul. He was later converted into an offensive lineman and became a perennial All-Pro.

Allen continued to stock his team with veterans, particularly on defense. His starting linebackers at the beginning of the season—Myron Pottios, Maxie Baughn and Jack Pardee—averaged 33 years of age. In the defensive backfield was Ed Meador, 33, Richie Petitbon, 32, and Kermit Alexander, 29.

Los Angeles breezed through the preseason schedule with a 6-0 record. The club then won its first three league games over St. Louis, 34-13, Buffalo, 19-0, and San Diego, 37-10. In its next six games, it lost three and tied one to post a 6-3-1 record.

The Rams faced a must-win situation against their next opponent, the first-place San Francisco 49ers. The surprising 49ers were 7-2-1. A win would virtually wrap up the western division title for San Francisco.

In the rain and fog at San Francisco's Kezar Stadium, the Rams were resurrected and thrown back into the race with a decisive, 30-13, win. The rushing yardage was evenly distributed between three Ram running backs. Les Josephson gained 54 yards, Willie Ellison had 51 yards and Larry Smith added 50 yards. Gabriel completed just seven of 21 passes for 70 yards. The win left San Francisco and Los Angeles deadlocked in the race for the league crown.

The Rams lost to Detroit a week later and dropped a game behind the 49ers. But on the last day of the season, they were still alive in the title chase. The Rams had to beat the New York Giants. More importantly, the Oakland Raiders had to beat the 49ers. A win by the Rams and a 49er loss would give the Rams their second straight division title.

The Rams did their part. They completely dominated New York, 31-3, to knock the Giants out of the Super Bowl competition. Los Angeles won be-

hind tough defense and Gabriel's accurate throwing arm. Gabriel was good on 13 of 21 passes for 158 yards and two touchdowns. Josephson was the game's leading ball carrier. He picked up 106 yards in 20 carries.

Oakland did not cooperate with the Rams, however. The 49ers destroyed the Raiders, 38-7, to win the league title. Los Angeles finished in second place with a 9-4-1 record.

1971 Despite five consecutive winning seasons, and an overall record of 49-17-4, George Allen's contract was not renewed for the 1971 season. He was replaced by Tommy Prothro, the former head coach at UCLA.

Prothro took the opposite approach of Allen and rebuilt the team with young players. Among the veterans he unloaded were Jack Pardee, Maxie Baughn, Myron Pottios, Richie Petitbon, Tommy Mason, Bob Brown and Billy Truax.

The Rams had two first-round picks in the 1971 college draft and Prothro used them to select linebacker Isiah Robertson from Southern University and defensive end Jack Youngblood from Florida. On the third round, he drafted Texas A&M defensive back Dave Elmendorf.

On April 15, 1971, team owner Dan Reeves died of cancer. His friend and business partner William Barnes took over as team president and general manager.

The Rams got off to a disastrous start in the league opener when they lost to the New Orleans Saints on the last play of the game. Rookie quarterback Archie Manning sparked the Saints to a 17-3 third quarter lead, but the Rams came back to take a 20-17 advantage in the fourth period.

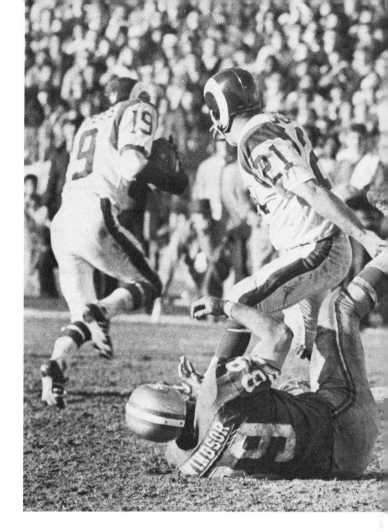

Linebacker Isiah Robertson was a first-round choice of Los Angeles in 1971. He teamed with Jim Youngblood and Jack Reynolds to give the Rams one of the top linebacking crews in the NFL. **Top, right:** Defensive back Jim Nettles (19), after a big interception, leaves intended receiver Bob Windsor (89) sprawled on the ground. **Bottom, right:** Jack Snow (84) goes high in the air against the Buffalo Bills to catch a pass from quarterback Roman Gabriel. Snow is third on the Rams' all-time reception list with 340 catches. He averaged 17.7 yards per reception.

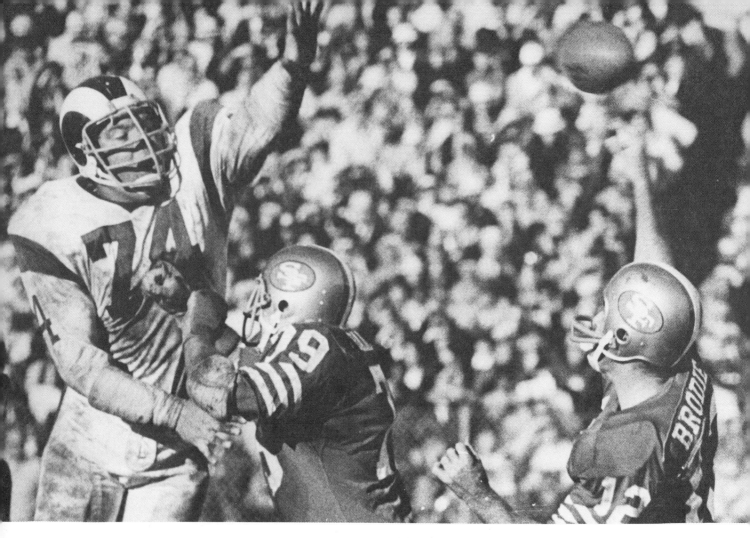

Merlin Olsen goes high in the air to block a pass by San Francsco's John Brodie. Cas Banaszek (79) attempts to keep Olsen away from Brodie. Olsen played in 208 games for Los Angeles, more than any other player. **Page 121:** Linebacker Jack ''Hacksaw'' Reynolds (64) stops San Francisco running back Vic Washington. Reynolds was drafted out of Tennessee on the first round in 1970. He anchored the Rams' defensive unit for 11 years until he migrated north to San Francisco.

Les Josephson paced the Rams with two touchdown runs.

The Saints took control of the ball at their own 30-yard line with 1:30 to play. Manning moved the Saints downfield with quick passes to receivers Dave Parks and Danny Abramowicz. With five seconds remaining in the game, the Saints had the ball on the one-yard line. A field goal would tie the game, but New Orleans decided to go for the win. Manning rolled out to his right looking for a receiver and decided to make a run for the end zone. As Manning crossed the goal line, he fumbled the ball and the Rams' Jack Youngblood pounced on it at the one-yard line. The officials ruled, however, that Manning had crossed the goal line before the fumble and awarded six points to the Saints. The ruling gave New Orleans a 24-20 win.

Things got worse the following week when the Atlanta Falcons tied Los Angeles, 20-20. In the third week of the season, the Rams finally got a win for their new head coach when they beat the Chicago Bears, 17-3.

One of Prothro's offseason acquisitions was wide receiver Lance Rentzel. Rentzel's speed was put to good use against Chicago. The wide receiver set up the Rams' first score after running 23 yards on a reverse to the Chicago six-yard line. Josephson powered his way in from there. Later in the game, Rentzel ran 50 yards on a reverse for a touchdown. Willie Ellison was the workhorse against Chicago. He gained 95 yards on 22 carries.

The Rams continued their winning streak with a 20-13 victory over first place San Francisco and a 30-13 thumping of Green Bay. The defense was superb against the Packers, allowing just 194 yards of total offense.

After beating the 49ers in their second meeting of the season, the Rams were in first place with a 6-3-1 record. San Francisco was directly behind them at 6-4. But the lead lasted only a week. Dallas beat Los Angeles, 28-21, and the 49ers moved back into first place.

The Rams remained just percentage points be-

hind the 49ers the rest of the year. The race came down to the final day of the season once again. Los Angeles had to beat Pittsburgh and hope the Detroit Lions could knock off San Francisco in order to win the conference title.

The Rams beat the Steelers, 23-14. Gabriel was on target, completing 13 of 22 passes for 148 yards and a touchdown. Willie Ellison needed 23 yards rushing to go over the 1,000 mark for the season. He gained exactly 23 yards on 11 carries.

Detroit could not help the Rams though. San Francisco defeated the Lions, 31-27, to finish 9-5 and win the western conference title. The Rams finished with an 8-5-1 record.

1972 In the offseason, Ram owner Robert Irsay, who purchased the club from the estate of Dan Reeves, made an unprecedented move. He traded the entire Los Angeles franchise to Carroll Rosenbloom for the Baltimore Colts franchise. Rosenbloom became the new Ram owner in July, 1972.

The 1972 college draft bolstered the Rams already potent running attack. Among the collegians selected were Texas running back Jim Bertelsen on the second round and Colorado State back Lawrence McCutcheon on the third round. Prothro then began to rebuild his defensive line by trading away All-Pro defensive end Deacon Jones and replacing him with young Fred Dryer.

Early in the season the Rams discovered another top-notch running back in Bob Thomas. In the league opener against New Orleans, Thomas gained 144 yards on 18 carries. Two weeks later, he ran 19 times for 142 yards against the San Francisco 49ers.

Thomas was an unheralded 11th-round draft choice of the Cincinnati Bengals in 1971. The Rams picked him up after he was cut loose by the Bengals. The 5-10, 200-pound Thomas earned a starting job after fullback Willie Ellison was sidelined with an injury. But Thomas was just part of the story against San Francisco. Los Angeles totaled 302 yards on the ground against the 49ers enroute to a 31-7 win.

At midseason, the Rams had a promising 5-2-1 mark. Then suddenly they collapsed. The Rams won just one game in their last six starts to finish

with a 6-7-1 record and in third place behind San Francisco and Atlanta. It was Los Angeles' first losing season in seven years.

Shortly after the season ended, Rosenbloom fired Prothro who had three years left on a five-year contract. Detroit Lion Assistant Coach Chuck Knox was hired to replace Prothro. Under Knox, the Rams began one of the most successful periods in team history.

1973 Knox began rebuilding immediately. He used his three second-round draft choices to pick Colorado running back Cullen Bryant, quarterback Ron Jaworski from Youngstown and Tennessee Tech linebacker Jim Youngblood. On the fourth round, he selected Terry Nelson, a tight end from Arkansas and on the fifth round he picked Cody Jones, a defensive end from San Jose State. All five players figured prominently in the Rams' future success.

Knox also engineered several bold trades before the 1973 season began. Veteran quarterback John Hadl was obtained from the San Diego Chargers for defensive end Coy Bacon and running back Bob Thomas. Roman Gabriel then was traded to Philadelphia for receiver Harold Jackson and two first-round draft choices. The trades would make Knox look like a genius by year's end.

The Rams were blessed with a covey of outstanding backs. Lawrence McCutcheon, Jim Bertelsen, Larry Smith, Les Josephson, Tony Baker and Cullen Bryant labored behind an excellent offensive line. In the league opener against Kansas City, Bertelsen rushed for 143 yards while McCutcheon gained 120. Quarterback John Hadl threw only nine passes, but he completed seven for 95 yards and two touchdowns. It was enough offense to beat the Chiefs, 23-13.

Los Angeles continued to score points everywhere it went. The club ran up wins over Atlanta, 31-0, Minnesota, 40-20, and Houston, 31-26, enroute to a 4-0 record.

In the fifth game of the season, nearly 82,000 fans packed the Coliseum to watch the Rams take on the Dallas Cowboys. They saw Hadl put on an unforgettable aerial show. He threw touchdown passes of 63, 67, 16 and 36 yards, all to wide receiver Harold Jackson. Hadl finished the day

Deacon Jones 1961–1971

Ask Deacon Jones about football's best defensive lineman and he doesn't hesitate to answer.

"Nobody in the history of the game was better at sacking the quarterback than Deacon," he said. "Call the Hall of Fame and ask them. I had more sacks in a 14-game season than these guys are getting now. There was no lineman that could consistently stop me. You can ask George Allen who the best lineman was and he'll tell you it was me."

No one ever accused Jones of being modest about his ability. But then the Rams' "Fearsome Foursome," which he was a part of in the 1960s, may have been the most dominant line in football history. Jones and Lamar Lundy were the defensive ends, while Merlin Olsen and Roosevelt Grier were the tackles. Roger Brown, an All-Pro

with the Detroit Lions, stepped into the lineup in 1967 when Grier retired. Two members of that group, Olsen and Jones, are already in Pro Football's Hall of Fame.

"We were an entity all our own," Jones said of the Fearsome Four-some. "We were a unique group. I'll go so far as to say we changed the nature of the game. I don't think that line will ever be duplicated. It was the best defensive line ever put together. It took a good collective effort on everyone's part to be successful."

The Rams' defensive line was made up of four outstanding individual talents. Jones played in his first Pro Bowl in 1964, and was selected to play every year after that until 1971. Merlin Olsen played in every Pro Bowl from 1962 until 1975. But each singular talent had to blend together to make the group effective,

Jones says. It was their ability to work together that was their greatest strength.

"We had a great relationship on the field and off the field," he said. "Even to this day we're friends. I consider Merlin one of my good buddies. It was a good group of individuals."

When Jones reported to the Rams' rookie camp in 1961 as a 14th-round draft choice from South Carolina State, he was one of the few people who believed he would win a spot with the club. Never short on confidence, Jones publicly announced he would be starting for the Rams come opening day.

"When I got to Los Angeles, I was a million-to-one shot to make the team," Jones said. "They didn't take many players from a black school like I attended. I told everybody I came to play and I was serious. I

wasn't supposed to say that as a rookie. I was supposed to keep quiet, but I knew what would happen if I kept my mouth shut. I'd probably be gone. I challenged veterans to race me in the 40 and did other things to get people's attention. I had to do that. You see, there was a quota system back then. They didn't want too many blacks playing in the NFL. I was controversial, and I know there was people who didn't like me, but you have to get people to take notice. There was no place else for me to go but the AFL.''

There is no doubt that Jones was one of the NFL's great physical specimens. At 6-5 and 265 pounds, Jones could still outsprint most running backs. In his prime, he could run the 40-yard dash in 4.5 seconds.

''I don't think there was anyone who went sideline to sideline faster than me,'' he said.

In his brash style, Jones claims there were no offensive linemen in the NFL that could detain him. They might slow him down, but they couldn't stop him.

''I don't think there is any lineman I could give credit to for being able to stop me,'' he said. ''Truthfully, they couldn't block me. In fact, very few linemen ever blocked me one-on-one anyway. I usually was confronted with a series of people. I didn't have that much respect for offensive linemen.''

The Fearsome Foursome was the cornerstone of the great Rams'

defensive teams of the 1960s. Between 1963 and 1970, they averaged 44 quarterback sacks per season. In 1967, the Rams were the hardest team in the league to score on, giving up just 196 points in 14 games.

Running backs did not have an easy time against the Los Angeles defense, either. Three times between 1964 and 1968, the Rams allowed the fewest rushing yards in the NFL. Jones says he had a special love for chasing running backs.

''Pound for pound, Jim Brown was the best back I ever played against,'' Jones said. ''He took some punishment because everybody was after him. But he was able to withstand the punishment and come away from the game uninjured. There was other guys, like Gale Sayers or O.J., that were good because they were so quick off the ball. You had to hit them before they were by you. But you have to understand what I am saying here. I faced some good backs, but there was no running back that was hard for me or any lineman to bring down if I had a shot at him.

''Right now I would say Walter Payton is probably the best running back around. There are few players that can match his level of skill.''

Jones played two seasons with the San Diego Chargers after leaving the Rams in 1971, then ended his career in 1974 with the Washington Redskins.

At Washington, he was reunited once again with former Ram head coach George Allen. In 1980, just six years after his retirement, Jones was elected to Pro Football's Hall of Fame.

''Making the Hall of Fame was my biggest thrill as a football player,'' he said. ''One thing I regret is that I never made it to the Super Bowl. I played my best for 11 years with the Rams and we had some outstanding teams, but something always seemed to get in the way of the Super Bowl.

''I'm also happy that I never had any serious injuries. I never had a knee operation or anything that seems so common among the players today. I was able to retire with my body still intact.

''I must say I enjoyed my career with the Rams,'' Jones said. ''I think I was controversial sometimes, but I had fun playing football. I played with the best defensive line in the game and in front of the best fans. We dominated opposing lines and I think that's what the fans paid to see. I think we gave them what they wanted.''

Jones is proud of his place in the Hall of Fame and his ranking among the greatest defensive linemen to play professional football. Despite those honors, he has one regret about his career.

''I wish I had killed more quarterbacks,'' he said jokingly.

completing 12 of 22 passes for 279 yards, as the Rams beat Dallas, 37-31. Jackson caught seven of those throws for 238 yards. His four touchdown receptions tied a team record set by Elroy Hirsch in 1951 and Bob Shaw in 1949.

After posting a 6-0 record, Los Angeles suffered its first loss of the season in a controversial game against the Minnesota Vikings. The Vikings had a 10-9 lead with three minutes left to play when they were forced to punt. The Rams prepared to retain the ball in good field position. Kicker Mike Eischeid took the snap and was apparently bumped by the Rams' Rich Saul after the punt. Eischeid went down and a penalty was called. Saul protested, claiming that no contact was made. Nevertheless, the officials let the penalty stand and Minnesota received a first down. The Vikings then were able to run out the clock to preserve the win.

Los Angeles was stopped again the following week by the Atlanta Falcons, 15-13, then went on a six-game winning streak to close out the year with a 12-2 record. The 12 wins set a club record for victories in a season.

The record-setting year was accomplished with outstanding play on both offense and defense. Los Angeles averaged 28 points per game while allowing just 12.7 points per contest. Fullback Lawrence McCutcheon was a major force in the offensive unit. He broke Dick Bass' single-season rushing record by gaining 1,097 yards. Quarterback John Hadl, who completed 52 percent of his 258 passes, was the unanimous choice as NFL Player of the Year. Chuck Knox, who coordinated the team's effort, was voted NFL Coach of the Year.

Los Angeles found itself in the NFC playoffs for the first time in three years. The club's opponent in the opening round was the Dallas Cowboys.

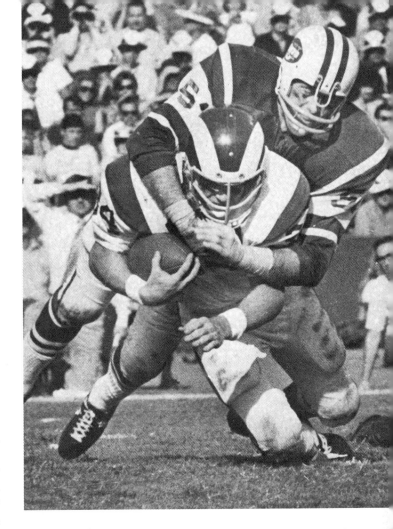

Top: Fullback Les Josephson is ridden to the turf by New York Jets linebacker John Ebersole. Josephson is fifth on the Rams all-time rushing list with 3,407 yards. **Bottom:** Tight end Bob Klein pulls down a pass from James Harris. Klein was drafted out of USC on the first round in 1969. His best year with the Rams was in 1972 when he caught 29 passes for 330 yards.

Dallas took a 17-0 lead early in the second quarter before Los Angeles could get on track. Kicker David Ray booted two field goals for the Rams from 33 and 37 yards, but he missed two others in the first half that would have closed the gap to 17-12.

Early in the final period Ray narrowed the margin to 17-9 after kicking a 40-yard field goal. On the Cowboys' next possession, Los Angeles defensive end Fred Dryer recovered a fumble on the Dallas 17-yard line. Two plays later Tony Baker scored on a five-yard run, making the score 17-16, and the Rams were back in the game with over 10 minutes to play.

Los Angeles had the momentum and seemed to be in command at that point. After the kickoff, the Rams stopped Dallas on two consecutive plays and Hadl prepared to take over again. Cowboy quarterback Roger Staubach faced a desperate third-and-14 situation from his own 17-yard line. But suddenly Staubach connected with wide receiver Drew Pearson on an 83-yard touchdown pass that stunned the Rams. Los Angeles was unable to score after that and Dallas added a field goal to win, 27-16.

1974 Nevada bookmakers made Los Angeles the preseason favorite to reach Super Bowl IX, but early in the 1974 season the club never seemed to jell. The Rams were upset by New England and Green Bay, and after five games had a 3-2 record. During that stretch they averaged just 15 points per game, so Knox went to his bench to generate more offensive power.

Ram quarterback Pat Haden tries to elude Minnesota Viking Carl Eller in the 1976 NFC Championship Game. Haden completed 54 percent of the 1,363 passes he threw for Los Angeles between 1976 and 1981. **Top right:** Rams wide receiver Harold Jackson outruns Bruce Taylor. **Bottom, right:** Ron Jessie (81) gets behind San Francisco's All-Pro cornerback Jimmy Johnson to grab a pass from James Harris. Jessie played with the Rams from 1975 to 1979.

A tackle by Deacon Jones (75) causes San Diego Charger running back Mike Garrett to lose the football. Merlin Olsen (74) assists Jones.

He traded starting quarterback John Hadl to Green Bay for five draft choices and turned the quarterback job over to James Harris.

In his first start, before 74,000 fans at the Coliseum, Harris blitzed the 49ers. He ran for one touchdown and threw for three more in the Rams, 37-14, victory. Harris led the club to seven wins in its final nine games and Los Angeles clinched its second western division title under Chuck Knox with a 10-4 record.

The Rams faced former skipper George Allen and the Washington Redskins in the first round of the playoffs. Earlier in the season, the Redskins defeated Los Angeles, 23-17. The Rams had the home field advantage against Washington and 80,118 fans showed up at the Coliseum, hoping they would make the most of it. Midway through the first period, they got their wish. Harris gave the Rams a 7-0 lead when he connected with Bob Klein on a 10-yard pass.

There was little else for Ram fans to cheer about in the first half. The Redskins, led by quarterback Bill Kilmer, scored 10 unanswered points and left the field at halftime with a 10-7 edge.

The Ram defense dominated the second half. Los Angeles took advantage of three intercepted passes and two recovered fumbles to put 12 points on the board and build a 19-10 lead. The big blow came in the fourth period when linebacker Isiah Robertson intercepted a Sonny Jurgensen pass and returned it 59 yards for a touchdown. Washington was unable to score on the stingy Ram defense in the second half and Los Angeles held on to win its first playoff game since 1951. It gave the Rams a chance to meet Minnesota in the NFL Championship Game.

The game matched two of the best defenses in football, and both units played up to championship standards. The first quarter was scoreless, although the Rams had one excellent opportunity to get on the board. Los Angeles marched to the Vikings' 19-yard line, but Lawrence McCutcheon lost the ball on a fumble. In the second quarter, Minnesota took a 7-3 lead.

Los Angeles put together a formidable drive in the third quarter. Starting from its own one-yard line, Harris moved the Rams 98 yards. The big

Lawrence McCutcheon 1972–1979

Appearing in the Super Bowl is a life-long dream for most NFL players. The Los Angeles Rams reached that pinnacle after the 1979 season. They posted a 9-7 league record, breezed through the playoffs and faced the Pittsburgh Steelers in Super Bowl XIV. But for Los Angeles running back Lawrence McCutcheon, the game produced mixed emotions.

"I always looked at that season as sort of a weird year," McCutcheon said. "We had better teams before that, but didn't get to the Super Bowl. Of the teams I played on at Los Angeles, that team won the least amount of games. It was just one of those up-and-down seasons."

Playing in the Super Bowl was McCutcheon's greatest thrill as a player. On a personal level, however, he was disappointed because he did not play a bigger role in the game. Earlier in the 1979 season, McCutcheon lost his starting position when Wendell Tyler and Cullen Bryant worked their way into the lineup. Tyler went on to gain 1,109 yards rushing that season.

McCutcheon carried the ball just five times for 10 yards in the Super Bowl, but he was involved in one of the game's biggest plays. Late in the third quarter, he fooled the Steelers by throwing a 24-yard touchdown pass to receiver Ron Smith. The score put Los Angeles in front, 19-17.

"After all those years of just missing the Super Bowl it was a thrill to finally make it,"

he said. "But at the same time I was a little disappointed to have a limited amount of playing time in that game. I would have liked to have played a bigger part, especially if it would have helped the team win."

McCutcheon played a large role in the club's success during the 1970s. Between 1973 and 1977, McCutcheon was nearly a cinch to gain 1,000 yards rushing per season. He missed the mark just once during those five years when he gained 911 yards in 1975. In his eight seasons with the Rams, he gained 6,186 yards and is the club's all-time leading rusher. When he retired after the 1981 season, he was 11th on the NFL's all-time rushing list.

"I always considered myself a complete back rather than just a runner," McCutcheon said. "Rather than excel in just one area, I tried to excel in all phases of the game. I took pride in being able to block and catch the ball too."

McCutcheon was always an effective receiver. He nabbed 184 passes between 1972 and 1979 to rank 10th on the club's all-time receiving chart.

McCutcheon joined the Rams as a third-round draft pick out of Colorado State in 1972. He was placed on the taxi squad his rookie season. When Chuck Knox took over the head coaching duties in 1973, he had a meeting with McCutcheon and asked why the big running back wasn't playing regularly.

"I told him that was a good question," McCutcheon said. "I thought I should have been playing more. He said he'd give me every opportunity to win a starting job in the preseason. I worked very hard in practice that year and Knox ended up trading a couple of the other backs. I like to think that he saw something in me and decided to make those trades because of my ability."

McCutcheon didn't let his coach down. In his first season as a starter, he gained 1,097 yards on 210 carries, an average of 5.2 yards per attempt. He was also the team's second leading receiver in 1973 with 30 receptions.

It was just the beginning of an outstanding career. McCutcheon went on to gain 1,109 yards in 1974, 911 yards in 1975, 1,168 yards in 1976 and 1,238 yards in 1977. The only man to gain more rushing yards in a single season for the Rams is Eric Dickerson.

"1973 was an important year for me," McCutcheon said. "I finally got to play and see what I could do. Knox showed he had confidence in me and that gave me the confidence I needed."

Although McCutcheon gives Chuck Knox credit for having faith in his running ability, he says there is one other coach who helped shape his career. Elijah Pitts, the Rams' backfield coach during the mid-1970s, and a former star runner with the Green Bay Packers, was McCutcheon's mentor.

"Those two guys probably had the most impact on me as a player," McCutcheon said. "Elijah always spent lots of time with the players. He let me know what was going on. He was an effective teacher, which was probably the most important thing. I wanted to be a well-rounded back and Elijah was able to help me improve on my blocking skills and other little things that people just don't notice. I found him to be an easy person to relate to."

McCutcheon credits Knox with the team's turnaround in the 1970s. In 1972, a year prior to Knox' arrival, the Rams had a 6-7-1 mark. The following year under Knox, the Rams finished in first place in the NFC Western Division with a 12-2 record. Los Angeles lost those two games by a total of three points.

"That was really a great team," McCutcheon said. "It was probably the best Ram team I played on. There was lots of talent already there. We just started blending it together that year. We had a pretty effective defense to start with and that was getting most of the attention. Chuck (Knox) put the offense together. It was kind of a conservative offense, but it got the job done."

The Rams' ball-control attack was centered around McCutcheon in 1973, but Jim Bertelsen also rushed for 854 yards. In addition, Tony Baker and Larry Smith both gained over 300 yards on the ground. Quarterback John Hadl threw only 258 passes all season, well below the league average of 353 passes. Still, the Rams led the NFC in scoring with 388 points.

When recalling the game's fiercest competitors, most running backs remember frightening collisions with the game's most feared linebackers. Men like Dick Butkus, Ray Nitschke and Sam Huff often come to mind. McCutcheon says the hardest hitters he played against were a pair of defensive backs.

"The Bears had a good one in Doug Plank," McCutcheon said. "But the hardest single hit I ever took during my career was from Kenny Houston. He played with the Washington Redskins at the time. He just knocked me flat.

"I only faced Butkus during the 1973 season and he was on the decline at that time. There were some other good linebackers around. Tommy Nobis, who was with Atlanta, and Jeff Siemon from the Minnesota Vikings were probably the best.

"I had a good career with the Rams. I'm very proud to have played for this organization. My eight years with Los Angeles were among the most enjoyable of my life. I was glad to have played on the west coast and just fortunate it was with such a fantastic organization."

Pat Haden (11) gives encouragement to Ram players as they come off the field.

play was a 73-yard pass from Harris to Harold Jackson. Jackson was downed at the one. Two plays later the drive ended when Harris' pass was intercepted by Minnesota linebacker Wally Hilgenberg.

The Vikings scored a fourth quarter touchdown on Dave Osborn's one-yard run to clinch the game, 14-10. The Rams were stopped short of the Super Bowl once more.

1975 The Rams had an outstanding player draft in 1975. Among the rookies who made the team were defensive tackle Mike Fanning of Notre Dame, guard Dennis Harrah of Miami, tackle Doug France of Ohio State, defensive back Monte Jackson of San Diego State, center Geoff Reece of Washington State, defensive back Rod Perry of Colorado and USC quarterback Pat Haden.

It turned out to be an exceptional year for the defense. In preseason play, Los Angeles shut out

Oakland and Philadelphia and limited the San Francisco 49ers and Kansas City Chiefs to just two field goals. After finishing the exhibition season with a 5-1 record, the Rams were once again pegged as favorites to reach the Super Bowl.

Los Angeles didn't look like a championship team in its opener at Dallas. Quarterback James Harris was unable to move the club for three quarters, completing just one of 10 passes for five yards. He had three passes intercepted. In the fourth period, Harris was replaced by Ron Jaworski. Jaworski completed three of seven passes and led the Rams to their only score after a 74-yard drive. Dallas won the game, 18-7. Only one other team would score that many points against the Rams during the regular season.

In the second week of the season, Los Angeles played up to its reputation with a 23-14 victory over San Francisco. It was the start of a six-game winning streak that included a 13-10 overtime win over San Diego and a 42-3 dumping of Philadelphia.

The 49ers handed the Rams their second loss of the year, a 24-23 heartbreaker, but Los Angeles rebounded to win its last six games. During that stretch they played the best defensive football in the NFL, allowing an average of five

points per game. They beat Atlanta, 16-7, Chicago, 38-10, Detroit, 20-0, New Orleans, 14-7, Green Bay, 22-5, and the Super Bowl champion Pittsburgh Steelers, 10-3.

The defense was anchored by linemen Jack Youngblood, Fred Dryer, Merlin Olsen and Cody Jones. The linebackers included Jim Youngblood, Isiah Robertson, Jack Reynolds and Ken Geddes. In the secondary were Dave Elmendorf, Monte Jackson, Ed McMillan, Rod Perry and Bill Simpson.

During the course of the season, the Rams allowed just 135 points, an average of nine points per game. The 1969 Minnesota Vikings are the only team to allow less points in a season with 133. On offense, the Rams averaged 26 points.

The Rams finished in first place in the NFC Western Division with a 12-2 record. It assured them of the home field advantage in their first round playoff game against the St. Louis Cardinals.

A crowd of 72,650 saw Chuck Knox' club knock the Cardinals out of Super Bowl contention by scoring four touchdowns in the first half. The defense scored two of the six-pointers. Jack Youngblood returned an intercepted pass 47 yards for one touchdown, while defensive back Bill Simpson raced 65 yards to score with another interception.

Los Angeles added one more touchdown in the second half to breeze to a 35-23 win. Ron Jaworski started at quarterback for the injured James Harris and completed 12 of 23 passes for 203 yards. Lawrence McCutcheon was the Rams' workhorse, gaining 202 yards on 37 carries to break Steve Van Buren's playoff rushing record. Van Buren gained 196 yards for the Philadelphia Eagles in the 1949 playoffs.

The Rams next faced the Dallas Cowboys in the NFC Championship Game. Dallas made its

Top: Running back Cullen Bryant, as a free safety might see him, blasts through a big hole. **Bottom:** Jack Youngblood tackles Vikings running back Chuck Foreman for no gain.

Marlin McKeever 1961–1966, 1971–72

Marlin McKeever was the last of a vanishing breed. In the age of specialization, McKeever played both offense and defense. He was one of the last NFL players to perform both ways.

When he joined the Los Angeles Rams in 1961, as the club's first-round draft choice, he was the heir apparent to popular linebacker Les Richter. The former USC star made a favorable impression as a rookie, but did not win the starting linebacker job until Richter retired a year later.

"When I first reported to the Rams, they still had good linebackers around, guys like Jack Pardee, Les Richter and Bill Jobko," McKeever said. "I played a lot at the beginning of the year, but got hurt in about the fifth game and didn't play much the rest of the season."

McKeever was content at linebacker, but due to circumstances beyond his control, he suddenly had his career change directions during the 1963 season. The Rams decided they could use his athletic skills on offense.

"About midway through the season the club had a lot of injuries and we were running out of men, especially on offense," he said. "They decided to use me as a tight end in a game against the 49ers and see what I could do. I ended up playing there the rest of the season."

McKeever had three receptions against the 49ers, including a key

29-yard catch from Roman Gabriel that set up a touchdown. He ended the season with just 11 catches for 152 yards. But a year later, in 1964, he really began to blossom. He grabbed 41 passes for 582 yards and was the club's leading receiver. He had found himself a new position. For the next several years he alternated between linebacker and tight end. In all, he caught 133 passes for 1,737 yards and six touchdowns during his career.

"I enjoyed being a receiver and getting my hands on the ball, but I think I was more suited to being a linebacker," he said. "That's where I mostly played in college, and that's where I felt most comfortable."

McKeever was traded to the Minnesota Vikings in 1967, but returned to the Rams in 1971, where he was used again as a linebacker. He never forgot his pass-catching skills, however, and intercepted four passes that year. In 1972 he intercepted two more passes. Both years he led the team's linebackers in interceptions.

Since McKeever is one of the few modern-day players who has seen action on both sides of the line of scrimmage, he has a unique perspective from which to judge opposing players.

"The best back I played against was Jim Brown," McKeever said. "He was quite fast for a big man. Jim Taylor was a tough one to bring down. He liked to run right at you. That guy

wasn't afraid of anyone. Jim Brown was different from Taylor in that respect. He wouldn't try to run over people. He used his speed to get around them.

"I was fortunate to play against Hugh McElhenny when I first got to the Rams. He was nearing the end of his career, but he was still something else. He had outstanding moves and was very elusive. He reminded me a lot of Jon Arnett. He didn't have great speed, but he was deceptive."

From the tight end position, McKeever not only caught passes, he opened holes for the Rams' running backs. In order to succeed at his new position, he needed the bruising strength of an offensive tackle and the speed and finesse of a wide receiver. As a blocker, he often found himself facing the meanest men in the NFL.

"I guess Dick Butkus was the one guy that I remember most," McKeever said. "He was every bit as tough as people said he was. He took it as a personal afront if you tried to block him.

"In practice, I often faced Deacon Jones. He was something to watch. It really helped your game when you practiced against an All-Pro like that. In a real game situation, Willie Davis from Green Bay was one of the best defensive linemen. He was strong and quick, and he was a smart player."

During his years as a Ram receiver, McKeever

generally caught his passes from quarterback Roman Gabriel. The two have kept in touch over the years and still remain good friends.

"Roman was an outstanding athlete," he said. "He was big enough to run over people if he had to, and he had an outstanding arm. He played at about 6-4 and 225 pounds. Gabriel was a good leader on the field."

McKeever had the opportunity to play under some outstanding coaches during his career, including John McKay at USC, Bob Waterfield, Harland Svare, George Allen and Tommy Prothro with the Rams, Vince Lombardi with the Redskins and Bud Grant at Minnesota. He finds it difficult to select one top coach over all of the others.

"John McKay was a great coach for us at USC," McKeever said. "I only played one year for him, but he was a good organizer. You could tell he was going to do good things with the football program there. Bob Waterfield was my first coach with the Rams. We didn't do too well on the field (4-10 in 1961), but I'll always remember him as a great person.

"We had the most success at Los Angeles when Tommy Prothro was the coach (8-5-1 in 1971). He always seemed to know exactly what he was doing. In 1971 we should have won the division, but we lost to New Orleans and tied Atlanta. San Francisco won the title that season and we beat them twice."

In his prime, McKeever played at 6-1 and 235 pounds. He had the physical skills to make it as a professional athlete, but he contends it was his mental attitude that helped him succeed in the NFL.

"When I got drafted out of USC, I had a great desire to achieve as a professional," he said. "I think that's what is most important to the success of any athlete at that level. I was big enough and I was quick for my size, but I wasn't overwhelmingly fast. It all comes down to desire."

McKeever is a native of Los Angeles who grew up watching the Rams and the USC Trojans play football. It was always a dream of his to play for the hometown teams.

"I was six years old when I saw my first football game at the Coliseum," McKeever said. "The Rams were new in town, but I remember watching guys like Elroy Hirsch and Tom Fears and Bob Waterfield. Later, I got to stay in the area and play football at USC. Then, when I got drafted by the Rams, it was like a dream come true. All of a sudden I was dealing with Bob Waterfield and Tom Fears and the same guys who I watched and admired as a kid. That was all pretty exciting for me.

"My biggest thrill as a football player was making the Pro Bowl while I was playing for the Rams. Since I grew up watching them play it was a great feeling to represent them."

way to the title game by defeating the Minnesota Vikings, 17-14, on a dramatic 50-yard pass from Roger Staubach to Drew Pearson with just 24 seconds left in the game.

Against the Cowboys, the Rams were unable to sustain the remarkable defensive play they exhibited throughout the season. Dallas jumped out to a 21-0 halftime lead on the brilliant passing of Staubach. He threw three touchdown passes in the first half, then started the second half by throwing another scoring pass to Preston Pearson. It was Pearson's third touchdown catch of the day. By the end of the third quarter, the Cowboys had built an insurmountable, 34-0, lead.

Quarterback James Harris started against Dallas, but after his first throw was intercepted by Cowboy linebacker D.D. Lewis, Los Angeles went with backup Ron Jaworski. Jaworski was under pressure all afternoon and was sacked four times.

The Dallas defense completely shut down Los Angeles. McCutcheon, who rushed for 202 yards a week earlier, gained just 10 yards on 11 carries. The Rams picked up only 22 yards on the ground and 118 yards of total offense.

1976 There was a season-long battle for the Ram quarterback job in 1976. James Harris opened the exhibition season as the starter, but Ron Jaworski and Pat Haden made strong bids to be the team's number-one signal caller. In the club's last preseason game, Harris broke the thumb on his throwing hand and Ron Jaworski was awarded the starting job.

Top, right: Lawrence McCutcheon (30) sweeps end for a short gain against the Dallas Cowboys. McCutcheon is the Rams all-time leading rusher with 6,186 yards. **Middle, right:** Merlin Olsen goes head-to-head with Atlanta Falcon guard Gregg Kindle in one of his final games with the Rams in 1976. Olsen played in 14 Pro Bowls during his 15 seasons with Los Angeles. **Bottom, right:** Lawrence McCutcheon runs over Jeff Wright to score a touchdown against the Minnesota Vikings in the 1976 NFC championship game. **Pages 136-137:** Jack Youngblood (85) prepares to pounce on a loose ball in the end zone during the 1979 NFC Championship Game in Los Angeles. Tony Dorsett (33) and Pat Donovan of the Cowboys watch helplessly as the ball bounces away. The Rams defeated Dallas, 21-19.

The Rams continued to play great defense in 1976, but added a strong offensive machine to go along with it. Despite quarterback injuries all season long, Los Angeles had the league's highest scoring offense. Most of the offensive punch was supplied by running backs Lawrence McCutcheon and John Cappelletti.

Among the rookies who were on the opening day roster were linebacker Kevin McLain from Colorado State, Pat Thomas, a defensive back from Texas A&M, guard Jackie Slater of Jackson State, linebacker Carl Eckern from San Jose State and Dwight Scales, a receiver from Grambling.

The Rams' quarterback woes continued in their first regular season game at Atlanta when Jaworski was also injured. Pat Haden was brought in to quarterback the club. It was his first game as a professional, yet Haden directed the Rams to a 30-14 win over the Falcons.

Haden relied on a pounding ground game to beat Atlanta. Lawrence McCutcheon gained 115 yards in 26 carries and John Cappelletti rushed for 102 yards in 22 chances. Haden threw just one pass in nearly two quarters of play and that was a 47-yard touchdown toss to Ron Jessie.

Haden got the starting call the next week at Minnesota. He completed 11 of 22 passes for 136 yards, but it was Cappelletti with 128 yards and McCutcheon with 110 yards, that carried the offense again. Although Los Angeles moved the ball on the ground, it was unable to put points on the scoreboard. Three times it was stopped inside the Vikings' 10-yard line.

The Rams came from behind to tie the game at 10-10 in the fourth quarter and force it into overtime. Neither team could score during the 15-minute overtime period and the game ended in a tie.

After two wins stretched their record to 3-0-1, the Rams were shut out for the first time in seven years by the San Francisco 49ers, 16-0. Los Angeles bounced back to win seven of its last nine games, including a 59-0 rout of Atlanta, and clinch its fourth straight league title under Chuck Knox. The 59-0 win was the largest margin of victory in team history.

McCutcheon finished the season as the league's second-leading ground gainer with 1,144 yards. It was enough to break the Ram single-season rushing record. John Cappelletti, a former Heisman Trophy winner at Penn State, gained 688 yards.

In the club's final regular season game, a 20-17 win over Detroit, Haden went down with an injured knee. Despite the severe sprain, Haden was ready to play a week later against Dallas in the playoffs.

Haden was still hobbling on a sore knee at Dallas, but he got the offense moving in the second quarter. He marched the club 72 yards and scored on a four-yard run to give the Rams a 7-3 edge. Dallas scored late in the second period to take a 10-7 lead at halftime, but that would be the extent of its offensive output.

In the second half, Haden was able to generate one more offensive drive. McCutcheon capped the drive with a one-yard plunge to give the Rams a 14-10 lead. That was all they needed. Dallas scored two points on a safety late in the game, but Los Angeles held on for a 14-12 victory. Los Angeles' defense was the difference in the game. It limited the Cowboys to 85 yards rushing and intercepted three Roger Staubach passes.

The next stop for Los Angeles was Minnesota for the NFC Championship Game. It was the second time in three years the Rams and Vikings were matched for the league title.

On their first possession of the game, the Rams marched at will down the field behind the powerful running of McCutcheon and Cappelletti. They were stopped at the one-foot line, and on fourth down, Coach Knox elected to have kicker Tom Dempsey attempt an eight-yard field goal. The kick was blocked, and Viking cornerback Bobby Bryant ran 90 yards with the loose ball to give Minnesota a 7-0 lead.

Disaster struck again in the second quarter. Minnesota's Matt Blair blocked a punt at the 10-yard line after kicker Rusty Jackson fumbled the snap. The Vikings recovered and added a field goal to take a 10-0 lead at halftime.

Minnesota scored another touchdown in the third quarter, then Haden began to rally the Rams. He led them to two third-quarter scores, bringing the Rams to within striking distance, 17-13. McCutcheon scored the club's first touchdown on a 10-yard run. Haden connected on a five-yard pass to Harold Jackson for the second score.

The Vikings clinched the game in the fourth period when running back Chuck Foreman took a Tarkenton screen pass 57 yards to set up an-

Bill Simpson sets sail with the first of three interceptions against the 49ers. **Page 140:** Kicker Tom Dempsey (10) after booting a 40-yard field goal in 1975. Dempsey kicked 31 field goals that season and led the team in scoring with 94 points. Ron Jaworski (16) is the holder.

other touchdown. Sammy White scored on a 12-yard run to put the game out of reach, 24-13.

Merlin Olsen, the last active member of the Rams' Fearsome Foursome, retired at the end of the season. Olsen played in 14 Pro Bowls while a member of the Rams, more than any player in the club's history.

1977 The Rams had their annual shakeup at quarterback prior to the 1977 season. Ron Jaworski was traded to the Philadelphia Eagles for the rights to tight end Charle Young, while James Harris signed with the San Diego Chargers. To replace them, the Rams picked up veteran Joe Namath from the waiver list, and selected Nebraska quarterback Vince Ferragamo on the fourth round of the college draft.

In addition to Ferragamo, the Rams made several excellent picks in the draft. Selected were linebacker Bob Brudzinski from Ohio State, defensive back Nolan Cromwell from Kansas, receiver Billy Waddy from Colorado and running back Wendell Tyler of UCLA.

Namath won the starting quarterback job over Haden and Ferragamo. In the opener against Atlanta, he completed 15 of 30 passes for 141 yards in a losing effort. The strong running game that had become a Los Angeles trademark was stopped by the Falcons. McCutcheon, Cappelletti and Tyler managed just 51 yards in 21 carries.

Knox got Los Angeles back on track the next week. The Rams shut out Philadelphia, 20-0. It was just the first of three shutouts by the Rams in 1977.

Pat Haden regained the starting quarterback spot in the fifth week of the season after the Rams suffered a tough loss to the Chicago Bears, 24-23. Namath was unable to get his aching knees to work against the Bears, and he was sacked several times. Knox decided to go with the more mobile Haden at quarterback for the rest of the season and it paid off. The Rams won eight of their last 10 games. Included in that streak was a

David Ray 1969–1974

Place kickers in professional football generally lead a lonely life. They are relegated to the sideline where they pace nervously awaiting that special moment when they have a chance to score. Most kickers play less than a minute per game.

That wasn't so with former Ram kicking star David Ray. Ray began his career with the Los Angeles Rams in 1969. He was originally signed as a wide receiver. Kicking was just an

additional skill. When he joined the Rams they were loaded with talented receivers like Jack Snow, Billy Truax and Wendell Tucker. Ray decided to sharpen his kicking ability although Bruce Gossett was the team's primary kicker. His potpourri of skills helped him land a spot on the Rams' roster.

"I wasn't merely a kicker," Ray said. "I usually got into every game as a receiver, although they didn't throw to me that much.

I shuttled in a lot of plays. I also worked out in the defensive back-field so I could play there if they needed me."

In the age of special-ization, Ray was one of the last kickers in football to play another position. It was for his toe, however, that most Los Angeles fans remember him.

A year after Ray joined the club, the Rams traded away kicker Bruce Gossett. Ray was handed the kicking job. He came on like gang-

busters, scoring 121 points in his initial year as a kicker. He made 29 of 45 field goal attempts and was perfect on his 34 extra point tries. Ray ended the season as the league's second leading scorer, just four points behind leader Fred Cox.

In five years as the team's kicker, from 1970 to 1974, Ray scored 497 points with his toe. He ranks third on the team's all-time scoring list behind Bob Waterfield, who has 573 points, and Gossett with 571.

Ray claims he got a good introduction to big time football at the University of Alabama where he played under the legendary Paul "Bear" Bryant. Bryant was instrumental in steering Ray into professional football. He also shaped Ray into a well-rounded person.

"Bear Bryant was just a great man to play for," Ray said with a hint of a southern drawl. "I loved him and everybody who played for him loved him. He was easily the greatest influence on me as a player and as a person. One of his best qualities was knowing how to get the most out of the kids he had playing for him. He would take kids at Alabama and turn them into men before they graduated. When you got to Alabama you may have been immature, but when you left, you were a man."

Ray came under the tutelage of another successful coach at Los Angeles in George Allen. Allen assumed the head coaching job after the 1965 season. Under

Harland Svare that year, the Rams finished in last place in the western division with a 4-10 record. Allen turned the team around in 1966. He guided them to a third place finish with an 8-6 record. A year later they won the western division title with an 11-1-2 record. In 1969, Ray's first year with the club, they finished in first place again with an 11-3 record.

"Allen was a hard worker and he expected everybody else around him to work just as hard," Ray said. "He was a good coach, but I didn't really like him as a person. As a coach he could definitely get the job done. His record speaks for itself.

"Allen was always more of a defensive-minded coach. That was just his philosophy. He didn't want the offense to win games, he wanted the defense to win it. His big thing was to minimize the turnovers."

The year 1973 is one that stands out in Ray's mind. It was Chuck Knox' first season as the Ram coach. The team went 12-2 that year and won the western division title.

"We had a great offensive team in 1973," Ray said. "John Hadl had taken over for Roman Gabriel at quarterback and John won the 'Player of the Year' award. The running game was on that year. McCutcheon gained over 1,000 yards. Actually it was a good all-around performance. The defense was pretty sharp that year, too."

Indeed, the defense allowed an average of 12.5 points per game. The Rams shut out two opponents and held five teams to a touchdown or less.

It was also Ray's best year as a kicker. He led the league in scoring with 130 points. It was the most points scored in a single season in Los Angeles' history. He also kicked 30 field goals to set another team single-season mark, breaking the record he established in 1970 with 29 field goals.

Although kickers are called on to deliver in many pressure-packed situations, Ray claims that the stress of kicking a last-minute field goal never bothered him. The mechanics of kicking are the same whether there are 20 seconds on the clock or 20 minutes.

"As a kicker, I didn't feel any added pressure," Ray said. "I did enough kicking in practice so that it didn't affect me to kick with the game on the line. I don't claim to have nerves of steel or anything, it's just that I was too wrapped up in the game to worry about it. But I don't think you'd want to have someone that is a flake doing your kicking.

"I think people are starting to realize that it's not just the kicker that matters in a situation like that. They now realize that the holder and the center also play an important role. If the ball doesn't get to the holder, or if the holder misses the placement, it doesn't matter how good of a kicker you are."

Running back Jeff Kordan (31) blocks a punt by Julian Fagan of the New Orleans Saints in a 1970 game.

20-14 win over the World Champion Oakland Raiders.

McCutcheon ended the regular season with 1,238 rushing yards. He also caught 25 passes and scored nine touchdowns. However, it was the defensive unit that was most impressive. Opponents scored just 146 points in 14 games against the Rams defense, an average of 10 points per contest.

The Rams' 10-4 record was good for first place in the NFC Western Division. They opened post-season play against the Minnesota Vikings. It was the third time in four years the two clubs were matched in the playoffs. Minnesota won both previous games. Los Angeles had the home field advantage and was a nine-point favorite at game time. Attendance at the Coliseum was 62,538.

The game was a defensive struggle most of the way. At the start of the fourth quarter, the Vikings held a 7-0 lead. Viking quarterback Bob Lee guided Minnesota to another touchdown in the fourth period and put the game out of reach for Los Angeles, 14-0. The Minnesota defense then held the Rams scoreless until the last minute of the game, when Harold Jackson caught a one-yard pass from Pat Haden.

Lawrence McCutcheon provided most of the offense for Los Angeles. He gained 102 yards on 16 carries. Haden played the entire game at quarterback and completed 14 of 32 passes for 130 yards. He had three passes intercepted.

It was Chuck Knox' last season with the Rams. He resigned to take a head coaching job with the Buffalo Bills. Knox was the most successful coach in Ram history. He led the club to a 54-15-1 record and five straight western division titles.

1978 With Knox' departure, Ram owner Carroll Rosenbloom rehired George Allen to direct the club in 1978. Allen had been the Ram head coach from 1966 to 1970 under former owner Dan Reeves.

In the 1978 draft, the Rams used their first choice to select Oklahoma running back Elvis Peacock. Kicker Frank Corral from UCLA was a third-round pick and defensive end Reggie Doss

Guard Dennis Harrah prepares to block down on 49er Willie Harper to spring Cullen Bryant. **Pages 146-147:** Willie Ellison springs around end for a five-yard gain against the Dallas Cowboys. Les Josephson (34) throws a block.

of Hampton Institute was chosen on the seventh round.

Los Angeles lost its first two preseason games to New England and San Diego, then George Allen suddenly was fired. Team owner Carroll Rosenbloom claimed Allen had over-extended his authority and could not work within the framework prescribed by Rosenbloom. Allen's assistant, Ray Malavasi, was hired as head coach.

With Namath gone, Haden beat out Ferragamo for the starting quarterback position. He was effective enough to lead Los Angeles to wins in its first seven league games. A midseason slump caused the Rams to lose to the New Orleans Saints and Atlanta Falcons, then Los Angeles finished the season with five wins in its last seven games.

The highlight of the year was a 27-14 win over the Super Bowl champion Dallas Cowboys. Los Angeles' defense flexed its muscle against Dallas, holding Tony Dorsett to just 38 yards in 19 carries. Staubach was sacked three times and harrased enough to throw four interceptions. The most important interception came with 3:21 left in the game. The Rams were clinging to a 20-14 lead, and Staubach was ready to stage one of his customary come-from-behind wins. But Ram cornerback Rod Perry picked off a Staubach pass at the 42-yard line and danced down the sidelines into the end zone. The touchdown clinched the 27-14 win.

Los Angeles ended the season with a 12-4 record to win its sixth consecutive western division title. It gave the club a chance to face the Minnesota Vikings in another divisional playoff. The Rams had failed to beat Minnesota in three previous post-season games. This time the ending would be different.

Before 69,631 happy fans at the Coliseum, Los Angeles buried the Vikings, 34-10. The game was tied 10-10 at halftime, but the Ram defense held Minnesota scoreless in the second half, while the offense rallied for 24 points.

Running back Cullen Bryant paced all rushers

with 100 yards on the ground and one touchdown. Haden completed 15 of 29 passes for 209 yards and two touchdowns. Frank Corral, the NFL's leading scorer, kicked two field goals and four extra points.

The only team keeping the Rams from Super Bowl XIII was the Dallas Cowboys. The Rams already defeated Dallas earlier in the season, but in post-season matchups with the Cowboys, Los Angeles was 1-2.

As expected, the first half was a defensive struggle. Neither team scored. But in the second half, things started going wrong for Los Angeles.

Midway through the third period, Charlie Waters picked off a Pat Haden pass and returned it to the Rams' 10-yard line. Dorsett scored from there to give Dallas a 7-0 edge, but the Rams never recovered.

After the interception, Haden was forced to leave the game with a broken finger. He was replaced by second-year quarterback Vince Ferragamo. Ferragamo was unable to mount any offensive attack and the Cowboys took advantage of seven turnovers to post a 28-0 win.

Dallas' "Doomsday Defense" limited the Rams to just 177 yards of total offense in the game. Cullen Bryant, the Rams' leading rusher, gained only 52 yards on 20 carries.

1979 Owner Carroll Rosenbloom died in a swimming accident prior to the 1979 season and his widow, Georgia, became majority owner of the club. Rosenbloom took control of the Rams in 1972 and presided over the team during its most successful era. In his seven years as the Rams' owner, they compiled a 72-26-4 record and had six consecutive first place finishes.

In the college draft, the Rams used their two first-round picks to select linebacker George Andrews from Nebraska and tackle Kent Hill of Georgia Tech. With their 12th-round pick they chose Drew Hill, a wide receiver from Georgia Tech.

The Rams concluded the exhibition season with an impressive 4-0 record, then opened the regular season against the Oakland Raiders. Los Angeles was a four-point favorite.

The Los Angeles special teams were a disaster all day. Two of Ken Clark's punts were blocked and both led to Raider touchdowns. The Rams also committed five turnovers, as Oakland defeated Los Angeles, 24-17. Pat Haden completed 21 of 41 passes for 229 yards, but had three passes intercepted.

The Rams bounced back with four wins in their next five games, including a 21-0 shutout of St. Louis. Midway through the season, Haden was injured and Ferragamo was given the starting assignment. The Ram offense was hampered by injuries to several other key starters, including fullback John Cappelletti and receivers Ron Jessie and Willie Miller. The retirement of perennial All-Pro tackle Tom Mack earlier in the year also left a hole in the offensive line.

Despite the adversity, Ferragamo and reserve quarterback Bob Lee led the club to five wins down the stretch. One victory came in a dramatic overtime game with long-time rival Minnesota.

The Vikings made that game interesting late in the fourth period when quarterback Tommy Kramer hit Ahmad Rashad on a 16-yard pass to tie the score at 21-21. In the overtime period, Lee guided the Rams to the five-yard line, where Frank Corral came on to attempt a 22-yard field goal. Corral never had a chance to kick. Holder Nolan Cromwell took the snap and ran untouched into the end zone. The touchdown gave the Rams a 27-21 win.

Los Angeles ended the year with a 29-14 loss to the New Orleans Saints. It was the Rams' final game at Memorial Coliseum before moving to Anaheim in 1980. They finished the season with a 9-7 record and their seventh-straight western division crown. Heading into the playoffs, Los Angeles was the only team that failed to win at least 10 league games.

Wendell Tyler ended the regular season with 1,109 yards rushing, despite the fact he did not start his first game until five weeks into the season. He replaced Lawrence McCutcheon in the starting lineup.

In the divisional playoffs, the Rams opened against the Dallas Cowboys. It marked the fifth time in seven years the two teams had met in post-season competition. The Cowboys had won three of the four previous games.

The 1979 playoff game with Dallas was one of the most exciting in recent memory. Dallas opened the game as a nine-point favorite and got on the board early by dropping Ferragamo in the end zone for a safety. Ferragamo came back to

throw two scoring passes before the half ended. Wendell Tyler was on the receiving end of a 32-yard pass, and Ron Smith hauled in a 43-yard toss, as the Rams took a 14-5 lead into the locker room. Smith's touchdown came with just two seconds left in the half.

Dallas dominated the second half. They took a 19-14 lead early in the fourth period, as running back Tony Dorsett methodically moved the ball downfield against the Rams. Meanwhile, the Cowboy defense held the Rams scoreless.

With 2:20 to play, the Cowboys were forced to punt. Ferragamo took over and on the first play from scrimmage, fired a pass to receiver Billy Waddy. The ball was deflected by Cowboy linebacker Mike Hegman, but it bounced directly into Waddy's hands. He grabbed the ball and took off down the sidelines to complete a 50-yard touchdown pass.

Despite the 21-19 lead, Los Angeles still had to contain quarterback Roger Staubach. The Cowboys had nearly two minutes left to get in range for a field goal that would win the game. The Ram defense did its job, pressuring Staubach into four consecutive incomplete passes. Ferragamo took over and ran out the clock to preserve the win.

The Rams' next stop was the NFC Championship Game with the Tampa Bay Bucs at Tampa. Both clubs had formidable defenses, and that was evident from the opening kickoff. Most of the action was on the line of scrimmage, with the Rams clearly the dominant force. Los Angeles' defensive line contained Tampa's running attack, allowing just 92 yards all day. Meanwhile, Ram running backs Cullen Bryant and Wendell Tyler picked up yardage in steady amounts. The Rams had trouble scoring, however, and put just six points on the scoreboard in the opening half.

Tampa's offense was shut down again in the second half and suffered a devastating blow

Page 148: Defensive end Fred Dryer battles San Francisco's Ron Singleton in an attempt to rush quarterback Steve DeBerg. **This page:** New Orleans Saints cornerback Maurice Spencer intercepts a Ron Jaworski pass to rob Harold Jackson of a touchdown reception.

when starting quarterback Doug Williams was forced to leave the game with an injured arm. Substitute quarterback Mike Rae could not get the offense moving either. Rae and Williams combined to complete just four of their 26 passes.

Frank Corral kicked another field goal in the fourth quarter to put the game away, 9-0, and lead Los Angeles to its first Super Bowl. Bryant was the team's leading ground gainer with 106 yards, while Tyler picked up 86.

It seemed unlikely that a team that went 9-7 in the regular season would make it to the Super Bowl, but the Rams swept through the playoffs with superb defense and timely offense. Few people gave them a chance to beat the Pittsburgh Steelers, winners of three previous Super Bowls. Nevada bookmakers listed the Steelers as 11-point favorites, despite the fact that the Rams were playing in their backyard at Pasadena.

A record Super Bowl crowd of 103,985 probably thought the oddsmakers were correct when the Steelers marched 79 yards on their first possession and scored on a 41-yard Matt Bahr field goal. But the Rams came right back. Los Angeles recovered Bahr's onside kickoff attempt to gain excellent field position at the Rams' 41-yard line. Ferragamo completed two clutch passes and Wendell Tyler broke free on a 39-yard run, moving the ball inside the 10-yard line. Cullen Bryant concluded the drive by pounding one yard through the Steeler line to score.

Los Angeles continued to surprise everyone. After three quarters of play they held a 19-17 lead. Ferragamo, who was starting only his eighth NFL game, was spectacular. He completed a 50-yard pass to Billy Waddy late in the third period to set up the go-ahead touchdown. That score came on McCutcheon's 24-yard pass to Ron Smith.

Then in the fourth quarter things began to change. The Steeler defense tightened up and began to put pressure on Ferragamo. He was sacked four times on the day. Meanwhile, Terry Bradshaw opened up the offense. He unloaded a 73-yard touchdown pass to Stallworth to put Pittsburgh in front, 24-19.

Ferragamo mounted one more drive. He marched the club 52 yards to the Pittsburgh 32-yard line. With five minutes to play, the Rams were in good position to score again and take the lead. But Steeler linebacker Jack Lambert made the play of the game. He intercepted a Ferragamo pass and the Steeler offense ran down the clock on a 70-yard touchdown drive to clinch a 31-19 triumph.

Ferragamo completed 15 of 25 passes for 212 yards. Wendell Tyler was the leading Ram rusher with 60 yards on 17 carries.

Page 152: Eric Dickerson weaves his way through and over Tampa Bay Buccaneer defenders as he makes a good gain for the Rams.

150

1980–1986

CHAPTER FIVE

THE NEW GENERATION

T he Olympic Games were held in Moscow in 1980, but at President Jimmy Carter's request, the U.S. Olympic team boycotted the games.

There was happier news in Los Angeles where the Lakers won the NBA title behind the effort of the league's Most Valuable Player, Kareem Abdul-Jabbar. Magic Johnson was voted MVP in the playoffs.

Bjorn Borg continued his domination of the men's tennis scene in 1980. He won his fifth French Open title and fifth straight Wimbledon Championship.

The Rams left Memorial Coliseum, their home since 1946, and moved to Anaheim Stadium for the 1980 season. Several veterans were absent from training camp that year. Among the holdouts were Jack Youngblood, Jim Youngblood, Larry Brooks and Bob Brudzinski. All four reported to camp a week before the league opener against the Detroit Lions. Running back Wendell Tyler also was lost for the first half of the season due to a car accident.

Pat Haden battled with Vince Ferragamo, the hero of the 1979 playoffs, for the starting quarterback job during the preseason. Haden was the signal caller on opening day.

Los Angeles began the year with a revamped secondary after selecting Texas defensive back Johnnie Johnson on the first round of the 1980 draft and Leroy Irvin, a defensive back from Kansas, on the third round. Among the Rams' other draft picks were tackle Irv Pankey and running backs Jewerl Thomas and Mike Guman.

The Rams played their first league game at Anaheim Stadium against the Detroit Lions. Detroit finished the 1979 season with a 2-14 record, the worst in pro football. But the Lions had a new weapon in their backfield, Heisman Trophy winner Billy Sims.

Sims showed the Orange County crowd his Heisman Trophy was not a fluke. He racked up 153 yards rushing and scored three touchdowns to lead the Lions to a 41-20 victory over the NFC champs. To make things worse, Pat Haden broke a finger on his passing hand and was lost to the club for four weeks.

The quarterback situation grew desperate in the second week of the season when Ferragamo skipped practice while his agent attempted to negotiate a new contract. Ferragamo returned to quarterback the team in its second game of the year against Tampa Bay, but the Rams were beaten 10-9 and seemed headed for a disastrous season.

In their next game, against the Green Bay Packers, the Rams suddenly caught fire. They ran up 37 points in the second quarter and demolished the Packers, 51-21. The game was a catalyst for the Rams, as they won five

of their next six games with Ferragamo playing superbly.

Los Angeles closed out the season with convincing victories over New Orleans, Dallas, Atlanta and the New York Jets. The only blemish on its record in the second half of the season came in an overtime loss to the Buffalo Bills. The Bills were coached by Chuck Knox.

The Rams lost more than a game at Buffalo, however. Ferragamo suffered brusied ribs and lung damage after a vicious tackle that left him spitting blood. Haden returned at quarterback for the first time since his opening game injury. He was ineffective, completing just five of 16 passes.

In addition, running back Elvis Peacock was sidelined for the season with knee ligament damage. The loss of Peacock left the Rams particularly short at running back because a week earlier Wendell Tyler was knocked out of action for the year. Tyler, who had just recovered from an offseason auto accident, dislocated an elbow.

The Rams ended the year with a 20-17 overtime win over Atlanta. It left the Rams in second place in the western division with an 11-5 record. Nevertheless, they won a wild card berth in the playoffs and faced the Dallas Cowboys in the opening round.

Ferragamo finished his first full season as a Ram starter by throwing for a club record 3,199 yards and 30 touchdowns. He completed 59 percent of his 404 passes and was ranked second among the league's signal callers.

The young quarterback did not have as much luck against the Cowboys in Irving, Texas. He guided the Rams to two touchdowns in the first half, including a 21-yard scoring pass to Preston Denard. But Los Angeles could manage only a 13-13 tie at intermission.

In the second half, the Cowboys moved the ball at will. Dallas scored three unanswered touchdowns to build a 34-13 lead while the Doomsday Defense stopped the Ram offense.

Linebacker Carl Ekern hauls in 49er Jerry Rice.

Ferragamo completed 14 of his 30 passes, but had three intercepted and was sacked once. The Los Angeles running game was limited to just 92 yards. Dallas ran all over the Rams, compiling a club record 338 yards on the ground. Tony Dorsett led all rushers with 160 yards.

1981 Los Angeles' chance for a winning year in 1981 was diminished long before the first snap of the season. The club lost its offensive and defensive leaders to salary disputes in the offseason. Linebacker Jack Reynolds migrated north to the San Francisco 49ers and quarterback Vince Ferragamo went to Montreal of the Canadian Football League. The defense suffered another blow with the departure of linebacker Bob Brudzinski.

To beef up the linebacking corps, the Rams selected Mel Owens of Washington with their first-round draft choice and Jim Collins of Syracuse on the second round. The starting quarterback job went to Pat Haden. His backup was second-year man Jeff Rutledge.

Los Angeles started the year on a sour note. In the league opener against Houston, quarterback Ken Stabler came out of his brief retirement and led the Oilers to a 27-20 win. Stabler missed all but the last week of training camp, yet still had enough savvy to complete 13 of 20 passes for 192 yards and two touchdowns.

The big news, however, was found on the Los Angeles sideline. Popular defensive end Fred Dryer was benched for the first time in his 14-year career. He had been unofficially cut two weeks before the season began, then rejoined the team a week later because of a contract clause which forbid the team to waive him without his permission. He sat on the bench throughout the game despite repeated cheers and chants by Dryer fans at Anaheim Stadium. It ended Dryer's string of playing in 174 straight games.

After suffering another loss at the hands of New Orleans, Malavasi tried to inject life into the offense by signing former Houston quarterback Dan Pastorini. Haden remained the starting quarterback, however, and guided the Rams to wins over Green Bay, Chicago and Cleveland.

In the sixth week of the season, Malavasi led his warriors to Atlanta. The physically intimidating Falcons went after Haden and knocked him out

of action in the second quarter. Haden was belted by Atlanta defensive tackle Wilson Fauminma on what appeared to be a late hit. He was carted off the field and was reported to have a broken left leg. X-rays later proved to be negative.

Rutledge came in to relieve Haden. He directed the offense like an old pro. The lead changed hands four times and with four minutes to play, Atlanta held a 35-34 advantage. It was then that Rutledge performed his final magic act. Starting from his own 28-yard line, Rutledge moved the Rams to the Atlanta eight in 14 plays. With 24 seconds left, Corral kicked a 25-yard field goal to give Los Angeles a 37-35 win.

LeRoy Irvin was a standout on the Ram special teams. He returned six punts for 204 yards, including touchdown runs of 75 and 84 yards. The win gave Los Angeles a 4-2 record and a tie for first place in the western division. Unfortunately, that was the high point of the year. The Rams lost eight of their remaining 10 games to finish with their worst record since 1965. It was the first time in nine years Los Angeles failed to make the playoffs.

Wendell Tyler rebounded from the injuries he suffered during the 1980 season to gain 1,074 yards. He also scored 17 touchdowns to tie a team record. Quarterback Dan Pastorini was disappointing as Haden's replacement. He completed just 42 percent of 152 passes and had 14 throws intercepted. It was the last season for veteran lineman Rich Saul. He retired after playing in 176 consecutive games during 12 years with the Rams.

1982 Although already deep at running back with Cullen Bryant, Wendell Tyler, Mike Guman and Jewerl Thomas, the Rams used their first choice in the 1982 draft to pick

Page 156: Washington Redskins running back John Riggins is unstoppable as he carries four Rams defenders into the end zone. **Top, right:** Jackie Slatter works against 49er Ted Vincent. **Bottom, right:** Rich Saul (61) blocks Archie Reese.

Eric Dickerson fends off Buffalo Bills cornerback Mario Clark as each entwines his fingers in the other's face mask. Dickerson gained 12 yards and a first down.

Barry Redden of Richmond. The quarterback situation also was strengthened by the return of Vince Ferragamo from the Canadian League. Meanwhile, standout quarterback Bert Jones was acquired from Baltimore.

Jones won the starting quarterback job and in the first half of the league opener he showed why. Los Angeles was matched with the Green Bay Packers at Milwaukee. Jones directed the Rams to a 23-0 halftime lead with clutch passes, including an eight-yard scoring toss to tight end Mike Barber.

In the second half, the momentum quickly changed. Packer quarterback Lynn Dickey threw a touchdown pass on Green Bay's first possession and tossed a 42-yard pass to set up a score on the club's second possession. Green Bay went on to post five unanswered touchdowns and stun the Rams 35-23. Dickey called it "the greatest comeback I've ever been a part of."

Jones was unable to move the Ram offense in the second half. He had two passes intercepted and was sacked four times. He finished the day by completing 17 passes in 34 attempts for 202 yards.

Los Angeles lost its second game of the season to the Detroit Lions, 19-14, then the NFL Players Association went on strike. When the strike was settled, league play resumed in late November. The Rams continued their losing streak with a 34-17 loss to Atlanta.

Los Angeles got its first win of the season a week later against the Kansas City Chiefs, 20-14. Bert Jones opened at quarterback again but threw only a dozen passes. He completed six for just 67 yards. Wendell Tyler carried the offense. He gained 138 yards on 25 carries and scored two touchdowns. Midway through the fourth period Jones was shaken up and Ferragamo entered the game to a loud ovation. He ran out the clock without throwing a pass.

The Rams suffered four consecutive losses to post a 1-7 record. The Super Bowl Champion San Francisco 49ers were the Rams' final opponent. San Francisco was battling for a playoff spot and a loss would knock them out of post-season play.

Nolan Cromwell 1977–

It was just a matter of time before Nolan Cromwell got the recognition he deserved. For years he labored quietly in the Rams' secondary. Only wide receivers and quarterbacks were aware of his presence.

Cromwell wasn't always a defensive specialist. He broke in with the Rams in 1977 after being selected on the second round of the college draft. At the University of Kansas he was a highly touted quarterback. As a junior he was named the Big 8 Player of the Year. That year he set an NCAA single-season rushing record for quarterbacks by gaining 294 yards. In addition to starring on the gridiron, Cromwell was an accomplished decathalon performer with the Kansas track squad.

But Los Angeles didn't want another quarterback. Joe Namath and Pat Haden were already on the Rams' roster. And Los Angeles used its fourth-round pick in 1977 to select Nebraska quarterback Vince Ferragamo. What the Rams needed was a defensive back, so Cromwell's athletic skill was used elsewhere. He worked out at safety, a position he had played for two years at Kansas. It was a move that eventually paid off for Los Angeles. It caused headaches for the rest of the NFL.

Cromwell did not win a starting position overnight. He competed with veteran secondary men Dave Elmendorf, Bill Simpson, Monte

Jackson and Pat Thomas during his rookie season. After seeing limited action mostly on special teams for two years, he broke into the starting lineup in 1979 as a free safety. He showed everybody he belonged there by intercepting five passes that season and returning them 109 yards.

Cromwell topped that performance in 1980 by intercepting eight passes to lead the NFC. He returned them an average of 17.5 yards and scored one touchdown. His outstanding play earned him a berth in the Pro Bowl. It was the first of four consecutive Pro Bowl appearances for Cromwell.

In 1983 Cromwell was moved from his free safety spot to strong safety to make room for Johnnie Johnson. It was a smooth transition for Cromwell. His outstanding play at strong safety earned him Football Digest's Defensive Back of the Year award. Johnson, a first-round draft pick in 1980 from Texas, then took over the free safety position. Together they anchor one of the best secondaries in the NFL. Both men credit Coach John Robinson and his staff for the club's recent success.

"Coach Robinson brought a positive attitude to the team and that has worn off on everyone else," said Cromwell. "The current management has done a great job since taking over." Johnson agrees with Cromwell.

"The current staff has really helped me develop as a player," Johnson said. "They helped me make the transition to free safety."

Cornerbacks LeRoy Irvin, Jerry Gray and Gary Green round out the starting defensive backfield. Green was acquired from the Kansas City Chiefs in 1984 for two top draft picks. He played in three consecutive Pro Bowls between 1981 and 1983 and was voted Kansas City's Most Valuable Player in 1982.

LeRoy Irvin was the Rams' third-round draft choice in 1980. Like Cromwell, he attended the University of Kansas. Irvin established himself as one of the elite cornerbacks in the league in 1984 when he intercepted five passes for 166 yards. Two of those interceptions were returned for touchdowns, including an 81-yard score against Cleveland and a 51-yard return against New Orleans. In the 1983 NFC playoff game against Dallas, Irvin returned an interception 93 yards to set a club record.

Cromwell is the acknowledged leader in the secondary, but he is also an important special teams player. In fact, he may be the only placekick holder who is a legitimate NFL scoring threat. Three times since 1979 he has rushed for touchdowns from field goal formation. He has also recovered a blocked punt for a touchdown and blocked a punt that was returned for a score.

After nine seasons in the NFL, Cromwell has formed some solid opinions on his opponents around the league.

"The San Diego Chargers have always been one of the toughest teams for me to play against," Cromwell said. "They have a great offensive scheme and passing attack. They put a lot of pressure on the secondary. The toughest individual player I've faced would probably be William Andrews from Atlanta. He's got tremendous determination."

Cromwell has already made his mark on the Los Angeles Rams' record book. He is second on the club's all-time interception list with 31. He has averaged nearly 19 yards per return and has scored three touchdowns. Ed Meador is the Rams' all-time leader with 46 interceptions. Cromwell also has one of the longest interception returns in club history. In 1980, he returned an interception 94 yards but was stopped short of the goal line. During that season, he intercepted a pass in four consecutive games.

Cromwell endured a slight setback near the end of the 1984 season when he injured his right knee in a game with the Chicago Bears. It was the first major injury he suffered as a Ram and ended his streak of playing in 84 straight games. He's already working on a new streak.

Los Angeles held a 21-20 lead late in the fourth period, but quarterback Joe Montana moved the 49ers into scoring position with less than two minutes on the clock. Kicker Ray Wersching attempted a 24-yard field goal, but Ivory Sully broke through the line and blocked it to preserve the Rams win.

1983 Ray Malavasi and his staff were relieved of their coaching duties after the 1982 season and former USC coach John Robinson was named the Rams new head man. Robinson brought in most of his staff from Southern Cal including Gil Haskell, Marv Goux and Hudson Houk.

In one of his first moves with the Rams, Robinson traded Wendell Tyler and Cody Jones to the 49ers for two top draft choices. With his first-round pick, he drafted SMU running back Eric Dickerson. Robinson then installed the single-back offense with Dickerson as the club's main cog.

Dickerson helped the club win its opening game by gaining 91 yards in a 16-6 win over the New York Giants. It was one of the few times the rookie was held to under 100 yards that season.

Ferragamo regained the starting quarterback job and completed 17 of 28 passes for 279 yards and two touchdowns. Tight end Mike Barber was on the receiving end of both touchdown passes. Rookie Henry Ellard also caught three passes for 91 yards.

The Rams' good fortune continued throughout the season. They won five of their first seven games before suffering consecutive losses to San Francisco and Miami.

Top: Defensive end Jack Youngblood drops Danny White for a loss. **Bottom:** Jack Youngblood (85) and Reggie Doss (71) confer with a line coach. **Page 162:** Preston Dennard (88) goes deep against the 49ers. Dennard was the club's leading receiver in 1981 when he caught 49 passes for 821 yards.

Eric Dickerson 1983–

It was near the end of the 1984 season that Eric Dickerson clearly established himself in the NFL record books. Under a warm winter sun at Anaheim Stadium, Dickerson rushed through the Houston Oiler defense for 215 yards. It gave him 2,006 yards in 15 games that year to eclipse O.J. Simpson's single-season rushing mark. Dickerson added another 99 yards in the final game of the season to finish the year with 2,105 yards.

Dickerson will always be remembered for his outstanding accomplishments that season, but people really began to take notice of the graceful running back a year earlier. In just his fourth professional game, he gained 192 yards against the New York Jets. A week later, he rushed for 199 yards against the Detroit Lions and became the NFC's· leading rusher. He

eventually gained 1,808 yards in 1983, the sixth highest in NFL history, and was the NFC Rookie of the Year.

Dickerson quickly became a subject of praise throughout the league. O.J. Simpson claimed that Dickerson could be the best running back to ever play the game of football. New York Giants Coach Bill Parcells said that Dickerson played like he was "superhuman." Even Jim Brown conceded that Dickerson was "a great runner."

Dickerson's talent lies in his unique blend of physical skills. At 6-3 and 220 pounds, he has the size and strength to run over potential tacklers. His power is combined with sprinter's speed. He has been clocked at 9.4 in the 100-yard dash. But what Coach John Robinson likes most about Dickerson are his courage and toughness. It is those two qualities that make him an outstanding back, Robinson says.

Robinson has been familiar with Dickerson's talents since the prized running back starred at Sealy High School in Sealy, Texas. While a coach at Southern California, Robinson ventured to Sealy in an effort to recruit Dickerson for the Trojans. Dickerson decided to stay near home and play at Southern Methodist. Four years later, after Robinson was named head coach of the Rams, he had another shot at Dickerson. This time he

wouldn't get away. The Rams made Dickerson their first-round draft pick in 1983. He was the second player picked overall that year behind quarterback John Elway of the Denver Broncos.

Dickerson had a distinguished playing career at SMU. Although he shared the backfield with another outstanding runner in Craig James, he was selected Southwest Conference Offensive Player of the Year in both 1981 and 1982. In 1981, Dickerson's junior year, he was a second team All-American.

As a senior, Dickerson rushed for 1,617 yards to rank third in the nation. He also scored 17 touchdowns. Six of his touchdown runs were over 60 yards. He was a consensus All-American that year and finished third in the Heisman Trophy voting.

When Dickerson left SMU, he had compiled 4,450 yards on 790 carries for a 5.6-yard rushing average. It was enough to break Earl Campbell's conference rushing record. His 48 touchdowns shattered Doak Walker's school scoring mark.

As good as Dickerson was in college, he has topped it as a professional. In just three seasons with the Rams, Dickerson has already become the NFL's premier offensive force. Despite playing in a single-back offense, and with little support from the passing game, Dickerson has shattered numerous team and NFL rushing marks. At his current pace, he threatens to break

virtually all existing rushing records.

Dickerson has already gained 5,147 yards, an average of 1,715 yards per season. He is ranked third on the Rams' all-time rushing list behind Lawrence McCutcheon with 6,186 yards and Dick Bass with 5,417 yards. At his current pace, he will pass Jim Brown and become the NFL's second leading all-time rusher behind Walter Payton after just seven seasons.

Even more remarkable is Dickerson's per game rushing average. While most backs regard 100 yards rushing as a mark of superiority, Dickerson has made the 100-yard game commonplace. He has averaged 111 yards per game in his three seasons with Los Angeles.

Since joining the Rams, Dickerson has also become a more rounded performer. At SMU, he was rarely used as a receiver. He caught just 19 passes in four years of collegiate play. In his rookie season with the Rams he not only led the league in rushing, he caught 51 passes and scored a team record 20 touchdowns.

It's no coincidence that the Ram's fortunes have soared since Dickerson joined the club. Prior to his arrival, the Rams finished 6-10 in 1981 and a disastrous 2-7 in 1982. With Dickerson leading the offense, Los Angeles finished 9-7 in 1983 and made the playoffs. They have been a contender ever since. And that is the mark of an outstanding player.

With just three games left in the season, Los Angeles was on top in the NFC West with an 8-5 mark. San Francisco and New Orleans were a game behind at 7-6. But the Rams picked a bad time for a slump. They lost two in a row to Philadelphia and New England and suddenly found themselves a game behind the 49ers. Going into the final game of the season, the Rams needed a win over the New Orleans Saints to secure a playoff spot.

The lead changed hands five times in the contest, but the Rams had it when it counted most. New Orleans was in front, 24-23, with two minutes to play when the Rams took over at their 20. Ferragamo drove Los Angeles 55 yards and with six seconds on the clock, Lansford came in to try a 42-yard field goal. The kick was successful and wrapped up a wild card berth for the Rams.

Dickerson ended the season with 1,808 yards, a rookie rushing record. He also set a team record by scoring 20 touchdowns. He was a unanimous selection as NFL Rookie of the Year.

Not surprisingly, the Rams faced an old nemesis, the Dallas Cowboys, in the first round of the playoffs. Dallas was a nine-point favorite. Early in the game, Ferragamo moved the club 85 yards. He completed four passes including an 18-yard scoring strike to David Hill to give the Rams a 7-0 lead. Dallas tied the score before the half and went in front, 10-7, in the third quarter. The Rams then took control of the ball game. Ferragamo connected on scoring passes to Preston Dennard and George Farmer, and Mike Lansford booted a 20-yard field goal, to clinch the 24-17 win.

Ferragamo completed 15 of 30 passes for 162 yards and Dickerson gained 99 yards on 23 carries. Farmer was the club's leading receiver with five catches.

The Rams traveled to the nation's capital to meet the Washington Redskins in the divisional

Top, right: Eric Dickerson holds up the football he carried to break the NFL season rushing record in 1984, beating O.J. Simpson's 1973 record by four yards. **Bottom, right:** Cullen Bryant leaps for two yards before being grabbed by Cowboy Randy White (54).

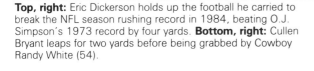

Linebacker Jack Reynolds (64) puts the stop on Earl Cooper of the San Francisco 49ers at the goal line. **Page 167:** Running back Cullen Bryant (32) was the Rams' leading ground gainer in 1978. He picked up 658 yards that season and scored seven touchdowns. **Pages 168-169:** Defensive end Jack Youngblood (85) sacks Seattle Seahawk quarterback Jim Zorn during a game in 1982.

playoff. They might as well have faced a runaway train. In one of the worst mismatches in playoff history, the Redskins destroyed Los Angeles, 51-7. It was the worst defeat ever suffered by the Rams.

Washington scored the first five times it had the ball and posted a 24-0 lead before Los Angeles got on the scoreboard. That touchdown came on a 32-yard pass from Ferragamo to Dennard. After that, it was all Redskins.

Dickerson was held to a season-low 16 yards on 10 carries. He caught six passes for just nine yards. Ferragamo was chased all day and sacked three times. He completed 20 of 43 passes, but was intercepted three times.

1984 Coach Robinson took a step toward improving his pass defense in 1984 by acquiring All-Pro cornerback Gary Green from Kansas City for a first-round draft choice. He also tried to strengthen the passing attack by installing the Shotgun Formation during the preseason.

The passing game was nowhere to be found in the opener against Dallas. Even while using the Shotgun, Ferragamo had trouble finding his receivers. He completed just 11 of 33 passes for 84 yards and threw four interceptions. The Rams took a 13-0 first quarter advantage, but that was all the points they would score. Dallas methodically chipped away at the lead and won the game, 20-13.

Dickerson supplied most of the offense, gaining 138 yards in 21 carries. The Rams totaled just 204 yards of offense in the game.

After a victory over the Cleveland Browns, the Rams lost to the Pittsburgh Steelers. More importantly, they lost quarterback Vince Ferragamo who broke the finger on his passing hand. Jeff Kemp replaced Ferragamo and played admirably in his absence. He guided the team to wins in four of its next five games.

At the midway point in the season, the Rams

had a 5-3 record when their northern rival, the San Francisco 49ers, visited Anaheim. San Francisco had a 7-1 record and continued its winning ways by beating the Rams, 33-0. It was the first time the Rams had been held scoreless in three years.

Dickerson got the Rams back on track a week later with an exceptional running performance. He gained 208 yards on 28 carries against the St. Louis Cardinals and led the Rams to a 16-13 win. Los Angeles won four of its last six games to secure a wild card spot in the playoffs with a 10-6 record.

Kemp proved to be a competent but unspectacular replacement at quarterback. He finished the season completing 50.4 percent of his 284 attempts for 2,021 yards. Henry Ellard was Kemp's favorite receiver. He grabbed 34 passes for 622 yards. Eric Dickerson set an NFL record by rushing for 2,105 yards in 379 carries. He averaged 5.6 yards per attempt and scored 14 touchdowns.

The Rams faced the New York Giants in the NFC wild card game. It was the first playoff game ever held at Anaheim Stadium and a record crowd of 66,037 was on hand to witness it.

In the regular season, the Rams dominated New York, 33-12. The results were different in the wild card game. The Giants took a 10-0 halftime lead and the Rams never recovered.

Dickerson gained his usual 100 yards. He totaled 107 yards in 23 carries and scored one touchdown. That came in the third quarter and put the Rams back in the game at 13-10. The rest of the game was a field goal match. Each side added three points with New York coming out ahead, 16-13.

1985 The Rams major concern in 1985 was to establish a passing attack that would match their powerful running game. Their first step was to sign Canadian Football League quarterback Dieter Brock. Brock spent 11 seasons in Canada and passed for 34,830 yards and 210 touchdowns. Twice he was the league's Most Valuable Player.

In the college draft, Los Angeles picked up Texas cornerback Jerry Gray on the first round, receiver Chuck Scott from Vanderbilt on the second round, and Clemson punter Dale Hatcher on the third round. Heisman Trophy winning quarterback Doug Flutie was picked on the 11th round although he was under contract to the

New Jersey Generals of the United States Football League.

During the exhibition season Brock won the starting quarterback position from Jeff Kemp. Although the quarterback situation was settled early, the Rams found themselves without star running back Eric Dickerson. Dickerson was an early season hold out.

With Dickerson out of action for the season opener against the Denver Broncos, Coach Robinson went to his bench. He found Charles White, who won the Heisman Trophy while playing under Robinson at USC, and Barry Redden. The two filled in admirably for Dickerson. Redden rushed for 46 yards on 13 carries before retiring with a sprained ankle. White ran for 83 yards in 18 rushes and scored the winning touchdown.

The Rams built an early 10-3 lead on Mike Lansford's 37-yard field goal and a two-yard touchdown pass from Brock to tight end David Hill. Bronco quarterback John Elway responded with two scoring tosses to give Denver a 16-10 halftime advantage.

Lansford added another field goal and midway through the final period, Los Angeles retained the ball again. As time dwindled away Brock completed five passes for 58 yards. With a little over two minutes to play, White scored on an eight-yard run to give Los Angeles a 20-16 win.

The 34-year-old Brock struggled in his first NFL game. He ended the contest with a respectable 16 completions in 29 attempts, but only three were completed to wide receivers. The remainder of his passes were short pitches to backs and tight ends.

Los Angeles' victory over Denver was a sample of things to come. The Rams chalked up seven consecutive wins including a decisive, 35-24, Monday night victory at Seattle, and a 16-0 win

Top: Defensive tackle Merlin Olsen was the Rams' first-round pick from Utah State in 1962. **Bottom:** Defensive back Johnnie Johnson was the Rams' first-round pick in 1980. The former Texas star had three interceptions that season.

Henry Ellard 1983–

In just three NFL seasons, Henry Ellard has become the league's most dangerous double threat. He has already appeared in the Pro Bowl as a punt returner and is quickly becoming one of the league's premier wide receivers.

Ellard's value lies in his ability to score at any time from any place on the field. He is a genuine game breaker. Seven of the touchdowns he has scored for the Rams have been over 60 yards. He averages nearly 15 yards every time he touches the football.

In 1984 Ellard personally accounted for 1,049 yards of offense. Although he caught just 34 passes, he gained 622 yards. Another 427 yards came on kickoff and punt returns. Ellard improved on that total in 1985. He posted 1,312 total yards with 811 coming on receptions and an additional 501 yards on punt returns.

Ellard has always been a dangerous man with a football tucked under his arm. The Rams made him their second-round draft choice in 1983—the 34th pick overall—after a remarkable collegiate career at Fresno State. In 1982 he caught 62 passes for 1,510 yards and 15 touchdowns. He averaged nearly 25 yards per catch. That season he was voted the Pacific Coast Athletic Association's Offensive Player of the Year. When he left Fresno State he had 138 catches for 2,947 yards and 39 touchdowns. Only five men have totaled more receiving yardage in NCAA history.

Ellard was not just a one sport star at Fresno State, however. He was also an outstanding intercollegiate triple jumper with a personal best of 56-5½. Willie Banks holds the United States indoor record with a jump of 57-1½. Ellard is also a speedster and has been timed at 4.45 in the 40-yard dash.

Ellard's athletic ability became apparent to players and coaches around the NFL in 1983. Although he was nagged by injuries, including a broken collarbone, he established himself as one of the league's top punt returners in his rookie season. He returned 16 punts that year an average of 13.6 yards. He also scored one touchdown on a 72-yard return. More importantly, Ellard's efforts helped turn the Rams' special teams into one of the league's most respected units.

Ellard has continued to sharpen his punt returning skills since that rookie season. He topped the league in 1985 with a 13.6-yard average and over the past three seasons he has averaged a league leading 13.5 yards per return. He has also returned four kicks for touchdowns during that period, including an 83-yard score, an 80-yard return and a 73 yarder. Twice he has been selected to the Pro Bowl as a return man.

Despite his importance on punt returns, Ellard's value as a receiver has also increased. He has been the club's leading pass catcher for two consecutive seasons. In his injury plagued rookie season, Ellard managed to catch 16 passes for 268 yards, but in 1984 he had 34 receptions for 622 yards to lead the club. He averaged 18.3 yards per catch and had six touchdown receptions. In 1985 Ellard improved on that figure by catching 54 balls for 811 yards and five touchdowns. He averaged 15 yards per catch that season.

The Rams made a move to complement Ellard's pass catching ability with the acquisition of Ron Brown in 1984. Brown was a gold medalist in the 1984 Olympics as a member of the United States' 400 meter relay team. He caught 23 passes in 1984 despite missing training camp to run in the Olympics. Brown has been timed at 4.28 in the 40. Together with Ellard they constitute one of the fastest receiving combinations in football. "Speed is a tremendous asset on the football field," Brown said. "The game is played on quickness and that helps me survive at this level. I also think we're lucky here because the coaching staff is so good. Everything the coaches preach, their philosophy, is geared toward the Super Bowl."

Running back Wendell Tyler scoring one of his 17 touchdowns during the 1981 season.

over Kansas City. It gave the Rams a four-game lead over the defending Super Bowl champion San Francisco 49ers. Despite the winning streak, critics claimed the Rams offense was sluggish. Against the Chiefs, Dickerson gained just 68 yards on 26 carries for an average of 2.6 yards. Brock completed nine of 20 passes for 68 yards and no touchdowns.

San Francisco, struggling with a 3-4 record, was the Rams' next opponent at Anaheim Stadium. The 49ers awoke from their season long slumber and jumped out to a 28-0 first half lead. It was all the points San Francisco needed as it coasted to a 28-14 win.

The Rams maintained their first place standing in the western division by winning four of their next seven games. It gave them a 11-4 record going into the final game of the season. That contest was against their cross-town rival, the Los Angeles Raiders. The Rams had already clinched

a playoff spot but a victory would give them local bragging rights until their next confrontation.

It was a defensive battle all the way. In the first half both teams exchanged field goals. Lansford tied the game at 3-3 with just 43 seconds left in the half, but the Raiders capitalized on a good kick return and three clutch passes to move the ball to the Rams 33-yard line with five seconds to play. Chris Bahr connected to give the Raiders a 6-3 halftime lead.

The Raiders scored the game's only touchdown late in the fourth quarter on a 21-yard pass from Marc Wilson to Dokie Williams. The score upped the Raiders advantage to 16-6. The Raider defense then shut down the Rams to clinch the win.

Brock completed 14 of 28 passes for 159 yards. Wilson connected on 19 of 29 for 188 yards. Marcus Allen was the game's leading rusher with 123 yards on 24 tries. Dickerson carried 25 times for 98 yards. He ended the regular season with 1,234 yards in 292 carries. Allen was the NFL's leading rusher with 1,759 yards in 380 carries.

The Dallas Cowboys were Los Angeles' opponent in the first round of the NFC playoffs. The NFC East champions finished the regular season

Jack Youngblood 1971–1984

When a back injury forced Jack Youngblood to miss a game against the Houston Oilers near the end of the 1984 season everyone was caught by surprise. Youngblood had become a fixture on the Rams' defensive line. He was as reliable as the sun in summer. The last time he missed a start for Los Angeles, Richard Nixon was living in the White House.

Youngblood's durability is legend. The New York Yankees' Lou Gehrig is known as the ironman, but he didn't knock heads with 270-pound tackles for a living, or fend off crack-back blocks. Surely Youngblood's stamina ranks alongside Gehrig's in the annals of sport. He appeared in 200 straight games for Los Angeles between 1972 and 1984, more than

anyone who ever strapped on a horned helmet. Only two men have played in more total games for the Rams, Merlin Olsen with 208 and Charlie Cowan with 206.

Youngblood reported to the Rams in 1971 as a first-round draft choice out of the University of Florida. Linebacker Isiah Robertson was also a first-round pick that year. Youngblood's job

was to wrest a starting position from all-pro defensive end Deacon Jones or Coy Bacon. It was a difficult assignment. Youngblood didn't receive his first starting call until midway through the 1972 season. Once in the starting lineup he couldn't be removed. Youngblood didn't miss a game until 1984.

Time and injury finally got to Youngblood that year. Much of his previous success could be attributed to freedom from injury. But his longevity finally came to a halt during the 13th game of the season at Tampa Bay. He felt his back twist when he was double-teamed on a block. The injury was diagnosed as a sciatic nerve condition in his lower back. It caused Youngblood to lose strength in his left leg. Nevertheless, he continued to play and was back in the starting lineup the following week against New Orleans. He left the game early, then had his streak broken the next week when he sat out a game against Houston.

Most Ram followers were surprised to see Youngblood sidelined by an injury. His ability to play with pain was legendary. During the first round of the 1979 playoffs, he fractured a fibula in his left leg. Youngblood refused to come out of the game. He was fitted with a brace and continued to perform. He went on to play every defensive down in the NFC Championship Game and the Super Bowl despite the leg fracture.

"Most of my durability and success was due to hard work and determination," Youngblood said. "I always worked hard to improve my performance. I feel if you're willing to go that extra mile to improve yourself, you'll be a success.

"I also am lucky in that I was blessed with physical skill. The good lord gave me the talent and tools necessary to play in the NFL."

Even with a back injury in 1984, Youngblood had another outstanding season. He led the team in sacks with 9.5 and had 43 tackles. His best game was against the St. Louis Cardinals when he had three sacks for 26 yards. More importantly, he won the game for Los Angeles when he jumped over a St. Louis blocker and batted down a last second field goal attempt that would have tied the game.

It was Youngblood's pride that finally compelled him to retire in 1985. He admits he probably could have played a few more seasons, but the back injury caused him to lose strength in his left leg. Youngblood has always relied on his quickness and the lack of leg strength would have affected his style of play. He preferred to retire than play at a level he found unacceptable.

At the time of his retirement, Youngblood was still the Rams' most complete defensive lineman. In a game of specialization, he was an anomaly. During his first 12 years

with the club, Youngblood was an outside end in the 4-3 defense. When Robinson took over the club in 1983, he installed the 3-4 defense and moved Youngblood to the inside position. Youngblood was now forced to line up opposite an offensive lineman rather than in a gap. He also was forced to adapt a style that required strength rather than the finesse and quickness that Youngblood had previously depended on.

Even at the new position, Youngblood was a standout. He was rarely replaced by pass rushing specialists because he was the pass rushing specialist. He led the club in sacks each of his last seven seasons.

Youngblood made an enormous contribution to the Rams. During his 14 seasons with the club he played in seven Pro Bowls. But a more telling statistic is the club's record during that time. The Rams had just two losing seasons while Youngblood was a member of the defensive unit. They had seven first place finishes in the NFC west and appeared in one Super Bowl. Two teams consistently stood between Los Angeles and the Super Bowl.

"Dallas was always the toughest team for us to beat," Youngblood said. "It seems like we always had to get past Dallas or Minnesota in the playoffs. Those teams turned out to be our nemesis on the road to the Super Bowl."

with a 10-6 record. They couldn't improve on that record against the Rams.

Eric Dickerson was a one-man offense against the Cowboys. He rushed 34 times for 248 yards as the Rams beat Dallas 20-0. Dickerson's performance set an NFL record for rushing yardage in a playoff game. It was also the best single-game rushing effort in Ram history.

Lansford got the scoring started in the first quarter on a 33-yard field goal that put Los Angeles in front 3-0. They were the only points scored in the first half. Early in the third quarter Dickerson scored the first of his two touchdowns on a 55-yard run. He added a 40-yard run later in the period.

Meanwhile the Rams' defense dismantled the Cowboys. Dallas quarterback Danny White was sacked five times and had three passes intercepted. Running back Tony Dorsett was held to just 58 yards on 17 carries.

The Rams' special teams also got in on the act. They forced fumbles on two Cowboy kick returns. Both fumbles resulted in Los Angeles scores. The 20-0 victory marked the first time Dallas had been held scoreless in 36 playoff games.

The NFC Championship Game was next for Los Angeles. The Rams were matched with the nearly invincible Chicago Bears. Chicago boasted a 15-1 regular season record and walloped the New York Giants, 21-0, in their first playoff game. They also had the home field advantage for their matchup with the Rams.

Chicago's Soldier Field was cold and windy for the game and it got even gloomier for Los Angeles as the afternoon progressed. The Bears built a 10-0 first quarter lead on Jim McMahon's 16-yard scramble and a 34-yard field goal by Kevin Butler. As it turned out, that was all the scoring they needed. The Bears impressive defense shut out Los Angeles.

The Rams had a golden opportunity to score and change the momentum of the game just before the first half ended. Coach Gil Haskell's special teams came through with a fumble recovery at the Bears' 21-yard line with 1:04 to play. Two running plays by Dickerson gained nine yards. Then with the clock running down Brock hit Dickerson on a screen pass. Dickerson battled to the five, but the Rams were unable to use their last time out as the half expired.

Eric Dickerson was held to just 46 yards rushing in the game and turned the ball over once on a fumble. Quarterback Dieter Brock was limited to 10 completions in 31 attempts and one interception. Meanwhile, the Bears posted two more touchdowns on the way to a 24-0 victory. Despite the loss it was a fine season for the Rams. They ended the year with a 12-6 record and their best finish since appearing in Super Bowl XIV.

Page 176: Rams safety Eddie Brown (25) battles Tampa Bay's Jimmie Giles (88) for the ball during the 1980 NFC title game.
Page 178: Fullback Les Josephson (34) races through a hole in the New Orleans Saint defense.

RECORDS

All-Time Rams Roster

NOTE: Players listed below (name, position, college, years with Rams) are those who have appeared in at least one regular season game (or on active roster) for the Rams since the club moved to Los Angeles in 1946.

A

Adams, John (TE), Cal State L.A., 1963
Agajanian, Ben (K), New Mexico, 1953
Agler, Bob (R), Otterbein, 1948-49
Alexander, Kermit (DB), UCLA, 1970-71
Alexander, Robert (RB), West Virginia, 1982-83
Allen, Duane (E), Santa Ana JC, 1961-64
Anderson, Bruce (DE), Williamette, 1966
Andrews, George (LB), Nebraska, 1979-85
Arnett, Jon (RB), USC, 1957-63
Arnold, Walt (TE), New Mexico, 1980-81
Atkins, Pervis (RB), New Mexico State, 1961-63

B

Bacon, Coy (DT), Jackson State, 1968-72
Bagarus, Steve (RB), Notre Dame, 1947
Bain, Bill (G), USC, 1979-85
Baker, John (DT), No. Car. College, 1958-61
Baker, Terry (QB-RB), Oregon State, 1963-65
Baker, Tony (RB), Oregon State, 1973-74
Banta, Jack (RB), USC, 1946-48
Barber, Mike (TE), Louisiana Tech, 1982-85
Barnett, Doug (DE), Azusa Pacific, 1982-83
Barry, Paul (RB), Tulsa, 1950-52
Bass, Dick (RB), Pacific, 1960-69
Battle, Ron (TE), North Texas State, 1981-82
Baughan, Maxie (LB), Georgia Tech, 1966-70
Beathard, Pete (QB), USC, 1972
Benton, Jim (E), Arkansas, 1946-47
Bertelsen, Jim (RB), Texas, 1972-76
Bighead, Jack (E), Pepperdine, 1955
Bishop, Richard (NT), Louisville, 1983
Bleeker, Mel (RB), USC, 1947
Boeke, Jim (T), Heidelberg, 1960-63
Bolinger, Russ (G), Long Beach State, 1983-85
Bouley, Gil (T), Boston College, 1946-50
Bowers, Bill (DB), USC, 1954
Boyd, Bob (E), Loyola (L.A.), 1950-57
Braatz, Tom (E), Marquette, 1958
Bradshaw, Charlie (T), Baylor, 1958-60
Brady, Ed (LB), Illinois, 1984
Bratkowski, Zeke (QB), Georgia, 1961-63
Bravo, Alex (DB), Cal Poly SLO, 1957-58
Breen, Gene (LB), Virginia Tech, 1967-68
Brink, Larry (DE), No. Illinois St., 1948-53
Brito, Gene (DE), Loyola (L.A.), 1959-60
Britt, Charley (DB), Georgia, 1960-63
Brock, Dieter (QB), Jacksonville State, 1985
Brooks, Larry (DT), VA. St.-Petersburg, 1972-82

Brown, Bob (T), Nebraska, 1969-70
Brown, Eddie (S-KR), Tennessee, 1978-79
Brown, Fred (LB), Miami (Fla.), 1965
Brown, Roger (DT), Maryland State, 1967-69
Brown, Ron (WR), Arizona State, 1984-85
Brown, Willie (E-RB), USC, 1964-65
Brudzinski, Bob (LB), Ohio State, 1977-80
Bruney, Fred (DB), Ohio State, 1958
Bryant, Cullen (DB-RB), Colorado, 1973-82
Budka, Frank (DB), Notre Dame, 1964
Bukich, Rudy (QB), USC, 1953-56
Burke, Mike (P), Miami (Fla.), 1974
Burman, George (C-G), Northwestern, 1967-70
Burroughs, Don (DB), Colorado A&M, 1955-59
Buzin, Rich (T), Penn State, 1971
Byrd, Mac (LB), USC, 1965

C

Cahill, Dave (DT), Northern Arizona, 1967
Cain, Lynn (RB), USC, 1985
Cappelletti, John (RB), Penn State, 1974-78
Carey, Bob (E), Michigan State, 1952, 1954, 1956
Carollo, Joe (T), Notre Dame, 1962-68, 1971
Carrell, Duane (P), Florida State, 1975
Carson, Howard (LB), Howard Payne, 1981-83
Casey, Bernie (WR), Bowling Green, 1967-68
Cash, Rick (DE), Northeast Missouri, 1969-70
Casner, Ken (T), Baylor, 1952
Cason, Jim (DB), LSU, 1955-56
Castete, Jesse (DB), McNeese State, 1956-57
Celotto, Mario (LB), USC, 1981
Champagne, Ed (T), LSU, 1947-50
Chapple, Dave (P), UC Santa Barbara, 1972-74
Childs, Henry (TE), Kansas State, 1981
Chuy, Don (G), Clemson, 1963-68
Clark, Al (CB), Eastern Michigan, 1972-75
Clark, Ken (P), St. Mary's (N.S.), 1979
Clarke, Leon (E), USC, 1956-59
Cobb, Bob (DE), Arizona, 1981
Collier, Bob (T), SMU, 1951
Collins, Jim (LB), Syracuse, 1982-85
Collins, Kirk (CB), Baylor, 1982-83
Cordileone, Lou (LB), Clemson, 1962
Corn, Joe (RB), No College, 1948
Corral, Frank (K-P), UCLA, 1978-81
Cothren, Paige (K), Mississippi, 1957-58
Cowan, Charlie (T), N. Mex. Highlands, 1961-75
Cowhig, Jerry (RB), Notre Dame, 1947-49
Cowlings, Al (DE), USC, 1975, 1977
Coyle, Ross (DB), Oklahoma, 1961
Crabb, Claude (DB), Colorado, 1966-68

Cromwell, Nolan (S), Kansas, 1977-85
Cross, Bobby (T), Kilgore JC, 1954-55
Cross, Irv (DB), Northwestern, 1966-68
Croudip, David (CB), San Diego State, 1984
Crow, Lindon (DB), USC, 1961-64
Crutchfield, Dwayne (RB), Iowa State, 1984
Curran, Pat (TE-RB), Lakeland, 1969-74
Currie, Dan (LB), Michigan State, 1965-66
Currivan, Don (DE), Boston College, 1948-49
Curry, Bill (C), Georgia Tech, 1974

D

Dahms, Tom (T), San Diego State, 1951-54
Dale, Carroll (E), VPI, 1960-64
Daniel, Willie (DB), Mississippi State, 1967-69
Daugherty, Dick (LB), Oregon, 1951-58
David, Bob (G), Villanova, 1947-48
Davis, Anthony (RB-KR), USC, 1978
Davis, Glenn (RB), Army, 1950-51
Davis, Roger (G), Syracuse, 1964
Dean, Hal (G), Ohio State, 1947-49
DeFruiter, Bob (NT), Nebraska, 1948
DeJurnett, Charles (DT), San Jose State, 1982-85
Delaney, Jeff (S), Pittsburgh, 1980
deLauer, Bob (C), USC, 1946
DeMarco, Bob (C), Dayton, 1975
Dempsey, Tom (K), Palomar JC, 1975-76
Dennard, Preston (WR), New Mexico, 1978-83
Dennis, Mike (RB), Mississippi, 1968-69
Dickerson, Eric (RB), SMU, 1983-85
Dickson, Paul (T), Baylor, 1959
Dils, Steve (QB), Stanford, 1984-85
Doll, Don (DB), USC, 1954
Doss, Reggie (DE), Hampton Institute, 1978-85
Dougherty, Bob (LB), Kentucky, 1957
Drake, Bill (DB), Oregon, 1973-74
Dryer, Fred (DE), San Diego State, 1972-81
Duckworth, Bobby (WR), Arkansas, 1985
Dunstan, Bill (DT), Utah State, 1979
Dwyer, Jack (DB), Loyola (L.A.), 1952-54
Dyer, Henry (RB), Grambling, 1966-68

E

Eason, Roger (G), Oklahoma, 1946-48
Ekern, Carl (LB), San Jose State, 1976-85
Ellard, Henry (WR), Fresno State, 1983-85
Ellena, Jack (MG), UCLA, 1955-56
Ellersick, Don (DB), Washington, 1960
Ellis, Ken (DB), Southern U, 1979
Ellison, Willie (RB), Texas Southern, 1967-72
Elmendorf, Dave (DB), Texas A&M, 1971-79
Evey, Dick (DT), Tennessee, 1970
Ezerins, Vilnis (RB), Whitewater State, 1968

F

Fanning, Mike (DT), Notre Dame, 1975-82
Fanning, Stan (DE), Idaho, 1963
Farmer, George (WR), Southern U, 1982-84
Farmer, Tom (RB), Iowa, 1946
Faulkner, Chris (TE), Florida, 1984
Fawcett, Jake (T), SMU, 1946
Fears, Tom (E), UCLA, 1948-56
Ferragamo, Vince (QB), Nebraska, 1977-80, 1982-84
Ferris, Neil (DB), Loyola (L.A.), 1953
Finch, Karl (E), Cal Poly Pomona, 1962
Finlay, Jack (G), UCLA, 1947-51
Fournet, Sid (DT), LSU, 1955-56
Fox, Tim (S), Ohio State, 1985
France, Doug (T), Ohio State, 1975-81
Franckhauser, Tom (DB), Purdue, 1959
Fry, Bob (T), Kentucky, 1953-58
Fuller, Frank (DT), Kentucky, 1953-58
Fuller, Steve (QB), Clemson, 1983
Fulton, Ed (G), Maryland, 1978

G

Gabriel, Roman (QB), No. Carolina State, 1962-72
Geddes, Ken (LB), Nebraska, 1971-75
Gehrke, Fred (RB), Utah, 1946-49
George, Bill (LB), Wake Forest, 1966
Geredine, Tom (WR), NE Missouri State, 1976
Gilbert, Lewis (TE), Florida, 1981
Gordon, Dick (WR), Michigan State, 1972-73
Gossett, Bruce (K), Richmond, 1964-69
Grant, Otis (WR), Michigan State, 1983-84
Gravelle, Gordon (T), BYU, 1979
Gray, Jerry (CB), Texas, 1985
Green, Gary (CB), Baylor, 1984-85
Greene, Kevin (LB), Auburn, 1985
Gremminger, Hank (DB), Baylor, 1966
Grier, Roosevelt (DT), Peenn State, 1963-66
Griffin, Bob (C), Arkansas, 1953-57
Griffin, John (DB), Memphis State, 1963
Guillory, Anthony (LB), Lamar Tech, 1965, 1967-68
Guman, Mike (RB), Penn State, 1980-85
Guzik, John (LB), Pittsburgh, 1959-60

H

Haden, Pat (QB), USC, 1976-81
Hadl, John (QB), Kansas, 1973-74
Hall, Alvin (DB), No College, 1961-63
Halliday, Jack (DT), SMU, 1951
Halverson, Dean (LB), Washington, 1968, 1972
Hamilton, Ray (E), Arkansas, 1946-47
Harding, Roger (C), California, 1946
Hardy, Jim (QB), USC, 1946-48
Harmon, Tom (RB), Michigan, 1946-47
Harrah, Dennis (G), Miami (Fla.), 1975-85
Harris, Eric (DB), Memphis State, 1983-85
Harris, James (QB), Grambling, 1973-76
Harris, Jim (DB), Oklahoma, 1958

All-Time Rams Roster

Harris, Joe (LB), Georgia Tech, 1979-81
Harris, Marv (LB), Stanford, 1964
Harrison, Dennis (DE), Vanderbilt, 1985
Hatcher, Dale (P), Clemson, 1985
Hauser, Art (DT), Xavier, 1954-57
Hayes, Larry (C), Vanderbilt, 1962-63
Haymond, Alvin (DB), Southern U, 1969-71
Haynes, Hall (DB), Santa Clara, 1954-56
Heckard, Steve (E), Davidson, 1965-66
Hecker, Bob (DB), Baldwin Wallace, 1952
Hecker, Norb (DB), Baldwin Wallace, 1951-53
Hector, Willie (T), Pacific, 1961
Henry, Mike (LB), USC, 1962-64
Henry, Urban (DT), Georgia Tech, 1961
Hickey, Howard (E), Arkansas, 1946-48
Hicks, Victor (TE), Oklahoma, 1980
Hill, David (TE), Texas A&I, 1983-85
Hill, Drew (WR-KR), Georgia Tech, 1979-84
Hill, Eddie (RB), Memphis State, 1979-80
Hill, Kent (G), Georgia Tech, 1979-85
Hill, Winston (T), Texas Southern, 1977
Hirsch, Elroy (E-RB), Wisconsin, 1949-57
Hock, John (G), Santa Clara, 1953-57
Hoerner, Dick (RB), Iowa, 1947-51
Hoffman, Bob (RB), USC, 1946-48
Holladay, Bob (RB), Tulsa, 1956
Holovak, Mike (RB), Boston College, 1946
Holtzman, Glenn (T), North Texas State, 1955-58
Hord, Roy (G), Duke, 1960-62
Horton, Greg (G), Colorado, 1976-78, 1980
Horvath, Les (RB), Ohio State, 1947-48
Houser, John (C-GO), Redlands, 1957-59
Howard, Gene (DB), Langston, 1971-72
Hubbell, Frank (DE-TE), Tennessee, 1947-49
Huffman, Dick (T), Tennessee, 1947-50
Hughes, Ed (DB), Tulsa, 1954-55
Humphrey, Buddy (QB), Baylor, 1959-60
Hunter, Art (C), Notre Dame, 1960-64
Hunter, Tony (TE), Notre Dame, 1985

I

Iglehart, Floyd (DB), Wiley, 1958
Iman, Ken (C), Southeast Missouri St., 1965-74
Irvin, LeRoy (CB-PR), Kansas, 1980-85

J

Jackson, Harold (WR), Jackson St., 1968, 1973-77
Jackson, Monte (CB), San Diego State, 1975-77
Jackson, Rusty (P), LSU, 1976
Janerette, Charlie (G), Penn State, 1960
Jaworski, Ron (QB), Youngstown, 1974-76
Jerue, Mark (LB), Washington, 1983-85
Jessie, Ron (WR), Kansas, 1975-79
Jeter, Gary (DE), USC, 1983-85
Jobko, Bill (LB), Ohio State, 1958-62

Jodat, Jim (RB), Carthage, 1977-79
Johns, Freeman (WR), SMU, 1976-77
Johnson, Clyde (T), Kentucky, 1946-47
Johnson, Johnnie (S), Texas, 1980-85
Johnson, Marvin (DB), San Jose State, 1951-52
Johnson, Mitch (T), UCLA, 1969-70
Jones, A.J. (RB), Texas, 1982-85
Jones, Bert (QB), LSU, 1982
Jones, Cody (DT), San Jose State, 1974-78,1980-82
Jones, David (DE), South Carolina State, 1961-71
Jones, Gordon (WR), Pittsburgh, 1983 84
Jones, Jimmy (RB), Washington, 1958
Jordan, Jeff (RB), Washington, 1970
Josephson, Les, (RB), Augustana, 1964-67,1969-74
Justin, Sid (CB), Long Beach State, 1979

K

Kalmanir, Tom (RB), Nevada, 1949-51
Kamana, John (RB), USC, 1984
Karras, Ted (G), Indiana, 1966
Karrlivacz, Carl (DB), Syracuse, 1959-60
Kay, Rick (B), Colorado, 1973,1975-77
Keane, Tom (DB), West Virginia, 1948-51
Kemp, Jeff (QB) Dartmouth, 1981-85
Kenerson, John (T), Kentucky State, 1960
Kersten, Wally (T), Minnesota, 1982
Kilgore, Jon (P), Auburn, 1965-67
Kimbrough, Elbert (DB), Northwestern, 1961
Klein, Bob (TE), USC, 1963
Klosterman, Don (QB), Loyola (L.A.), 1952
Kowalski, Gary (T), Boston College, 1983
Ksionyak, John (QB), St. Bonaventure, 1947

L

LaHood, Mike (G), Wyoming, 1969, 1971-72
Lamson, Chuck (DB), Wyoming, 1965-67
Lane, Dick (DB), Scottsbluff JC, 1952-53
Lang, Israel (RB), Tennessee State, 1969
Lange, Bill (G), Dayton, 1951-52
Lansford, Buck (G), Texas, 1958-60
Lansford, Mike (PK), Washington, 1982-85
Lapka, Myron (DT), USC, 1982-83
Larsen, Gary (DT), Condordia, 1964
Latin, Jerry (RB-KR), Northern Illinois, 1978
Laughlin, Jim (LB), Ohio State, 1985
Lazetich, Milan (MG), Michigan, 1946-50
Lear, Les (G), Manitoba, Canada, 1946
Lee, Bob (QB), Pacific, 1979-80
Leggett, Earl (DT), LSU, 1966
Lear, Les (G), Manitoba, Canada, 1946
Lee, Bob (QB), Pacific, 1979-80
Leggett, Earl (DT), LSU, 1966
Levy, Len (G), Minnesota, 1946

Lewis, David (LB), USC, 1983
Lewis, Woodley (DB-E), Oregon, 1950-55
Lilja, George (C), Michigan, 1982-83
Lipscomb, Gene (DT), No College, 1953-55
Livingston, Cliff (LB), UCLA, 1963-65
Locklin, Kerry (TE), New Mexico State, 1982
Long, Bob (LB), UCLA, 1960-61
Long, Bob (WR), Wichita State, 1970
Lothridge, Billy (P), Georgia Tech, 1965
Love, Duval (G), UCLA, 1985
Love, John (WR), North Texas State, 1972
LoVetere, John (DT), Compton JC, 1959-62
Lundy, Lamar (DE-TE), Purdue, 1957-69

M

Mack, Tom (G), Michigan, 1966-78
Magnani, Dante (RB), St. Mary's, 1947-48
Marchlewski, Frank (C), Minnesota, 1965,1968-69
Marconi, Joe (RB), West Virginia, 1956-61
Marshall, Larry (WR-KR), Maryland, 1978
Martin, Aaron (DB), No. Car. College, 1964-65
Martin, John (C), Navy, 1947-49
Maslowski, Matt (WR), U. of San Diego, 1971
Mason, Tommy (RB), Tulane, 1967-70
Matheson, Riley (G-LB), Tex. Sch./ Mines, 1946-47
Matson, Ollie (RB-E), USF, 1959-62
Mayes, Carl (RB), Texas, 1952
McCormick, Tom (RB), Pacific, 1953-55
McCutcheon, Lawrence (RB), Colo. St., 1972-79
McDonald, James (TE), USC, 1983-85
McDonald, Mike (LB), USC, 1983-84
McDonald, Tommy (WR), Oklahoma, 1965-66
McFadin, Bud (DT-T), Texas, 1952-56
McGee, Willie (WR), Alcorn A&M, 1974-75
McGlasson, Ed (C), Youngstown State, 1980
McIlhany, Dan (DB), Texas A&M, 1965
McKeever, Marlin (LB-TE), USC, 1961-66, 1971-72
McKinnely, Phil (T), UCLA, 1981
McLain, Kevin (LB), Colorado State, 1976-79
McLaughlin, Leon (C), UCLA, 1951-55
McMillan, Eddie (CB), Florida State, 1973-75
Meador, Ed (DB), Arkansas Tech, 1959-70
Meisner, Greg (DE), Pittsburgh, 1981-85
Mello, Jim (RB), Notre Dame, 1948
Mergenthal, Art (G), Notre Dame, 1946
Michaels, Lou (DE), Kentucky, 1958-60
Miller, Clark (DE), Utah State, 1970
Miller, Paul (DE), LSU, 1954-57
Miller, Ron (E), USC, 1956
Miller, Ron (QB), Wisconsin, 1962

Miller, Shawn (NT), Utah State, 1984-85
Miller, Willie (WR), Colorado State, 1978-82
Misko, John (P), Oregon State, 1982-84
Mitchell, Lydell (RB), Penn State, 1980
Molden, Frank (DT), Jackson State, 1965
Moore, Jeff (WR), Tennessee, 1980-81
Moore, Tom (RB), Vanderbilt, 1966
Morris, Jack (DB), Oregon, 1958-60
Morris, Larry (LB), Georgia Tech, 1955-57
Morrow, John (C), Michigan, 1956-59
Munson, Bill (QB), Utah State, 1964-67
Murphy, Phil (DT), South Carolina State, 1980-81
Myers, Brad (RB), Bucknell, 1953-56
Myers, Jack (RB-DB), UCLA, 1952

N

Namath, Joe (QB), Alabama, 1977
Naumetz, Fred (LB-C), Boston College, 1946-50
Nelson, Bill (DT), Oregon State, 1971-75
Nelson, Chuck (K), Washington, 1983
Nelson, Terry (TE), Arkansas AM&N, 1973-80
Nettles, Jim (DB), Wisconsin, 1969-72
Newsome, Vince (S), Washington, 1983-85
Nichols, Bob (T), Stanford, 1966-67
Nuzum, Rick (C), Kentucky, 1977

O

Odom, Ricky (DB), USC, 1979
Olsen, Merlin (DT), Utah State, 1962-76
Olsen, Phil (DT-DE), Utah State, 1971-74
O'Steen, Dwayne (CB), San Jose State, 1978-79
Owens, Mel (LB), Michigan, 1981-85

P

Panfil, Ken (T), Purdue, 1956-58
Pankey, Irv (T), Penn State, 1980-85
Pardee, Jack (LB), Texas A&M, 1957-70
Parish, Don (LB), Stanford, 1971
Pasqua, Joe (T), SMU, 1946
Pasquariello, Ralph (RB), Villanova, 1950
Pastorini, Dan (QB), Santa Clara, 1981
Paul, Don (LB), UCLA, 1948-55
Peacock, Elvis (RB), Oklahoma, 1979-80
Penaranda, Jairo (RB), UCLA, 1981
Pergine, Jon (LB), Notre Dame, 1969-72
Perkins, Art (RB), North Texas St., 1962-63
Perry, Rod (CB), Colorado, 1975-82
Peterson, Jim (LB), San Diego State, 1974-75
Petibon, Richie (DB), Tulane, 1969-70
Phillips, Jim (E), Auburn, 1958-64
Phillips, Rod (RB), Jackson State, 1975-78
Pifferini, Bob (LB), UCLA, 1977
Pillath, Roger (T), Wisconsin, 1965
Pitts, Elijah (RB), Philander Smith, 1970
Pitts, Hugh (LB), TCU, 1956
Pivec, Dave (TE), Notre Dame, 1966-68
Pleasant, Mike (CB), Oklahoma, 1984

All-Time Rams Roster

Plum, Milt (QB), Penn State, 1968
Plummer, Tony (DB), Pacific, 1974
Pope, Bucky (WR), Catawba, 1964, 1966-67
Pottios, Myron (LB), Notre Dame, 1966-70
Powell, Tim (DE), Northwestern, 1965
Preece, Steve (S), Oregon State, 1973-76
Pritko, Steve (DE), Villanova, 1946-47
Purnell, Jim (LB), Wisconsin, 1969-72
Putnam, Duane (G), Pacific, 1952-59, 1962

Q

Quinlan, Skeet (RB), San Diego State, 1952-56

R

Ray, David (K-WR), Alabama, 1969-74
Redden, Barry (RB), Richmond, 1982-85
Reece, Geoff (C), Washington State, 1976
Reed, Doug (DE), San Diego State, 1984-85
Reese, Booker (DE), Bethune-Cookman, 1984-85
Reid, Joe (LB), LSU, 1951
Reilly, Mike (LB), Oklahoma, 1982
Reinhard, Bob (T-DT), California, 1950
Reisz, Albie (QB), LSU, 1946
Rentzel, Lance (WR), Oklahoma, 1971-72, 1974
Repko, Joe (DT), Boston College, 1948-49
Reynolds, Jack (LB), Tennessee, 1970-80
Rhome, Jerry (QB), Tulsa, 1971
Rich, Herb (DB), Vanderbilt, 1951-53
Richardson, Jerry (DB), West Texas St., 1964-65
Richter, Les (LB), California, 1954-62
Rickards, Paul (QB), Pittsburgh, 1948
Robertson, Isiah (LB), Southern U., 1971-78
Robustelli, Andy (DE), Arnold, 1951-55
Rogers, Mel (LB), Florida A&M, 1976
Rucker, Conrad (G-T), Southern U., 1980
Ruthstrom, Ralph (RB), SMU, 1946
Rutledge, Jeff (QB), Alabama, 1979-81
Ryan, Frank (QB), Rice, 1958-61
Ryczek, Dan (C), Virginia, 1978-79

S

Saul, Rich (C), Michigan State, 1970-81
Scales, Dwight (WR), Grambling, 1976-78
Schuh, Harry (T), Memphis State, 1971-73
Schultz, Eberle (T), Oregon State, 1946-47
Schumacher, Gregg (DE), Illinois, 1967-68
Scibelli, Joe (G), Notre Dame, 1961-75
Scribner, Rob (RB), UCLA, 1973-76
Selawski, Gene (T), Purdue, 1959
Septien, Rafael (K), SW Louisiana, 1977
Severson, Jeff (DB), Long Beach State, 1979
Sewell, Harley (G), Texas, 1963

Shannon, Carver (DB-RB), So. Illinois, 1962-64
Shaw, Bob (E), Ohio State, 1946-49
Shaw, Glenn (RB), Kentucky, 1962
Shaw, Nate (DB), USC, 1969-70
Shearin, Joe (G), Texas, 1983
Sherman, Rod (WR), USC, 1973
Sherman, Will (DB), St. Mary's, 1954-60
Shiver, Ray (DB), Miami (Fla.), 1956
Shofner, Del (E), Baylor, 1957-60
Simensen, Don (T), St. Thomas, 1951-52
Simmons, Jeff (WR), USC, 1983
Simpson, Bill (DB), Michigan State, 1974-78
Sims, George (DB), Baylor, 1949-50
Slater, Jackie (T), Jackson State, 1976-85
Slaton, Tony (C), USC, 1984-85
Smith, Billy Ray (DE), Arkansas, 1957
Smith, Bobby (DB), UCLA, 1962-65
Smith, Bruce (RB), Minnesota, 1948
Smith, Doug (C), Bowling Green, 1978-85
Smith, Larry (RB), Florida, 1969-73
Smith, Lucious (CB), Cal State Fullerton, 1980-82
Smith, Ron (QB), Richmond, 1965
Smith, Ron (DB), Wisconsin, 1968-69
Smith, Ron (WR), San Diego State, 1978-79
Smith, V.T. (RB), Abilene Christian, 1949-53
Smyth, Bill (T-TE), Cincinnati, 1947-50
Snow, Jack (WR), Notre Dame, 1965-75
Sparkman, Alan (DT), Texas A&M, 1948-49
Stalcup, Jerry (LB), Wisconsin, 1960
Statuto, Art (C), Notre Dame, 1950
Stein, Bob (LB), Minnesota, 1973-74
Stephens, Larry (DT), Texas, 1962
Stephenson, Dave (G), West Virginia, 1950
Stiger, Jim (RB), Washington, 1965-67
Stokes, Tim (T), Oregon, 1974
Strode, Woody (E), UCLA, 1946
Strofolino, Mike (LB), Villanova, 1965
Strugar, George (DT), Washington, 1957-61
Studstill, Pat (WR-P), Houston, 1968-71
Stukes, Charlie (CB), Maryland East Sh., 1973-74
Sucic, Steve (RB), Illinois, 1946
Sully, Ivory (DB), Delaware, 1979-84
Svare, Harland (LB), Washington State, 1953-54
Swain, Bill (LB), Oregon, 1963
Sweet, Joe (WR), Tennessee State, 1972-73
Sweetan, Karl (QB), Wake Forest, 1969-70

T

Talbert, Diron (DT), Texas, 1967-70
Tarbox, Bruce (G), Syracuse, 1961
Taylor, Cecil (RB), Kansas State, 1955-57
Teeuws, Len (T), Tulane, 1952-53

Thomas, Bob (RB), Arizona State, 1971-72
Thomas, Clendon (DB), Oklahoma, 1958-61
Thomas, Jewerl (RB), San Jose State, 1980-82
Thomas, Pat (CB), Texas A&M, 1976-82
Thomason, Bob (QB), VMI, 1949
Thompson, Harry (G), UCLA, 1950-54
Toogood, Charley (DT-T), Nebraska, 1951-56
Towler, Dan (RB), Wash. & Jefferson, 1950-55
Truax, Billy (TE), LSU, 1964-70
Tucker, Wendell (WR), South Carolina St., 1967-70
Tyler, Wendell (RB), UCLA, 1977-82

V

Valdez, Vernon (DB), U of San Diego, 1960
Van Brocklin, Norm (QB), Oregon, 1949-57
Vann, Norwood (LB), East Carolina, 1984-85
Varrichione, Frank (T), Notre Dame, 1961-65
Vasicek, Vic (LB), Texas, 1950
Villanueva, Danny (P-K), New Mexico St., 1960-64
Von Sonn, Andy (LB), UCLA, 1964

W

Waddy, Billy (WR), Colorado, 1977-81
Wade, Bill (QB), Vanderbilt, 1954-60
Walker, Glen (P), USC, 1977-78
Wallace, Jackie (DB), Arizona, 1977-79
Waller, Ron (RB), Maryland, 1955-58
Wardlow, Duane (DE), Washington, 1954-56
Washington, Ken (RB-DB), UCLA, 1946-48
Waterfield, Bob (QB-DB-K), UCLA, 1946-52
Wendryhoski, Joe (C), Illinois, 1964-66
West, Pat (RB), USC, 1946-48
West, Stan (MG), Oklahoma, 1950-54
Westbrooks, Greg (LB), Colorado, 1979-80
White, Charles (RB), USC, 1985
White, Lee (RB), Weber State, 1971
Whitmyer, Nat (DB), Washington, 1963
Whittenton, Jesse (DB), Texas Western, 1956-57
Whittingham, Fred (LB), Cal Poly SLO, 1964
Wilbur, John (G), Stanford, 1970
Wilcher, Mike (LB), North Carolina, 1983-85
Wilkins, Roy (LB), Georgia, 1958-59
Wilkinson, Jerry (DE), Oregon State, 1979
Williams, Charlie (WR), Prairie View, 1970
Williams, Clarence (DB), Washington St., 1965-72
Williams, Eric (LB), USC, 1982-83
Williams, Frank (RB), Pepperdine, 1961-64

Williams, Henry (DB), San Diego State, 1983
Williams, Jeff (T), Rhode Island, 1977
Williams, Jerry (DB), Washington State, 1949-52
Williams, John (T), Minnesota, 1972-79
Williams, Mike (DB), LSU, 1983
Williams, Roger (DB), Grambling, 1971-72
Williams, Sam (DE), Michigan State, 1959
Williams, Travis (RB), Arizona State, 1971
Wilson, Ben (RB), USC, 1963-65
Wilson, Jack (RB), Baylor, 1946-47
Wilson, Jim (T), Georgia, 1968
Wilson, Tom (RB), No College, 1956-61
Winkler, Jim (DT), Texas A&M, 1951-52
Winston, Kelton (DB), Wiley, 1967-68
Wojcik, Greg (DT), USC, 1971
Woodlief, Doug (LB), Memphis State, 1965-69

Y

Yagiello, Ray (G), Catawba, 1948-49
Yary, Ron (T), USC, 1982
Young, Charlie (TE), USC, 1977-79
Young, Michael (WR), UCLA, 1985
Youngblood, George (DB), Cal State L.A., 1966
Youngblood, Jack (DE), Florida, 1971-84
Youngblood, Jim (LB), Tennessee Tech., 1973-84
Younger, Paul (RB-LB), Grambling, 1949-57

Z

Zilly, Jack (TE-DE), Notre Dame, 1947-51

Joe Marconi

Rams All-Time Draft

1946 CHOICES

1. Emil Sitko, B, Notre Dame
2. Don Samuel, B, Oregon State
3. Don Paul, C, UCLA
4. Newell Oestreich, B, California
5. Lafayette King, E, Georgia
6. Joe Waisler, B, Ohio State
7. Mike Schumchyk, G, Arkansas
8. Joe Signaigo, G, Notre Dame
9. Tom Phillips, B, Ohio State
10. Ted Strojny, T, Holy Cross
11. George Strohmeyer, C, Notre Dame & Texas A&M
12. Bob Palladino, B, Notre Dame
13. Dick Lorenz, E, Oregon State
14. Larry Bouley, B, Boston College & Georgia
15. Gasper Urban, G, Notre Dame
16. Bob Wise, C, Colorado & Nevada
17. Jerry Ford, B, Notre Dame
18. Rob Albrecht, B, Dartmouth & Marquette
19. Cliff Lewis, B, Duke
20. Bob Richardson, T, Marquette
21. Derald Lebow, B, Oklahoma
22. Bill Lippincott, B, Washington State
23. Kay Jamison, E, Florida
24. D.J. Gambrell, C, Alabama
25. Joe Dickey, B, Kansas & Colorado
26. Marty Grievas, E, San Francisco
27. J. Parrin, T, Southern California
28. Frank Plant, C, Georgia
29. Dale Cowan, T, Kansas State
30. Johnny West, B, Oklahoma

1947 CHOICES

1. Herman Wedemeyer, B, St. Mary's
2. Don Paul, C, UCLA
3. Gordon Gray, B, Southern California
4. Paul Evenson, T, Oregon State
5. Bill Smyth, T, Cincinnati
6. Bill McGovern, C, Washington
7. Max Partin, B, Tennessee
8. Carl Samuelson, T, Nebraska
9. Russ Stegar, B, Illinois
10. Dante Lavelli, E, Ohio State
11. Mike Dimitro, G, UCLA
12. John Kissell, T, Boston College
13. George Fuchs, B, Wisconsin
14. Ralph Chubb, B, Michigan
15. Don Hardy, E, Southern California
16. Ed Champagne, T, LSU
17. Jimmy Dewar, B, Indiana
18. Bernie Rieges, B, UCLA
19. Leon McLaughlin, C, UCLA
20. Charley Elliot, T, Oregon
21. Lou Levanti, C, Illinois
22. J.D. Cheek, T, Oklahoma A&M
23. Bob Dal Porto, B, California
24. Gene Standefer, B, Texas Tech
25. Bob David, B Villanova
26. Jim Hunnicutt, B, South Carolina
27. John Comer, B, Holy Cross
28. Dean Hall, G, Ohio State
29. Jim Atwell, B, South Carolina
30. Bob Prymuski, G, Illinois

1948 CHOICES

1. Choice to Detroit
2. Tom Keane, B, West Virginia
3. Bruce Bailey, B, Virginia
4. George Grimes, B, Virginia
5. Noel Cudd, T, West Texas State
6. Bob Alker, B, Colorado Mines
7. Mike Graham, B, Cincinnati
8. Glenn Johnson, T, Arizona State
9. Johnny Zisch, E, Colorado
10. Atherton Phleger, T, Stanford
11. Bob Heck, E, Purdue
12. Bill Schroll, B, LSU
13. Bob Dement, T, Mississippi Southern
14. Charley Schoenherr, B, Wheaton
15. Larry Brink, E, Northern Illinois
16. Bill O'Connor, G, Notre Dame
17. Bill Nelson, B, Montana State
18. Jim Reis, T, North Carolina State
19. Ray Borneman, B, Texas
20. Ray Yagiello, T, Catawba
21. John Pesek, B, Nebraska
22. Charlie Deautremont, B, So. Oregon
23. Bob Levenhagen, G, Washington
24. Leon Cooper, T, Mardin-Simmons & Albright
25. Jim Wade, B, Oklahoma City University
26. Ken Sinofsky, G, Nevada
27. Bobby Jack Stuart, B, Tulsa & Army
28. Hilliard Grim, E, Arizona
29. Tony Kunkiewicz, B, Trinity (Conn.)
30. Bill Taylor, E, Rice

1949 CHOICES

1. Bobby Thomason, B, VMI
2. George Sims, B, Baylor
3. Jim Winkler, T, Texas A&M
4. Norm Van Brocklin, QB, Oregon
5. Earl Howell, B, Mississippi
6. Charles Reynolds, B, Texas Tech
7. John Baker, G, California
8. John Waldrum, G, Sal Ross State (Tex.)
9. Johnny Smith, E, Arizona
10. Max Minnich, B, Bowling Green
11. Jim Cozad, T, Iowa
12. Bill Renna, G, Santa Clara
13. Paul Barry, B, Tulsa
14. Ed Carmichael, T, Oregon State
15. J.C. Dodd, B, Sal Ross State (Tex.)
16. Joe Morgan, G, Mississippi Southern
17. Dick Sheffield, E, Tulane
18. Hilalry Chollet, B, Cornell
19. Joe Leonard, T, Virginia
20. Lloyd Eisenberg, T, Duke
21. George Teufel, B, Lock Haven St. (Penn.)
22. Ed Hamilton, E, Arkansas
23. Walt Kersulis, E, Illinois
24. Fred Klenenok, B, San Francisco
25. Clay Matthews, T, Georgia Tech

1950 CHOICES

1. Stan West, G, Oklahoma
2. Bob Fuchs, G, Missouri
3. Don Murray, T, Penn State
4. Ben Proctor, E, Texas
5. Dick McKissack, B, SMU
6. Orville Langrell, T, Oklahoma City Univ.
7. Cliff Coggin, E, Mississippi Southern
8. Woodley Lewis, B, Oregon
9. Les Cowan, E, McMurry State (Tex.)
10. Jay Van Noy, B, Utah State
11. Fred Stuvek, G, West Virginia
12. John Lunney, G, Arkansas
13. Tom Hinbigler, B, College of Idaho
14. Bill Trautwein, T, Ohio State
15. Dave Stephenson, C, West Virginia
16. Jim Maloney, E, Fordham
17. Harry Haugold, T, Rensselaer Poly (N.Y.)
18. Bobby Collier, T, SMU
19. John Smith, E, Arizona
20. Bill Young, B, Hillsdale (Mich.)
21. Bill Klein, E, Hanover (Ind.)
22. Doug Barber, B, Dakota Wesleyan
23. Jim Bird, T, USC
24. Joe Joiner, E, Austin College (Tex.)
25. Dan Towler, B, Washington & Jefferson
26. Otto Haldy, T, Mankato State
27. Hal Kilman, T, TCU
28. Junior Morgan, E, San Jose State
29. Bob Hack, E, College of Pacific
30. Bill Lange, G, Dayton

1951 CHOICES

1. Bud McFadin, G, Texas
2. Herb Rich, B, Vanderbilt
3. Charley Toogood, T, Nebraska
4. George Kinek, B, Tulane
5. Tony Momsen, C, Michigan
6. Norb Hecker, E, Baldwin Wallace
7. Alan Egler, B, Colgat
8. Hugo Primiani, T, Boston Univ.
9. Nolan Lang, B, Oklahoma
10. Roland Kirkby, B, Washington
11. John Natyshak, B, Tampa Univ.
12. Don Hardey, B, College of Pacific
13. Joe Reid, C, LSU
14. Rob McCoy, B, Georgia Tech
15. Obie Posey, B, Southern Univ.
16. Bill Robertson, E, Memphis State
17. Hal Riley, E, Baylor
18. Dick Daugherty, G, Oregon
19. Andy Robustelli, E, Arnold (Conn.)
20. Jim Nutter, E, Wichita
21. Earl Stelle, B, Oregon
22. Billy Baggett, B, LSU
23. Dean Thomas, T, Michgan State
24. Harry Abeltin, G, Colgate
25. Jackie Calvurt, T, Clemson
26. Howie Ruetz, T, Loras College (Iowa)
27. Al Brosky, B, Illinois
28. Sterling Wingo, B, VPI
29. Earl Jackson, B, Texas Tech
30. Alvin Hanley, B, Kentucky State

1952 CHOICES

1. Bill Wade, B, Vanderilt (Bonus Choice)
1. Bob Carey, E, Michigan State
2. Bob Griffin, T, Arkansas
3. Dewey McConnell, E, Wyoming
4. Volney Quinlen, B, San Diego State
5. Gordon Polofsky, B, Tennessee
6. Jerrell Price, T, Texas Tech
7. Burt Delaven, T, College of Pacific
8. Tom McCormick, B, College of Pacific
9. Byron Townsend, B, Texas
10. Luke Welch, T, Baylor
11. Sam Baker, B, Oregon State
12. Jake Roberts, B, Tulsa
13. Red Phillips, C, Texas Tech
14. Joe Moss, T, Maryland
15. Bill Hegarty, T, Villanova
16. Bob Hooks, E, USC
17. John Griggs, C, Kentucky
18. Bob Dees, T, Southwest Missouri St.
19. Harry Geldien, B, Wyoming
20. Ed Weber, B, William & Mary
21. Art Preston, B, San Diego State
22. Joe Pahr, B, Illinois
23. Don Green, T, Miami (Ohio)
24. Rich Keinhofer, G, St. Ambrose (Iowa)
25. Len Teeuws, T, Michigan State
26. Frank Fuller, T, Kentucky
27. Hugh Meyer, C, Texas A&M
28. Granville Hart, B, Mississippi Southern
29. Gerry Perry, T, California

1953 CHOICES

1. Ed Barker, E, Washington State
2. Rudy Bukich, B, USC
3. Bob Fry, T, Kentucky
4. Willie Roberts, E, Tulsa
5. Tom Scott, E, Virginia
6. Howie Waugh, B, Tulsa
7. Bobby Reynolds, B, Nebraska
8. Bob Morgan, T, Maryland
9. Brad Myers, B, Bucknell
10. Mick Lakos, B, Vanderbilt
11. Jim Bailey, B, Miami (Ohio)
12. Chuck Doad, G, Notre Dame
13. Andy Matto, T, Cincinnati
14. Frank James, G, Houston
15. Tom Carroll, B, Oklahoma
16. Ben DeLoe, T, Mississippi State
17. Harland Svare, E, Washington State
18. Lew James, T, Wabash (Ind.)
19. Jack Ellena, T, UCLA
20. Bob Morford, B, College of Idaho
21. Dick Gordon, T, Toledo
22. George Porter, T, Southwest Texas St.
23. Larry Willoughby, B, Fresno State
24. Marlow Gudmundson, B, N. Dakota St.
25. Ed Clemens, C, Dayton
26. Louie Yourkowski, T, Washington
27. Lou Welsh, C, USC
28. Jim Murray, T, Montana
29. Ray Lewis, E, Boise J.C. (Idaho)
30. Fritz Phren, B, Col. of the Ozarks (Ark.)

Rams All-Time Draft

1954 CHOICES

1. Ed Beatty, C, Mississippi
2. Maurice Gillioz, T, Houston
3. Henry Hair, E, Georgia Tech
4. Norm Mygaard, B, San Diego State
5. Art Hauser, T, Xavier
6. Ken Panfil, T, Purdue
7. Charley Weeks, T, USC
8. George Black, E, Washington
9. Alex Bravo, B, California Poly
10. Joe Katchik, E. Notre Dame
11. Duane Wardlow, T, Washington
12. Jack Maultsby, T, North Carolina
13. Sam Hensley, E, Georgia Tech
14. Mitchell Johnson, B, Bishop Col. (Tex.)
15. Ed Elliot, B, Richmond
16. Roger Frey, T, Georgia
17. Ed Wilhelm, G, Houston
18. Stan Shariff, G. California Poly
19. Frank Givens, T, Georgia Tech
20. Bob Dougherty, B, Cincinnati
21. Jerry Cooper, T, West Virginia
22. Ray Pacer, T, Purdue
23. Don Marks, B, California
24. Ed Brookman, T, West Virginia
25. Dick Miller, B, Baldwin Wallace
26. Glen Holtzman, T, North Texas State
27. Entee Shine, E, Notre Dame
28. Dick Mann, B, Western Reserve
29. Dick Dietrick, E, Pittsburgh
30. Frank Metzke, T, Marquette

1955 CHOICES

1. Larry Morris, C, Georgia Tech
2. Cecil Taylor, B, Kansas City
3. Choice to New York Giants
4. Ed Fouch, T, USC
5. Ed Kelley, B, Texas
6. Tom Tharp, B, Alabama
7. Frank Clayton, B, USC
8. Billy Teas, B, Georgia Tech
9. John Witte, T, Oregon State
10. Claude Harland, E, Texas Tech
11. Joe Ray, T, UCLA
12. Jim Hanifan, E, California
13. Dave Parkinson, B, Texas
14. George Elliott, B, N.E. St. (Okla.)
15. Robert Hoerning, B, St. Norbert
16. Charles Coates, T, Tulane
17. Gene Mitcham, E, Arizona State
18. Clyde Sweeney, T, West Virginia
19. John Davis, E, Miles College
20. Jack Muldowney, T, Dayton & Mt. Union
21. Jerome Cvengros, T, Wisconsin
22. Ken Elmore, T, Texas Tech
23. George Medved, T, Florida
24. Bill Andrews, B, Trinity & Tyler Jr.
25. Ralph Cook, T, Wabash & Ball State
26. Lou Hallow, C, Wake Forest
27. Bruce Nevitt, C, Washington State
28. James Hoffman, B, Ohio State & Cincinnati
29. Bob Howe, B, Cincinnati
30. K.C. Jones, E, San Francisco

1956 CHOICES

1. Charles Horton, B, Vanderbilt
2. Hugh Pitts, C-B, Texas Christian
3. John Marshall, B, SMU
4. Jim Carmichael, E, California
5. Jess Whittenton, B, Texas Western
6. Eddie Vincent, B, Iowa
7. Jack Morris, B, Oregon
8. George Boyer, LB, Florida State
9. Maury Wolford, T, Louisville
10. Charles Sticka, B, Trinity Col. (Conn.)
11. Jim Decker, B, UCLA
12. Em Lindbeck, B, Illinois
13. Mike Norcia, B, Kent State
14. Tommy Runnels, B, North Texas State
15. Dick Shatte, B, Kentucky
16. Arnie Pelluer, E, Washington State
17. Jack Butler, T, Kentucky
18. John Klotz, T, Penn. Military Col.
19. Charles Dees, T, McNeese St.
20. John Coyne, T, Chester State (Pa.)
21. Milton Robichaux, E, Trinity (Tex.)
22. Dick Fouts, E, Missouri
23. Al Paulson, B, Washington State
24. Sam Williams, DE, Michigan State
25. Glen Tunning, G, Pittsburgh
26. Hardiman Cureton, T, UCLA
27. Roger Seisel, T, Miami (Ohio)
28. John Morrow, T, Michigan
29. Melvin Bates, B, Illinois
30. Dick Kackmeister, C, Central Michigan

1957 CHOICES

1. Jon Arnett, B, USC
2. John Pardee, B, Texas A&M
3. Billy Ray Smith, T, Arkansas
4. George Strugar, DT, Washington
4. Bobby Cox, B, Wash. & Minn.
5. Dean Derby, B, Washington
6. Roy Wilkens, E, Georgia
7. Ed Gray, T, Oklahoma
8. Roy Hord, T, Duke
9. John Mitchell, C, TCU
10. Warren Spragg, T, Hillsdale Col. (Mich.)
11. Don Smith, T, Miami (Ohio)
12. Donald Klochak, B, North Carolina
13. Bob Wolfenden, B, Virginia Poly
14. Joe Lazzarino, T, Maryland
15. Ed Hinman, B, Wichita
16. John Luck, T, Georgia
17. David Tripett, T, Hillsdale Col. (Mich.)
18. Clarence Cook, E, Nebraska
19. Bill Zuhowski, T, Georgia & Ariz. St.
20. Byron Beams, T, Notre Dame
21. Pat Pinkston, E, UCLA
22. Paige Cothern, B, Mississippi
23. Dalva Allen, B, Houston
24. Darryl Rogers, B, Fresno State
25. Jimmy Orr, B, Clemson & Georgia
26. Dick Blakley, B, Minnesota
27. Clancy Osborne, E, Arizona State
28. Bob Gudath, E, Compton Jr. Col. (Cal.)
29. Dean Maas, C, Minnesota
30. Lee Williams, B, Ohio State

1958 CHOICES

1. Jim Phillips, E, Auburn
2. Clendon Thomas, B, Oklahoma
3. Jim Jones, B, Washington
4. John Guzik, G, Pittsburgh
5. John Baker, T, North Carolina College
6. Floyd Iglehart, B, Wiley Col. (Tex.)
7. Bill Jobko, G, Ohio State
8. Bobby Marks, B, Texas A&M
9. Gene Salawaski, T, Purdue
10. Al Jacks, QB, Penn State
11. Gerry Schweitzer, E, Pacific Col.
12. Ronald Claiborne, T, Kansas
13. Anthony Kolodziej, E, Michigan St.
14. Bill Mason, B, UCLA
15. Richard Johnston, C, Mississippi South
16. Clint Westemeyer, E, St. Ambrose
17. William Thomas, C, Clemson
18. Coy Scott, T, McNeese State
19. Dick Dorsey, E, USC
20. George Colbert, B, Denver
21. Ron Parrish, QB, Linfield College (Oreg.)
22. Bill Steiger, E, Washington State
23. Gary Barry, B, East Texas State
24. Larry Harding, E, Michigan State
25. Bill Atkins, T, San Jose State
26. Lonald Bridges, B, Cent. Washington
27. Alonzo Vereen, B, Florida A&M
28. Gordy Morrow, E, Michigan
29. O'Jay Bourgeois, B, Arizona State
30. Walter Fondren, B, Texas

1959 CHOICES

1. Dick Bass, RB, Pacific
1. Paul Dickson, T, Baylor
2. Don Brown, B, Houston
3. Larry Hickman, B, Baylor
4. Blanche Martin, B, Michigan State
5. John Lands, E, Montana State
6. David Painter, C, Tulane
7. Eddie Meador, B, Arkansas Tech
8. Bill Conner, E, Jackson State
9. Larry Cundiff, T, Michigan State
10. Alan Goldstein, E, North Carolina
11. Joe Kelly, B, New Mexico A&M
12. Mike Connelly, C, Utah State
13. Al Witcher, E, Baylor
14. Peter Davidson, T, The Citadel
15. Walt Kelly, B, Houston
16. Ted Royal, C, DUke
17. David Wilemon, T, SMU
18. Dave Van Metre, E, Colorado College
19. Carver Shannon, B, Southern Illinois
20. Ross Coyle, E, Oklahoma
21. Marv Bergmann, T, Washington
22. Bill Meglen, G, Utah State
23. George Deiderich, G, Vanderbilt
24. Tom Campbell, B, Indiana
25. Bob Borah, E, Houston
26. Bill Strumke, B, Georgia
27. Alex Kroll, C, Yale
28. Rafer Johnson, B, UCLA
29. Ernie Moore, E, Alabama State
30. Donald Millich, B, Washington

1960 CHOICES

1. Billy Cannon, B, LSU
2. Choice to Cardinals
3. Charles Britt, QB, Georgia
4. Choice to Cardinals
5. Charles Janerette, T, Penn State
6. Jerry Stalcup, G, Wisconsin
7. Ron Morrison, T, New Mexico
8. Carroll Dale, E, VPI
9. Marvin Luster, E, UCLA
10. Curtis McClinton, HB, Kansas
11. Ken Young, HB, Valparaiso
12. Doug Brown, G, Fresno State
13. James Jones, E, SMU
14. Harold Stanger, C, North Texas State
15. Harry Rakowski, C, Citadel
16. Donald Kaczmarek, T, North Dakota
17. Emanuel Congedo, E, Villanova (Col.)
18. Tom Gates, B, San Bernardino Valley College
19. James Boeke, T, Heidelburg
20. Royce Shelton, HB, Stephen Austin

1961 CHOICES

1. Marlin McKeever, LB, USC
2. Elbert Kimbrough, E, Northwestern
3. Harold Beaty, G, Oklahoma State
4. Traded to New York
5. Willie Hector, G, College of the Pacific
6. Bruce Olderman, T, Allegheny Col.
7. Robert Lee Smith, B, UCLA
8. Reginald Carolan, E, Idaho
9. Duane Allen, E, Mt. San Antonio
10. Joseph Scibelli, T, Notre Dame
11. Bob A. Lane, E, Baylor
12. Walter Mince, B, University of Arizona
13. Mike McKeever, G, USC
14. David Jones, T, South Carolina State
15. Ernie Wright, T, Ohio State
16. Mike Zeno, G, VPI
17. Charles Allen, G, Washington
18. Bill Williamson, T, Bakersfield J.C.
19. Lou Zivkovich, T, New Mexico State
20. Al Lederle, E, Georgia Tech
21. Charles Cowan, T, N.M. Highlands
22. Larry Wood, B, Northwestern
23. Ron Miller, QB, Wisconsin

1962 CHOICES

1. Roman Gabriel, QB, N.C. State
2. Merlin Olsen, T, Utah State
2. Joe Carollo, T, Notre Dame
3. John Meyers, T, Washington
3. John Cornett, T, Rice
4. Art Perkins, FB, N. Texas State
5. Choice traded to New York
5. Jim Smith, T, Penn State
5. Ben Wilson, FB, USC
6. Choice traded to New York
7. Sherwyn Thorson, G, Iowa
7. Jim Bakken, QB, Wisconsin
8. Richard Farris, G, N. Texas State

Rams All-Time Draft

9. Isaac Lassiter, T, St. Augustine's
10. James Norris, T, Houston
11. Bert Wilder, T, N.C. STate
12. Marv Marinovich, T, USC
13. Robert Fernside, HB, Bowling Green
14. Gary Henson, E, Colorado
15. Walter Nikirk, T, Houston
16. Ron Skufea, T, Purdue
17. David Steadman, T, Georgia Tech
18. Charles Furlow, QB, Miss. State
19. Gerard Barto, T, Drake
20. Foster Anderson, T, UCLA

1963 CHOICES

1. Terry Baker, RB, Oregon State
1. Rufus Guthrie, G, Georgia Tech
2. Tom Nomina, T, Miami (Ohio)
3. Dave Costa, G, Utah
3. John Baker, LB, Mississippi State
4. John Griffin, DB, Memphis State
5. Joe Auer, B, Georgia Tech
5. Roland Benson, T, Miami (Fla.)
5. Don Chuy, T, Clemson
6. George Saimes, RB, Michigan State
6. Terry Monaghan, T, Penn State
7. William Zorn, T, Michigan State
8. Anton Peters, T, Florida
9. Mel Profit, WR, UCLA
10. Curtis Farrier, T, Montana State
11. Dave Theisen, B, Stanford
12. Bill Joe Moody, B, Arkansas
13. Al Hildebrand, T, Stanford
14. Alan Arbuse, T, Rhode Island
15. Larry Campbell, WR, Toledo
16. Walter Burden, LB, McNeese State
17. Jarrell Wilson, LB-K, Miss. South.
18. Buddy Soefker, B, LSU
19. Dornel Nelson, B, Arizona State
20. Bill Redell, DB, Occidental

1964 CHOICES

1. Bill Munson, QB, Utah State
2. Choice traded to Chicago
3. Jerry Richardson, DB, West Texas State
3. John Mims, T, Rice
3. Willie Brown, RB, USC
3. Roger Pillath, T, Wisconsin
4. Choice traded to New York
5. Ken Henson, C, TCU
6. Herman Johnson, HB, Michigan State
7. John Varnell, T, West Texas State
8. Frank Pope, WR, Catawba
9. Jerry Burton, B, N.W. Louisiana State
10. Gary Larsen, T, Concordia (Minn.)
10. Ron Smith, QB, Richmond
11. John Farris, T, San Diego State
12. William Dawson, WR, Florida State
13. Marvin Harris, C, Stanford
14. John Garrett, LB, Oklahoma
15. Mike Mayne, WR, Idaho
16. Phil Zera, RB, St. Joseph's
17. James Galmin, WR, Tampa
18. Thomas Smith, G, Villanova

19. Bob Cherry, WR, Wittenberg
20. Bob Hohn, RB, Nebraska

1965 CHOICES

1. Clarence Williams, RB, Washington State
2. Choice traded to Cleveland
3. Fred Brown, LB, Miami (Fla.)
4. Michael Strofolino, LB, Villanova
5. Douglas Woodlief, LB, Memphis State
5. Frank Marchlewski, C, Minnesota
6. William Harrison, WR, Elon College
7. Anthony Guillory, G, Lamar Tech
8. Stan Dzura, T, California
9. Ron Caveness, LB, Arkansas
10. Jim Burt, HB, W. Kentucky
11. Merlin Walet, FB, McNeese State
12. Bob Werl, WR, Miami (Fla.)
13. Brent Berry, T, San Jose State
14. Bill Robertson, WR, Austin College
15. Marvin Davis, WR, Wichita
16. Charlie Brown, T, Tulsa
17. Ed Blecksmith, B, USC
18. Leo Lowery, FB, Texas Tech
19. Bill Anderson, QB, Tulsa
20. Billy Scott, WR, N.E. St. (Okla.)

1966 CHOICES

1. Tom Mack, T, Michigan
2. Mike Garrett, HB, USC
3. Richard Tyson, G, Tulsa
4. Henry Dyer, FB, Grambling
5. Diron Talbert, T, Texas
5. Richard Arndt, T, Idaho
6. Bruce Anderson, T, Williamette
7. George Youngblood, DB, Los Angeles St.
8. Vilnis Ezerins, HB, Whitewater (Wis.)
9. Burton Matthies, HB, Nebraska State
10. Mike Capshaw, T, Abilene Christian
11. Darrell Hoover, HB, Arizona
12. George Clayton, DB, Fairmont State
13. Jake David, HB, Lamar Tech
14. Terry Parks, T, Los Angeles State
15. Mike Sullivan, WR, Oregon State
16. Joe O'Brien, WR, Arlington State
17. Daniel Gilbert, T, Arkansas Tech
18. Ray Johnson, LB, Whitworth
19. Homer Williams, WR, USC
20. Bud Harrington, FB, Tulsa

1967 CHOICES

1. Choice to Minnesota
2. Willie Ellison, HB, Texas Southern
2. Choice to Green Bay
3. Choice to Philadelphia
4. Choice to Chicago
5. Nate Shaw, DB, USC
6. Choice to Atlanta
7. Choice to Philadelphia
8. Choice to Chicago
9. Tommie Smith, HB, San Jose State
10. Leon Moore, DB, Tennessee A&I
11. Frank Horak, DB, TCU
12. Pat Badjek, LB, Franklin (Ind.)

13. John Erisman, WR, Miami (Ohio)
14. Walt Richardson, DT, Fresno State
15. Steve Bunker, TE, Oregon
16. Allen Sack, LB, Notre Dame
17. Bill Barnes, C, Washington

1968 CHOICES

1. Choice to Detroit
2. Gary Beban, QB, UCLA
2. Mike LaHood, G, Wyoming
3. Choice to Pittsburgh
4. Choice to Chicago
5. Don Martin, K, Washington
6. Bobby Webb, C, Southern Mississippi
7. Choice to Pittsburgh
8. Joe Williams, FL, Florida A&M
9. Bob Richardson, T, Washington
10. Allen Marcelin, FL, Parsons
11. John Pergine, LB, Notre Dame
12. Harold Jackson, WR, Jackson State
13. Dean Halverson, LB, Washington
14. Cephus Jackson, DB, Jackson State
15. Dennis Yell, T, Moorhead (Minn.)
16. Jimmy Raye, QB-DB, Michigan State
17. Choice to Philadelphia

1969 CHOICES

1. Larry Smith, RB, Florida
1. Jim Seymour, WR, Notre Dame
1. Bob Klein, TE, USC
2. Choice to Detroit
3. Choice to St. Louis thru Detroit
4. John Zook, DE, Kansas
5. Choice to Dallas
6. Pat Curran, LB, Lakeland (Wis.)
7. James Hawkins, DB, Nebraska
8. Richard Harvey, DB, Jackson State
9. Mike Foote, LB, Oregon State
10. Jerry Gordon, T, Auburn
11. Dave Svendsen, FL, E. Wash. St.
12. Tim Carr, QB, C.W. Post
13. Roger Williams, DB, Grambling
14. Ray Stephens, RB, Minnesota
15. George Jugum, LB, Washington
16. Henry Hipps, LB, North Carolina State
17. Jim Thorpe, DB, Hofstra

1970 CHOICES

1. Jack Reynolds, LB, Tennessee
2. Charles Williams, WR, Prairie View A&M
2. Choice to San Francisco thru Philladelphia
3. Choice to Baltimore thru Philadelphia
4. Choice to Chicago
5. Choice to New Orleans
6. Choice to Atlanta
7. Ted Provost, DB, Ohio State
7. Bill Nelson, DT, Oregon State
7. Choice to Washington
8. Rich Saul, LB, Michigan State
9. David Graham, T, N.M. Highlands
10. Vince Opalsky, RB, Miami (Fla.)
11. David Bookert, RB, New Mexico

12. Larry Arnold, QB, Hawaii
13. Melvin Jones, WR, Florida A&M
14. Bob Geddes, LB, UCLA
15. Dag Azam, G, West Texas State
16. Roland Reichardt, K, West Texas State
17. Don Crenshaw, DB, USC

1971 CHOICES

1. Isiah Robertson, LB, Southern
1. Jack Youngblood, DE, Florida
2. Choice to Green Bay
3. Dave Elmendorf, DB, Texas A&M
3. Choice to Chicago
4. Steve Worster, RB, Texas
4. Choice to New Orleans
5. Choice to Green Bay thru Washington
6. Choice to Detroit thru Philadelphia
7. Choice to Chicago
8. Tony Garay, DE, Hofstra
9. Joe Schmidt, WR, Miami (Fla.)
10. Don Popplewell, C, Colorado
11. Charlie Richards, QB, Richmond
12. Kurt Behrendt, T, Whitewater (Wis.)
13. Russell Harrison, RB, Kansas State
14. Lionel Coleman, DB, Oregon
15. Gary Kos, G, Notre Dame
16. Ross Boice, LB, Pacific Lutheran
17. Randy Vataha, WR, Stanford
17. Joe Sweet, WR, Tennessee State

1972 CHOICES

1. Choice to N.Y. Giants thru New England
2. Jim Bertelsen, RB, Texas
2. Choice to Oakland
3. Choice to New York Giants
3. Lawrence McCutcheon, RB, Colorado St.
4. John Saunders, DB, Toledo
4. Eddie Phillips, DB, Texas
5. Bob Childs, G. Kasas
5. Choice to N.Y. Giants thru Washington
5. Bob Christiansen, TE, UCLA
6. Choice to Green Bay
6. Edward Herbert, DT, Texas Southern
7. Choice to Oakland
8. Tom Graham, WR, Baldwin Wallace
9. Harry Howard, DB, Ohio State
10. Jim Massey, DB, Linfield
11. Choice to Oakland
11. Albert Schmidt, RB, Pittsburgh (Kan.)
12. David Hoot, DB, Texas A&M
13. Jaime Nunez, K. Weber State
14. Larry Brooks, T, Virginia State
15. Kenny Page, LB, Kansas
16. Jim Kirby, WR, Long Beach State
17. Luther Palmer, TE, Virginia Union
17. John McKean, C, Oregon

Rams All-Time Draft

1973 CHOICES
1. Choice to New England
2. Cullen Bryant, DB, Colorado
2. Ron Jaworski, QB, Youngstown
2. Jim Youngblood, LB, Tennessee Tech
3. Tim Stokes, T, Oregon
3. Choice to St. Louis
4. Choice to Oakland
4. Eddie McMillian, DB, Florida State
4. Terry Nelson, TE, Arkansas AM&N
5. Steve Jones, RB, Duke
6. Cody Jones, DE, San Jose State
6. Jim Peterson, DE, San Diego State
6. Jason Caldwell, WR, N.C. Cent.
7. Steve Brown, LB, Oregon State
7. Bill Dulac, G, Eastern Michigan
8. Choice to Washington
9. Jim Nicholson, T, Michigan
10. Choice to Washington
11. Jeff Inmon, RB, North Carolina Cent.
11. Willie Jackson, WR, Florida
12. Robert Storck, DT, Wisconsin
13. Rod Milburn, WR, Southern
13. Clinton Spearman, LB, Michigan
14. Walter Rhone, DB, Central Missouri
15. Jerry Bond, DB, Weber State
15. Kurt Matter, DE, Washington
16. Fuller Cherry, DB, Arkansas-Monticello
17. Fred Henry, RB, New Mexico

1974 CHOICES
1. John Cappelletti, RB, Penn State
1. Choice to Baltimore
2. Bill Simpson, DB, Michigan State
3. Al Oliver, T, UCLA
4. Norris Weese, DB, Mississippi
4. Frank Johnson, T, Cal-Riverside
5. Choice to Atlanta thru Minnesota and Philadelphia
6. Choice to Houston
7. John Harvey, RB, Texas Arlington
7. Choice to Washington
8. Choice to San Diego
9. Don Hutt, WR, Boise State
9. Derek Williams, DB, Cal-Riverside
9. Choice to Washington
10. Choice to Baltimore
11. Rick Hayes, T, Washington
12. Roger Freberg, G, UCLA
13. Pete Solverson, T, Drake
14. Ananias Carson, WR, Langston (Okla.)
15. Bob Thomas, K, Notre Dame
16. Dave Ottmar, P, Stanford
17. Willie Townsend, WR, Notre Dame

1975 CHOICES
1. Mike Fanning, DT, Notre Dame
1. Dennis Harrah, G, Miami (Fla.)
1. Doug France, T, Ohio State
2. Monte Jackson, DB, San Diego State
2. Leroy Jones, DE, Norfolk State
3. Choice to San Diego thru Chicago

3. Geoff Reece, C, Washington State
3. Dan Nugent, TE, Auburn
4. Rod Perry, DB, Colorado
5. Wayne Hammond, DT, Montana State
5. Rick Nuzum, C, Kentucky
6. Choice to Chicago thru San Diego
6. Darius McCarthy, WR, S. Carolina
7. Pat Haden, QB, USC
8. John Washington, DB, Tulane
9. Gordon Reigel, LB, Stanford
10. Choice to Chicago
11. Howard Strickland, RB, California
12. Chandler Williams, WR, Lincoln
13. A.J. Jacobs, DB, Louisville
14. Arthur Allen, WR, Clark
15. Alvin White, QB, Oregon State
16. Francis Reynolds, RB, Alcorn A&M
17. Skip Boyd, P, Washington

1976 CHOICES
1. Kevin McLain, LB, Colorado State
2. Pat Thomas, DB, Texas A&M
2. Ron McCartney, LB, Tennessee
3. Jackie Slater, G, Jackson State
4. Gerald Taylor, WR, Texas A&I
4. Choice to Houston thru Philadelphia and Green Bay
5. Carl Ekern, LB, San Jose State
5. Ken Bordelon, DE, LSU
5. Dwight Scales, WR, Grambling
6. Choice to Washington
7. Larry Buie, DB, Mississippi State
8. Choice to Washington
9. Jeb Church, DB, Stanford
10. Freeman Johns, WR, SMU
11. Brian Nemeth, TE, South Carolina
12. Jim Jodat, RB, Carthage
13. Steve Hamilton, QB, Emporia
14. Al Burleson, DB, Washington
15. Malcolm Campbell, WR, Cal-State L.A.
16. Rick Gage, WR, Arkansas Tech
17. Gary Shaw, DB, Brigham Young

1977 CHOICES
1. Bob Brudzinski, LB, Ohio State
2. Nolan Cromwell, DB, Kansas
2. Billy Waddy, RB-WR, Colorado
2. Choice to Seattle
3. Ed Fulton, G, Maryland
3. Wendell Tyler, RB, UCLA
4. Vince Ferragamo, QB, Nebraska
4. Eary Jones, DE, Memphis State
5. Donnie Hickman, G, USC
5. Jeff Williams, G, Rhode Island
6. Art Best, RB, Kent State
6. Choice to New Orleans
7. Choice to Washington
8. Rod Bockwoldt, DB, Weber State
9. Choice to Washington
10. Don Peterson, TE, Boston College
11. Carson Long, K, Pittsburgh
12. Barry Caudill, C, Southern Mississippi

1978 CHOICES
1. Elvis Peacock, RB, Oklahoma
1. Choice to Cleveland
2. Stan Johnson, DT, Tennessee State
2. Ronnie Smith, WR, San Diego State
3. Frank Corral, P-K, UCLA
3. Leon White, C, Colorado
4. Mark Manges, QB, Maryland
5. Choice to San Diego
6. Choice to Tampa Bay
7. Reggie Doss, DE, Hampton Institute
8. Choice to Washington
9. Andre Anderson, DE, New Mexico State
10. Charles Peal, T, Indiana
11. Ron Hostetler, LB, Penn State
12. Gus Coppens, T, UCLA

1979 CHOICES
1. George Andrews, LB, Nebraska
1. Kent Hill, T, Georgia Tech
2. Eddie Hill, RB, Memphis State
3. Jeff Moore, WR, Tennessee
3. Mike Wellman, C, Kansas
3. Choice to Tampa Bay thru Washington
4. Derwin Tucker, DB, Illinois
4. Jerry Wilkinson, DT, Oregon State
5. Choice forfeited
5. Victor Hicks, TE, Oklahoma
6. Choice to Cleveland
7. Jeff Delaney, DB, Pittsburgh
8. Choice to Kansas City
9. Jeff Rutledge, QB, Alabama
10. Larry Willis, WR, Alcorn State
10. Grady Ebensberger, DT, Houston
11. Jesse Deramus, DT, Tennessee St.
12. Drew Hill, WR, Georgia Tech

1980 CHOICES
1. Johnnie Johnson, DB, Texas
1. Choice to Cleveland
2. Irv Pankey, T, Penn State
2. Choice to Washington
3. Jewerl Thomas, RB, San Jose State
3. Leroy Irvin, DB, Kansas
3. Phillip Murphy, DT, North Carolina St.
4. Choice to Cleveland
5. Choice to Atlanta thru Washington
6. Mike Guman, RB, Penn State
6. Choice to Kansas City
7. Kirk Collins, DB, Baylor
7. Gerry Ellis, RB, Mississippi
8. Tom Pettigrew, T, Eastern Illinois
9. George Farmer, WR, Southern
10. Bob Gruber, T, Pittsburgh
11. Terry Greer, WR, Alabama State
12. Kevin Scanlon, QB, Arkansas

1981 CHOICES
1. Mel Owens, LB, Michigan
1. Choice to Washington

2. Choice to Minnesota thru Washington
2. Jim Collins, LB, Syracuse
3. Choice to Kansas City
3. Greg Meisner, DT, Pittsburgh
4. Robert Cobb, DE, Arizona
4. George Lilja, C, Michigan
4. Choice to Green Bay thru Washington
5. Choice to Washington
6. William Daniels, DT, Alabama State
7. Ron Battle, TE, North Texas State
7. Mike Clark, DE, Florida
8. Art Plunkett, T, Nevada-Las Vegas
9. Ron Seawall, LB, Portland State
10. Robert Alexander, RB, West Virginia
11. Marcellus Greene, DB, Arizona
12. Jairo Penaranda, RB, UCLA

1982 CHOICES
1. Choice to Baltimore
1. Barry Redden, RB, Richmond
2. Choice to Baltimore
3. Choice to Washington
3. Bill Bechtold, C, Oklahoma
4. Jeff Gaylord, LB, MIssouri
5. Wally Kersten, T, Minnesota
5. Doug Barnett, DE, Azusa Pacific
6. Kerry Locklin, TE, New Mexico State
7. Choice to Pittsburgh
7. Joe Shearin, G, Texas
8. A.J. Jones, RB, Texas
8. Mike Reilly, LB, Oklahoma
9. Bob Speight, T, Boston University
10. Miles McPherson, DB, New Haven Col.
11. Ricky Coffman, WR, UCLA
12. Raymond Coley, DT, Alabama A&M

1983 CHOICES
1. Eric Dickerson, RB, SMU
1. Choice to Seattle
2. Henry Ellard, WR, Fresno State
2. Mike Wilcher, LB, North Carolina
3. Choice to San Francisco
4. Chuck Nelson, K, Washington
4. Choice to Houston
4. Vince Newsome, DB, Washington
4. Doug Reed, DE, San Diego State
5. Choice to Detroit
5. Otis Grant, WR, Michigan State
6. Gary Kowalski, T, Boston College
7. Jeff Simmons, WR, USC
8. Troy West, DB, USC
9. Jack Belcher, C, Boston College
10. Choice to Minnesota
11. Danny Triplett, LB, Clemson
12. Clete Capser, QB, Washington State

1984 CHOICES
1. Choice to Kansas City
2. Choice to Cleveland
3. Choice to Detroit
4. Choice to Houston
5. Hal Stephens, DE, East Carolina

Rams All-Time Draft

6. Choice to Houston
7. George Radachowsky, CB, Boston College
8. Ed Brady, LB, Illinois
9. George Reynolds, P, Penn State
10. Norwood Vann, LB, East Carolina
10. Joe Dooley, C, Ohio State
11. Michael Harper, RB, USC
11. Dwayne Love, FB, Houston
12. Moe Bias, LB, Illinois
12. Roderick Fisher, CB, Oklahoma State

1985 CHOICES

1. Jerry Gray, DB, Texas
2. Chuck Scott, WR, Vanderbilt
3. Dale Hatcher, P, Clemson
4. Choice to Minnesota
5. Choice to Kansas City
5. Kevin Greene, LB, Auburn
6. Michael Young, WR, UCLA
6. Damone Johnson, TE, Cal Poly SLO
7. Danny Bradley, RB, Oklahoma
8. Marlon McIntyre, FB, Pittsburgh

9. Gary Swanson, LB, Cal Poly SLO
10. Duval Love, G, UCLA
11. Doug Flutie, QB, Boston College
11. Kevin Brown, S, Northwestern
12. Choice to Tampa Bay

1986 CHOICES

1. Mike Schad, T, Queen's (Canada)
2. Tom Newberry, G, Wisconsin-LaCrosse

3. Hugh Millen, QB, Washington
6. Robert Cox, T, UCLA
6. Lynn Williams, RB, Kansas
8. Steve Jarecki, LB, UCLA
8. Hank Goebel, T, Cal State Fullerton
9. Elbert Watts, CB, USC
10. Garrett Breeland, LB, USC
11. Chul Schwanke, RB, South Dakota
12. Marcus Dupree, RB, Oklahoma

All-Time Ram Coaches Roster

NOTE: Coaches listed below (name, college, years with Rams) are those who have been either head or assistant coaches of the Rams since the club moved to Los Angeles in 1946.

Allen, George, Michigan, 1957,1966-70
Alsman, Ed, Washington, 1974-75
Andersen, Foster, UCLA, 1978
Austin, Bill, Oregon State, 1965
Baker, Bob, Ball State, 1983-84
Battles, Bill, Brown, 1953-54
Bennett, Leeman, Kentucky, 1973-76
Brooks, Larry, Virginia State, 1983-85
Brooks, Rich, Oregon State, 1971-72
Campbell, Marion, Georgia, 1967-68
Carson, Bud, North Carolina, 1978-81
Catlin, Tom, Oklahoma, 1966-77
Coley, Max, San Jose State,1978
Crow, Lindon, USC, 1963
David, Jm, Colorado State, 1960-62
Dixon, Hewritt, Florida A&M, 1980-81
Doll, Don, USC, 1965
Dowler, Boyd, Colorado, 1970
Durden, Earnel, Oregon State, 1971-72
Erber, Lew, Montclair State, 1985
Evans, Clyde, Carbillo JC, 1978-82
Faulkner, Jack, Miami (O.), 1955-59, 1973-79
Fears, Tom, UCLA, 1960-61
Gillman, Sid, Ohio State, 1955-59
Goux, Marv, USC, 1983-85
Hadl, John, Kansas, 1982
Hall, Sid, COP, 1971-72
Haskell, Gil, San Francisco State, 1983-85
Hein, Mel, Washington State, 1950
Heinrich, Don, Washington, 1963-64
Hickey, Howard "Red", Arkansas, 1950-54
Hickman, Bill, Duke, 1978-80
Houck, Hudson, USC, 1983-85
Knox, Chuck, Juniata, 1973-77
Lanham, Paul, Glenville State, 1978-82
Lauterbur, Frank, Mt. Union, 1978-81
Levy, Marv, Coe, 1970
Lindskog, Vic, Stanford, 1960-62
Madro, Joe, Ohio State, 1955-59
Malavasi, Ray, Mississippi State, 1973-82

Marchibroda, Ted, Detroit, 1966-70
McKittrick, Bobb, Oregon State, 1971-72
McLaughlin, Leon, UCLA, 1971-72
Meyer, Ken, Denison, 1973-76
Patera, Jack, Oregon, 1963-66
Paterra, Herb, Michigan State, 1980-82
Paul, Don, UCLA, 1959-61
Pitts, Elijah, Philander Smith, 1974-77
Pool, Hampton, Stanford, 1950-54, 1960-62
Prochaska, Ray, Nebraska, 1966-70, 1973-77
Prothro, Tommy, Duke, 1971-72
Radakovich, Dan, Penn State, 1979-81
Rapp, Vic, Missouri, 1984
Raye, Jimmy, Michigan State, 1983-84
Richards, Ray, Nebraska, 1951-52
Ringo, Jim, Syracuse, 1982
Robinson, John, Oregon, 1983-85
Rymkus, Lou, Notre Dame, 1958
Sauer, John, Army, 1953-54
Schnelker, Bob, Bowling Green, 1963-65
Schnellenberger, Howard, Kentucky, 1966-69
Schwenk, Vic, Occidental, 1964-65
Shafer, Steve, Utah State, 1983-85
Shaughnessy, Clark, Minnesota, 1948-49
Shurmur, Fritz, Albion, 1982-85
Snow, Jack, Notre Dame, 1982
Snyder, Bob, Ohio U, 1946-49
Snyder, Bruce, Oregon, 1983-85
Stephenson, Kay, Florida, 1977
Storm, Lowell, Cincinnati, 1955-57
Stydahar, Joe, West Virginia, 1947-52
Sullivan, Joe, No College, 1966-70
Summerall, Pat, Arkansas, 1963-
Svare, Harland, Washington, State, 1962-65
Swiacki, Bill, Columbia, 1958
Taylor, Lionel, NM Highlands, 1977-81
Thomas, Joe, Oho Northern, 1955-56
Torgeson, LaVern, Washington State, 1969-70, 1978-80
Trafton, George, Notre Dame, 1946-49
Turner, Norval, Oregon, 1985
Vechiarella, Jim, Youngstown, 1981-82
Vermeil, Dick, San Jose State, 1969, 1971-73

Voris, Dick, San Jose State, 1954
Wagstaff, Jim, Idaho State, 1973-77
Waller, Charlie, Georiga, 1978
Walsh, Adam, Notre Dame, 1946
Waterfield, Bob, UCLA, 1958, 1960-62

Weaver, Larrye, Adams State, 1971-72
Weaver, Ralph, Newberry, 1954
Whittingham, Fred, Cal Poly, SLO, 1982-84
Wietecha, Ray, Northwestern, 1963-64

Rams All-Time Leaders

CAREER RUSHING

	Years	No.	Yds.	Avg.	LG	TD
1. Lawrence McCutcheon	1973-79	1,435	6,186	4.3	48	23
2. Dick Bass	1960-69	1,218	5,417	4.5	73t	34
3. Eric Dickerson	1983-85	1,061	5,147	4.9	85t	44
4. Dan Towler	1950-55	672	3,493	5.2	79t	44
5. Les Josephson 1964-67,	1969-74	797	3,407	4.3	75	17
6. Paul Younger	1949-57	682	3,296	4.8	75t	31
7. Wendell Tyler	1977-82	720	3,266	4.5	69t	33
8. Cullen Bryant	1973-81	801	3,117	3.9	26	20
9. Willie Ellison	1967-72	656	2,901	4.4	80t	20
10. Jon Arnett	1957-63	688	2,852	4.2	80t	19
11. Jim Bertelsen	1972-76	614	2,466	4.0	49	16
12. John Cappelletti	1974-78	632	2,246	3.6	38	15
13. Tom Wilson	1956-61	389	2,130	5.1	60	8
14. Dick Hoerner	1947-51	450	2,020	4.6	64	28
15. Larry Smith	1969-73	473	1,908	4.1	68	11
16. Joe Marconi	1956-61	398	1,769	4.4	75t	21
17. Ron Waller	1955-58	285	1,564	5.4	76	8
18. Skeet Quinlan	1952-56	246	1,489	5.6	74	10
19. Ollie Matson	1959-62	249	1,214	4.0	69t	9
20. Mike Guman	1980-85	303	1,185	3.9	18	10
21. Fred Gehrke	1946-49	244	1,150	4.6	53	8
22. Roman Gabriel	1962-72	315	1,146	3.6	23	28
23. Ben Wilson	1963-65	328	1,136	3.5	39	7
24. Barry Redden	1982-85	215	1,023	4.8	41	2
25. Elvis Peacock	1979-80	216	1,001	4.5	36	7

SEASON RUSHING

	Year	No.	Yds.	Avg.	LG	TD
1. Eric Dickerson	1984	379	2,105	5.6	66	14
2. Eric Dickerson	1983	390	1,808	4.6	85t	18
3. Lawrence McCutcheon	1977	294	1,238	4.2	48	7
4. Eric Dickerson	1985	292	1,234	4.2	43	12
5. Lawrence McCutcheon	1976	291	1,168	4.0	40	9
6. Lawrence McCutcheon	1974	236	1,109	4.7	23	3
7. Wendell Tyler	1979	218	1,109	5.1	63t	9
8. Lawrence McCutcheon	1973	210	1,097	5.2	37	2
9. Dick Bass	1966	248	1,090	4.4	50	8
10. Wendell Tyler	1981	260	1,074	4.1	69t	12
11. Dick Bass	1962	196	1,033	5.3	57	6
12. Willie Ellison	1971	211	1,000	4.7	80t	4
13. Lawrence McCutcheon	1975	213	911	4.3	42	2
14. Dan Towler	1952	156	894	5.7	55	5
15. Jim Bertelsen	1973	206	854	4.1	49	4

CAREER PASSING

	Years	Att.	Comp.	Yds.	Pct.	TD	Int.
1. Roman Gabriel	1962-72	3,313	1,705	22,223	.515	154	122
2. Norm Van Brocklin	1949-57	1,897	1,011	16,114	.534	118	127
3. Bob Waterfield	1945-52	1,618	814	11,893	.503	99	128
4. Vince Ferragamo	1977-84	1,268	730	9,376	.575	70	71
5. Pat Haden	1976-81	1,363	731	9,296	.536	52	60
6. Bill Wade	1954-60	1,116	602	8,572	.540	56	68
7. James Harris	1973-76	652	361	5,220	.554	33	27
8. Parker Hall	1939-42	721	329	4,013	.456	30	67
9. Zeke Bratkowski	1961-63	531	279	3,559	.525	20	35
10. Bill Munson	1964-67	550	287	3,556	.521	21	33
11. John Hadl	1973-74	373	188	2,688	.504	27	17
12. Frank Ryan	1958-61	373	181	2,674	.458	15	23
13. Jeff Kemp	1981-85	353	173	2,395	.490	14	10
14. Jim Hardy	1946-48	332	159	2,063	.479	21	21
15. Ron Jaworski	1974-76	124	54	719	.435	1	8
16. Dan Pastorini	1981	152	64	719	.421	2	14
17. Joe Namath	1977	107	50	606	.467	3	5

SEASON PASSING
(Based on Completions)

	Year	Att.	Comp.	Yds.	Pct.	TD	Int.
1. Vince Ferragamo	1983	464	274	3,276	59.1	22	23
2. Vince Ferragamo	1980	404	240	3,199	59.4	30	19
3. Pat Haden	1978	444	229	2,995	51.6	13	19
4. Dieter Brock	1985	365	218	2,658	59.7	16	13
5. Roman Gabriel	1966	397	217	2,540	54.7	10	16
6. Roman Gabriel	1969	399	217	2,549	54.4	24	7
7. Roman Gabriel	1970	407	211	2,552	52.0	16	12
8. Roman Gabriel	1967	371	196	2,779	52.8	25	13
9. Roman Gabriel	1968	366	184	2,364	50.3	19	16
10. Bill Wade	1958	341	181	2,875	53.1	18	22

CAREER PUNT RETURNS
(Minimum 50)

	Years	No.	Yds.	Avg.	LG	TD
1. Henry Ellard	1983-85	83	1,121	13.5*	83t	4
2. Jackie Wallace	1977-79	52	618	11.9	58	0
3. Jim Bertelsen	1972-76	59	821	11.1	60	0
4. Verda Smith	1949-53	75	972	10.9	85	1
5. LeRoy Irvin	1980-85	144	1,449	10.1	84t	4
6. Cullen Bryant	1973-82	71	707	10.0	40	0
7. Jon Arnett	1957-63	75	728	9.7	71t	1
8. Alvin Haymond	1969-71	110	934	9.4	36	0
9. Dave Elmendorf	1971-79	57	502	8.8	41	0
10. Eddie Brown	1978-79	57	345	6.1	28	0

SEASON PUNT RETURNS
(Minimum One Per Game)

	Year	No.	Yds.	Avg.	LG	TD
1. Woodley Lewis	1952	19	351	18.5	82	2
2. Verda Smith	1949	27	427	15.8	85	1
3. Les Horvath	1948	13	203	15.6	27	0
4. Jim Bertelsen	1972	16	232	14.5	60	0
5. Tom Harmon	1947	27	392	14.5	88	1
6. Henry Ellard	1983	16	217	13.6	72t	1
7. Henry Ellard	1985	37	501	13.5	80t	1
8. Henry Ellard	1984	30	403	13.4	83t	2
9. LeRoy Irvin	1981	46	615	13.4	84t	3
10. Alvin Haymond	1969	33	435	13.2	52	0

CAREER KICKOFF RETURNS
(Minimum 50)

	Years	No.	Yds.	Avg.	LG	TD
1. Tom Wilson	1956-61	51	1,383	27.1	103t	1
2. Cullen Bryant	1973-81	66	1,760	26.7	93	3
3. Alvin Haymond	1969-71	60	1,604	26.7	98	2
4. Dick Bass	1960-69	54	1,415	26.2	64	0
5. Verda Smith	1949-53	57	1,453	25.5	55	0
6. Ron Smith	1968-69	53	1,303	24.6	94t	1
7. Woodley Lewis	1950-55	109	2,602	23.9	88t	1
8. Jon Arnett	1957-63	107	2,554	23.9	105t	2
9. Pervis Atkins	1961-63	51	1,182	23.2	40	0
10. Barry Redden	1982-85	64	1,390	21.7	85	0

SEASON KICKOFF RETURNS
(Minimum One Per Game)

	Year	No.	Yds.	Avg.	LG	RD
1. Verda Smith	1950	22	742	33.7	97	3
2. Ron Brown	1985	28	918	32.8	98t	3
3. Tom Wilson	1957	11	475	26.4	98t	1
4. Dick Bass	1961	23	698	30.3	64	0
5. Travis Williams	1971	25	743	29.7	105t	1
6. Carver Shannon	1963	28	823	29.4	99t	1

Rams All-Time Leaders

	Year	No.	Yds.	Avg.	LG	TD
7. Alvin Haymond	1970	35	1,022	29.2	98	1
8. Cullen Bryant	1976	16	459	28.7	90	1
9. Clarence Williams	1966	15	420	28.0	81	0
10. Jon Arnett	1957	18	504	28.0	98t	1
11. Ron Smith	1968	26	718	27.6	94t	1
12. Fred Gehrke	1948	17	464	27.3	92	1
13. Ron Walter	1955	16	430	27.0	39	0
14. Bob Smith	1965	17	457	26.9	56	0
15. Cullen Bryant	1974	23	617	26.8	84	1
16. Woodley Lewis	1954	34	836	24.6	88t	1

CAREER RECEIVING

	Years	No.	Yds.	Avg.	LG	TD
1. Tom Fears	1948-56	400	5,397	13.4	80t	38
2. Elroy Hirsch	1949-57	343	6,289	18.3	91t	53
3. Jack Snow	1965-75	340	6,012	17.7	84t	45
4. Jim Phillips	1958-64	316	4,708	14.9	93t	27
5. Jim Benton 1938-40, 1942,	1944-47	275	4,566	16.6	84t	42
6. Dick Bass	1960-69	214	1,846	8.6	53	7
7. Harold Jackson 1968,	1973-77	200	3,591	17.9	69t	36
8. Les Josephson 1964-67,	1969-74	194	1,570	10.2	58	11
9. Preston Dennard	1978-83	189	3,066	16.2	64	21
10. Lawrence McCutcheon	1972-79	184	1,683	9.2	50	12
11. Billy Truax	1964-70	180	2,177	12.1	59t	18
12. Bob Boyd	1950-57	176	3,611	20.5	80t	28
13. Carroll Dale	1960-64	149	1,663	17.9	80t	17
14. Ron Jessie	1975-79	144	2,386	16.8	58	15
15. Cullen Bryant	1973-82	142	1,149	8.1	39	3
16. Bob Klein	1969-76	128	1,606	12.5	44	15
17. Larry Smith	1969-73	126	1,039	8.3	38	4
18. Tom McDonald	1965-66	122	1,750	14.3	62	11
19. Wendell Tyler	1977-82	120	1,146	9.6	71t	10
20. Mike Guman	1980-85	119	1,102	9.3	60	4

SEASON RECEIVING

	Year	No.	Yds.	Avg.	LG	TD
1. Tom Fears	1950	84	1,116	13.3	53	7
2. Jim Phillips	1961	78	1,092	14.0	69t	5
3. Tom Fears	1949	77	1,013	13.2	51	9
4. Tom McDonald	1965	67	1,036	15.5	51	9
5. Elroy Hirsch	1951	66	1,495	22.7	91	17
6. Elroy Hirsch	1953	61	941	15.4	70	4
7. Jim Phillips	1962	60	875	14.6	65t	5
8. Tom Moore	1966	60	433	7.2	30t	3
9. Tom McDonald	1966	55	714	12.9	62	2
10. Mike Barber	1983	55	657	11.9	42t	3

CAREER SCORING

	Years	TD	PAT	FG	Pts.
1. Bob Waterfield	1945-52	13	315	60	573
2. Bruce Gossett	1964-69	0	211	120	571
3. David Ray	1969-74	0	167	110	497
4. Frank Corral	1978-81	0	154	75	379
5. Elroy Hirsch	1949-57	55	9	0	339
6. Eric Dickerson	1983-85	46	0	0	276
7. Jim Benson 1938-40, 1942,	1944-47	45	0	0	270
8. Jack Snow	1965-75	45	0	0	270
9. Dan Towler	1950-55	44	0	0	264
10. Wendell Tyler	1977-82	43	0	0	258
11. Dick Bass	1960-69	42	0	0	252
12. Tom Fears	1948-56	39	12	1	249
13. Danny Villanueva	1960-64	0	111	44	243
14. Harold Jackson 1968,	1973-77	36	0	0	216
15. Lawrence McCutcheon	1973-79	35	0	0	210
16. Les Richter	1954-62	0	106	29	193
17. Dick Hoerner	1947-51	32	0	0	192
18. Tom Dempsey	1975-76	0	67	38	181

19. Roman Gabriel	1962-72	28	0	0	168
20. Jim Phillips	1958-64	27	0	0	162

SEASON SCORING

	Year	TD	PAT	FG	Pts.
1. David Ray	1973	0	40	30	130
2. David Ray	1970	0	34	29	121
3. Eric Dickerson	1983	20	0	0	120
4. Frank Corral	1978	0	31	29	118
5. Bruce Gossett	1966	0	29	28	113
6. Mike Lansford	1984	0	37	25	112
7. Bruce Gossett	1967	0	48	20	108
8. David Ray	1972	0	31	24	103
9. Mike Lansford	1985	0	38	22	104
10. Bruce Gossett	1969	0	36	22	102
11. Elroy Hirsch	1951	17	0	0	102
12. Wendell Tyler	1981	17	0	0	102

CAREER INTERCEPTIONS

	Years	No.	Yds.	Avg.	LG	TD
1. Ed Meador	1959-70	46	547	11.9	38t	5
2. Nolan Cromwell	1977-85	30	542	18.1	94	3
3. Rod Perry	1975-82	28	386	13.8	83t	4
4. Will Sherman	1954-60	28	515	18.4	95t	3
5. Clarence Williams	1965-72	28	428	15.3	65t	2
6. Dave Elmendorf	1971-79	27	421	15.6	57t	2
7. Pat Thomas	1976-82	26	292	11.2	64	1
8. Woodley Lewis	1950-55	23	416	18.1	45t	1
9. Bill Simpson	1974-78	22	391	17.8	42	0
10. LeRoy Irvin	1980-85	20	389	19.5	81t	3

SEASON INTERCEPTIONS

	Year	No.	Yds.	Avg.	LG	TD
1. Dick (Night Train) Lane	1952	14*	298	21.3	38	0
2. Woodley Lewis	1950	12	136	11.3	27	0
3. Will Sherman	1955	11	101	9.2	36	0
4. Monte Jackson	1976	10	173	17.3	46	3
5. Don Burroughs	1955	9	103	11.4	34	0
6. Clancy Williams	1966	8	97	12.1	32t	1
6. Ed Meador	1967	8	103	12.9	30t	2
6. Rod Perry	1976	8	79	9.9	43	0
6. Rod Perry	1978	8	117	14.6	44t	3
6. Pat Thomas	1978	8	96	12.0	33t	1
6. Nolan Cromwell	1980	8	140	17.5	34	1

Charles Toogood

Rams Individual Records

* NFL Record
** Playoff Record
† Ties NFL Record

RUSHING

MOST ATTEMPTS (Career)
1,435	Lawrence McCutcheon: 1973-1979	
1,218	Dick Bass: 1960-1969	
1,061	Eric Dickerson: 1983-1985	
797	Les Josephson: 1964-1967,1969-1974	

MOST ATTEMPTS (Season)
390	Eric Dickerson: 1983
379	Eric Dickerson: 1984
294	Lawrence McCutcheon: 1977
292	Eric Dickerson: 1985
291	Lawrence McCutcheon: 1976
260	Wendell Tyler: 1981

MOST ATTEMPTS (Game)
36	Charles White: 1985 vs. Philadelphia (Gained 144 yards)
34	Eric Dickerson: 1983 vs. Chicago Bears (Gained 127 yards)
33	Eric Dickerson: 1984 vs. New Orleans (Gained 149 yards)
32	Eric Dickerson: 1983 vs. Buffalo (Gained 125 yards)
31	Ollie Matson: 1959 at Chicago Bears (Gained 199 yards)
31	Lawrence McCutcheon: 1976 at S.F. (Gained 97 yards)
30	Three times (Most recent: Cullen Bryant: 1978 vs. Green Bay, 121 yards)

MOST YARDS GAINED (Career)
6,186	Lawrence McCutcheon: 1973-1979
5,417	Dick Bass: 1960-1969
5,147	Eric Dickerson: 1983-1985
3,493	Dan Towler: 1950-1955

MOST YARDS GAINED (Season)
*2,105	Eric Dickerson: 1984 (379 atts., 5.6 avg.)
1,808	Eric Dickerson: 1983 (390 atts., 4.6 avg.)
1,238	Lawrence McCutcheon: 1977 (294 atts., 4.2 avg.)
1,234	Eric Dickerson: 1985 (292 atts., 4.2 avg.)
1,168	Lawrence McCutcheon: 1976 (291 atts., 4.0 avg.)
1,109	Lawrence McCutcheon: 1974 (236 atts., 4.7 avg.)
1,109	Wendell Tyler: 1979 (218 atts., 5.1 avg.)
1,097	Lawrence McCutcheon: 1973 (210 atts., 5.2 avg.)
1,090	Dick Bass: 1966 (24 atts., 4.4 avg.)

MOST YARDS GAINED (Game)
**248	Eric Dickerson: 1985 vs. Dallas (34 atts., 7.3 avg.)
247	Willie Ellison: 1971 vs. New Orleans (26 atts., 9.5 avg.)
223	Tom Wilson: 1956 vs. Green Bay (23 atts., 9.7 avg.)
215	Eric Dickerson: 1984 vs. Houston (27 atts., 8.0 avg.)
208	Eric Dickerson: 1984 at St. Louis (21 atts., 9.9 avg.)
205	Dan Towler: 1953 at Baltimore (14 atts., 14.6 avg.)

LONGEST RUN FROM SCRIMMAGE
92	Kenny Washington: 1946 at Chicago Cardinals
85	Eric Dickerson: 1983 at New York Jets
84	Tom Harmon: 1946 at Chicago Bears
82	Tom Wilson: 1958 at Detroit

PASSING

MOST PASSES ATTEMPTED (Career)
3,313	Roman Gabriel: 1962-1972
1,897	Norm Van Brocklin: 1949-1957
1,618	Bob Waterfield: 1945-1952

MOST PASSES ATTEMPTED (Season)
464	Vince Ferragamo: 1983
444	Pat Haden: 1978
407	Roman Gabriel: 1970
404	Vince Ferragamo: 1980

MOST PASSES ATTEMPTED (Game)
53	Jim Hardy: 1948 vs. Chicago Cardinals
51	Dieter Brock: 1985 vs. San Francisco
48	Roman Gabriel: 1970 vs. New York Jets
46	Vince Ferragamo: 1982 vs. Chi. Bears

MOST PASSES COMPLETED (Career)
1,705	Roman Gabriel: 1962-1972
1,011	Norm Van Brocklin: 1949-1957
814	Bob Waterfield: 1945-1952

MOST PASSES COMPLETED (Season)
274	Vince Ferragamo: 1983 (464 atts., .591 pct.)
240	Vince Ferragamo: 1980 (404 atts., .594 pct.)
229	Pat Haden: 1978 (444 atts., .516 pct.)
218	Dieter Brock: 1985 (365 atts., .597 pct.)
217	Roman Gabriel: 1966 (397 atts., .547 pct.)
217	Roman Gabriel: 1969 (399 atts., .544 pct.)

MOST PASSES COMPLETED (Game)
35	Dieter Brock: 1985 vs. San Francisco (51 atts.)
30	Vince Ferragamo: 1982 vs. Chi. Bears (46 atts.)
28	Jim Hardy: 1948 vs. Chicago Cardinals (53 atts.)
27	Norm Van Brocklin: 1951 vs. N.Y. Yanks (41 atts.)
27	Roman Gabriel: 1970 vs. Detroit (42 atts.)

MOST CONSECUTIVE PASSES COMPLETED
13	Pat Haden: 1979 at Seattle
11	Norm Van Brocklin: 1950 at Detroit (10), Baltimore (1)
11	Zeke Bratkowski: 1963 at Cleveland (7), Green Bay (4)
11	Roman Gabriel: 1971 at Detroit
11	Vince Ferragamo: 1980 vs. S.F.

MOST YARDS GAINED (Career)
22,223	Roman Gabriel: 1962-1972
16,114	Norm Van Brocklin: 1949-1957
11,893	Bob Waterfield: 1945-1952

MOST YARDS GAINED (Season)
3,276	Vince Ferragamo: 1983 (464 atts., 274 comp.)
3,199	Vince Ferragamo: 1980 (404 atts., 240 comp.)
2,995	Pat Haden: 1978 (444 atts., 229 comp.)
2,875	Bill Wade: 1958 (341 atts., 181 comp.)

MOST YARDS GAINED (Game)
*554	Norm Van Brocklin: 1951 vs. N.Y. Yanks (41 atts., 27 comp.)
509	Vince Ferragamo: 1982 vs. Chi. Bears (46 atts., 30 comp.)
436	James Harris: 1976 at Miami (29 atts., 17 comp.)

MOST TOUCHDOWN PASSES (Career)
154	Roman Gabriel: 1962-1972
118	Norm Van Brocklin: 1949-1957
99	Bob Waterfield: 1945-1952

MOST TOUCHDOWN PASSES (Season)
30	Vince Ferragamo: 1980
25	Roman Gabriel: 1967
24	Roman Gabriel: 1969

MOST TOUCHDOWN PASSES (Game)
5	Bob Waterfield: 1949 vs. N.Y. Bulldogs
5	Norm Van Brocklin: 1950 vs. Detroit
5	Norm Van Brocklin: 1951 vs. N.Y. Yanks
5	Roman Gabriel: 1965 vs. Cleveland
5	Vince Ferragamo: 1980 vs. New Orleans
5	Vince Ferragamo: 1983 vs. San Francisco

BEST PASSING EFFICIENCY (Career—500 att.)
57.0%	Vince Ferragamo: 1977-80; 1982-1984 (1,280 atts., 730 comp.)
55.4%	James Harris: 1973-1976 (652 atts., 361 comp.)
54.0%	Bill Wade: 1954-1960 (1,116 atts., 602 comp.)

BEST PASSING EFFICIENCY (Season—100 att.)
59.7%	Dieter Brock: 1985 (365 atts., 218 comp.)
59.4%	Vince Ferragamo: 1980 (404 atts., 24 comp.)
59.1%	Vince Ferragamo: 1983 (464 atts., 274 comp.)
58.6%	Bill Wade: 1959 (261 atts., 153 comp.)
58.2%	Bill Wade: 1960 (182 atts., 106 comp.)

BEST PASSING EFFICIENCY (Game—20 or more)
81.8%	Roman Gabriel: 1967 vs. Baltimore (22 atts., 18 comp.)
81.0%	Pat Haden: 1979 at Seattle (21 atts., 17 comp.)
77.3%	Norm Van Brocklin: 1956 vs. Green Bay (22 atts., 17 comp.)
77.3%	Bill Wade: 1958 vs. Cleveland (22 atts., 17 comp.)
77.3%	Roman Gabriel: 1971 at Detroit (22 atts., 17 comp.)

LONGEST PASSING GAIN
96	Frank Ryan to Ollie Matson: 1961 vs. Pittsburgh
95	Bill Munson to Bucky Pope: 1964 vs. Green Bay
93	Bill Wade to Jim Phillips: 1958 at Green Bay
93	Roman Gabriel to Wendell Tucker: 1969 vs. San Francisco

MOST PASSES HAD INTERCEPTED (Career)
128	Bob Waterfield: 1945-1952
127	Norm Van Brocklin: 1949-1957
112	Roman Gabriel: 1962-1972

MOST PASSES HAD INTERCEPTED (Season)
24	Bob Waterfield: 1949
23	Vince Ferragamo: 1983
22	Bill Wade: 1958
21	Norm Van Brocklin: 1955,1957

MOST PASSES HAD INTERCEPTED (Game)
7	Bob Waterfield: 1948 at Green Bay
6	Four Players (Most recent: Bill Wade: 1958 vs. Detroit)

MOST CONSECUTIVE PASSES ATTEMPTED, NONE INTERCEPTED
206	Roman Gabriel: 1968-1969
119	Jeff Kemp: 1984
114	Jim Hardy: 1948
106	Pat Haden: 1977

Rams Individual Records

FEWEST PASSES HAD INTERCEPTED (Season—100 att.)
2	Roman Gabriel: 1962 (101 atts.)
4	Pat Haden: 1976 (105 atts.)
5	Roman Gabriel: 1965 (173 atts.)

LOWEST PERCENTAGE, PASSES HAD INTERCEPTED (Career—500 att.)
3.4	Roman Gabriel: 1962-1972

LOWEST PERCENTAGE, PASSES HAD INTERCEPTED (Season—100 att.)
1.8	Roman Gabriel: 1969 (7-399)
1.9	Roman Gabriel: 1962 (2-101)

PASS RECEIVING

MOST PASS RECEPTIONS (Career)
400	Tom Fears: 194-1956
343	Elroy Hirsch: 1949-1957
340	Jack Snow: 1965-1975

MOST PASS RECEPTIONS (Season)
84	Tom Fears: 1950
78	Jim Phillips: 1961
77	Tom Fears: 1949

MOST PASS RECEPTIONS (Game)
*18	Tom Fears: 1950 vs. Green Bay
13	Jim Phillips: 1961 vs. Green Bay
12	Jim Benton: 1946 at New York Giants

MOST YARDS GAINED (Career)
6,289	Elroy Hirsch: 1949-1957
6,012	Jack Snow: 1965-1975
5,397	Tom Fears: 1948-1956

MOST YARDS GAINED (Season)
1,495	Elroy Hirsch: 1951
1,212	Bob Boyd: 1954
1,116	Tom Fears: 1950
1,097	Del Shofner: 1958
1,092	Jim Phillips: 1961
1,067	Jim Benton: 1945
1,036	Tommy McDonald: 1965
1,013	Tom Fears: 1949

MOST YARDS GAINED (Game)
*303	Jim Benton: 1945 at Detroit
238	Harold Jackson: 1973 vs. Dallas
220	Ron Jessie: 1976 at Miami

MOST TOUCHDOWNS (Career)
53	Elroy Hirsch: 1949-1957
45	Jack Snow: 1965-1975
42	Jim Benton: 1938-40, 1942, 1944-1947

MOST TOUCHDOWNS (Season)
17	Elroy Hirsch: 1951
13	Harold Jackson: 1973
10	Bucky Pope: 1964

MOST TOUCHDOWNS (Game)
4	Bob Shaw: 1949 vs. Washington
4	Elroy Hirsch: 1951 vs. New York Yanks
4	Harold Jackson: 1973 vs. Dallas

MOST CONSECUTIVE GAMES, PASS RECEPTIONS
68	Jim Phillips: 1958-1963
51	Tom Fears: 1947-1951
32	Henry Ellard: 1983-1985
31	Jon Arnett: 1958-1960

MOST CONSECUTIVE GAMES, TOUCHDOWNS
†11	Elroy Hirsch: 1950-51
5	Jack Snow: 1967-68
5	Harold Jackson: 1973

PUNTING

MOST PUNTS (Career)
356	Norm Van Brocklin: 1949-1957
315	Bob Waterfield: 1945-1952
298	Pat Studstill: 1968-1971

MOST PUNTS (Season)
93	Ken Clark: 1979 (40.1 avg.)
89	Frank Corral: 1981 (42.0 avg.)
87	Danny Villanueva: 1962 (45.5 avg.)
87	Dale Hatcher: 1985 (43.2 avg.)

MOST PUNTS (Game)
12	Parker Hill: 1939 vs. Green Bay (39.3 avg.)
12	Rusty Jackson: 1976 at San Francisco (36.1 avg.)
11	Danny Villanueva: 1962 vs. Dallas (50.0 avg.)
11	Danny Villanueva: 1965 at Pittsburgh (40.5 avg.)

HIGHEST AVERAGE DISTANCE (Season)
45.5	Danny Villanueva: 1962 (87 punts)
45.4	Danny Villanueva: 1963 (81 punts)
44.6	Bob Waterfield: 1946 (39 punts)
44.6	Norm Van Brocklin: 1955 (60 punts)

HIGHEST AVERAGE DISTANCE (Game—4 punts or more)
52.5	Parker Hall: 1939 vs. Green Bay (6 punts, 315 yards)
52.5	Danny Villanueva: 1962 vs. S.F. (6 punts, 315 yards)
51.6	Bob Waterfield: 1946 at Chicago Bears (4 punts, 206 yards)
51.6	Jon Kilgore: 1967 vs. San Francisco (5 punts, 258 yards)

LONGEST PUNT
88	Bob Waterfield: 1948 at Green Bay
86	Bob Waterfield: 1947 at Green Bay
72	Norm Van Brocklin: 1956 vs. Chi. Bears

POINTS

MOST POINTS (Career)
573	Bob Waterfield: 1945-1952
571	Bruce Gossett: 1964-1969
497	David Ray: 1970-1974

MOST POINTS (Season)
130	David Ray: 1973 (30 FG, 40 PAT)
121	David Ray: 1970 (29 FG, 34 PAT)
120	Eric Dickerson: 1983 (20 Touchdowns)
118	Frank Corral: 1978 (29 FG, 31 PAT)

MOST POINTS (Game)
24	Bob Shaw: 1949 vs. Washington
24	Elroy Hirsch: 1951 vs. New York Yanks
24	Harold Jackson: 1973 vs. Dallas

TOUCHDOWNS

MOST TOUCHDOWNS (Career)
55	Elroy Hirsch: 1949-1957
46	Eric Dickerson: 1983-1985
45	Jim Benton: 1938-1940, 1942, 1944-1947
45	Jack Snow: 1965-1975

MOST TOUCHDOWNS (Season)
20	Eric Dickerson: 1983
17	Elroy Hirsch: 1951
17	Wendell Tyler: 1981
14	Eric Dickerson: 1984
13	Harold Jackson: 1973
13	Wendell Tyler: 1982
12	Eric Dickerson: 1985
11	Dick Hoerner: 1950
11	Dan Towler: 1954
11	Lawrence McCutcheon: 1976

MOST TOUCHDOWNS (Game)
4	Bob Shaw: 1949 vs. Washington
4	Elroy Hirsch: 1951 vs. New York Yanks
4	Harold Jackson: 1973 vs. Dallas

FIELD GOALS

MOST FIELD GOALS (Career)
120	Bruce Gossett: 1964-1969
110	David Ray: 1969-1974
75	Frank Corral: 1978-1981

MOST FIELD GOALS (Season)
30	David Ray: 1973
29	David Ray: 1970
29	Frank Corral: 1978

MOST FIELD GOALS (Game)
5	Bob Waterfield: 1951 vs. Detroit
3	Fourteen times (Most recent: Mike Lansford: 1985 vs. N.Y. Giants)

LONGEST FIELD GOAL
52	Mike Lansford: 1985 vs. Atlanta
52	Mike Lansford: 1985 vs. L.A. Raiders
51	Lou Michaels: 1960 at Baltimore
51	Danny Villanueva: 1962 vs. Dallas
51	Tom Dempsey: 1975 at San Francisco

MOST CONSECUTIVE FIELD GOALS
13	Mike Lansford: 1984
11	Tom Dempsey: 1976
9	Frank Corral: 1978 (6), 1979 (3)
8	Frank Corral: 1979 (2), 1980 (6)

POINTS AFTER TOUCHDOWN

MOST POINTS AFTER TOUCHDOWN (Career)
315	Bob Waterfield: 1945-1952
211	Bruce Gossett: 1964-1969
167	David Ray: 1969-1974

MOST POINTS AFTER TOUCHDOWN (Season)
54	Bob Waterfield: 1950
51	Frank Corral: 1980
48	Bruce Gossett: 1967

MOST POINTS AFTER TOUCHDOWN (Game)
†9	Bob Waterfield: 1950 vs. Baltimore
8	Paige Cothren: 1958 vs. San Francisco
7	Bob Waterfield: 1948 at N.Y. Giants
7	Bruce Gossett: 1966 vs. N.Y. Giants

MOST CONSECUTIVE POINTS AFTER TOUCHDOWN
165	Bruce Gossett: 1965-1969
102	David Ray: 1970-1972
87	Frank Corral: 1980-1981

SAFETIES

MOST SAFETIES (Career)
2	Fred Dryer: 1972-1981
2	Jack Youngblood: 1971-1984

MOST SAFETIES (Season)
†2	Fred Dryer: 1973

MOST SAFETIES (Game)
*2	Fred Dryer: 1973 vs. Green Bay

INTERCEPTIONS

MOST INTERCEPTIONS BY (Career)
46	Ed Meador: 1959-1970
30	Nolan Cromwell: 1977-1985
28	Will Sherman: 1954-1960
28	Clarence Williams: 1965-1970
28	Rod Perry: 1975-1982

Rams Individual Records

MOST INTECEPTIONS BY (Season)
*14   Dick (Night Train) Lane: 1952
12   Woodley Lewis: 1950
11   Will Sherman: 1955

MOST INTERCEPTIONS BY (Game)
3   Fifteen times (Most recent: Pat Thomas: 1979 at New Orleans)

MOST YARDS GAINED (Career)
547   Ed Meador: 1959-1970
542   Nolan Cromwell: 1977-1985
515   Will Sherman: 1954-1960
428   Clarence Williams: 1965-1972

MOST YARDS GAINED (Season)
298   Dick Lane: 1952
275   Woodley Lewis: 1950
201   Ilerb Rich: 1952

MOST YARDS GAINED (Game)
107   Aaron Martin: 1964 vs. San Francisco
99   Johnnie Johnson: 1980 vs. Green Bay
97   Herb Rich: 1952 vs. Dallas Texans
97   Bobby Smith: 1964 vs. San Francisco

MOST CONSECUTIVE GAMES, PASSES INTERCEPTED BY
6   Will Sherman: 1954-55
5   Dick (Night Train) Lane: 1952
4   Nolan Cromwell: 1980
4   Kirk Collins: 1983

LONGEST INTERCEPTED PASS RETURN
99   Johnnie Johnson: 1980 vs. Green Bay
97   Herb Rich: 1952 vs. Dallas Texans
97   Bobby Smith: 1964 vs. San Francisco
95   Will Sherman: 1956 vs. Green Bay

PUNT RETURNS

MOST PUNT RETURNS (Career)
144   LeRoy Irvin: 1980-1985
110   Alvin Haymond: 1969-1971
106   Woodley Lewis: 1950-1955

MOST PUNT RETURNS (Season)
56   Eddie Brown: 1979
53   Alvin Haymond: 1970
52   Jackie Wallace: 1978

MOST PUNT RETURNS (Game)
7   Alvin Haymond: 1970 vs. Atlanta
7   Cullen Bryant: 1976 at New Orleans
7   Eddie Brown: 1979 at Tampa Bay
7   Eddie Brown: 1979 vs. St. Louis
7   LeRoy Irvin: 1981 at San Francisco

MOST YARDS GAINED (Career)
1,449   LeRoy Irvin: 1980-85
1,121   Henry Ellard: 1983-1985
934   Alvin Haymond: 1969-1971
821   Jim Bertelsen: 1972-1976

MOST YARDS GAINED (Season)
618   Jackie Wallace: 1978
615   LeRoy Irvin: 1981
501   Henry Ellard: 19851
435   Alvin Haymond: 1969

MOST YARDS GAINED (Game)
*207   LeRoy Irvin: 1981 at Atlanta
127   LeRoy Irvin: 1981 at San Francisco
120   Woodley Lewis: 1953 at Detroit

MOST TOUCHDOWNS (Career)
4   LeRoy Irvin: 1980-1985
4   Henry Ellard: 1983-1985
3   Woodley Lewis: 1950-1955
2   Tom Kalmanir: 1949-1951
2   V.T. Smith: 1949-53

MOST TOUCHDOWNS (Season)
3   LeRoy Irvin: 1981
2   Woodley Lewis: 1952
2   Henry Ellard: 1984

MOST TOUCHDOWNS (Season)
†2   LeRoy Irvin: 1981 at Atlanta

HIGHEST AVERAGE PUNT RETURN (Career—75 ret.)
*13.5   Henry Ellard (83): 1983-1985
10.9   V.T. Smith (75): 1949-1953
10.4   LeRoy Irvin (144): 1980-1985
9.1   Jon Arnett (75): 1957-1963

HIGHEST AVERAGE PUNT RETURN (Season—one per game average)
18.5   Woodley Lewis: 1952
15.8   V.T. Smith: 1949
15.6   Les Horvath: 1948

LONGEST PUNT RETURN
90   Dick Bass: 1961 vs. Green Bay
88   Tom Harmon: 1947 vs. Detroit
85   V.T. Smith: 1949 at Green Bay
83   Henry Ellard: 1984 vs. N.Y. Giants

KICKOFF RETURNS

MOST KICKOFF RETURNS (Career)
171   Drew Hill: 1979-1984
109   Woodley Lewis: 1950-1955
104   Jon Arnett: 1957-1963

MOST KICKOFF RETURNS (Season)
*60   Drew Hill: .1981
43   Drew Hill: 1980
40   Drew Hill: 1979

MOST KICKOFF RETURNS (Game)
6   Woodley Lewis: 1953 at Green Bay
6   Carver Shannon: 1963 vs. Chicago
6   Carver Shannon: 1964 at Detroit
6   Jim Jodat: 1978 at Cleveland
6   Drew Hill: 1979 at Dallas
6   Drew Hill: 1980 vs. Miami
6   Drew Hill: 1981 at New Orleans
6   Drew Hill: 1981 at Dallas

MOST YARDS GAINED (Career)
3,438   Drew Hill: 1979-1984
2,603   Woodley Lewis: 1950-1955
2,590   Jon Arnett: 1957-1963

MOST YARDS GAINED (Season)
1,170   Drew Hill: 1981
1,022   Alvin Haymond: 1970
918   Ron Brown: 1985
880   Drew Hill: 1980

MOST YARDS GAINED (Game)
202   Carver Shannon: 1963 vs. Chicago
182   Alvin Haymond: 1970 vs. St. Louis
174   Woodley Lewis: 1953 at Detroit

MOST TOUCHDOWNS (Career)
3   Ron Brown: 1984-1985
3   V.T. Smith: 1949-1953
3   Cullen Bryant: 1973-1981
2   Jon Arnett: 1957-1963

MOST TOUCHDOWNS (Season)
3   V.T. Smith: 1950
3   Ron Brown: 1985

MOST TOUCHDOWNS (Game)
*2   Ron Brown: 1985 vs. Green Bay

HIGHEST AVERAGE KICKOFF RETURN (Season—one per game average)
33.7   V.T. Smith: 1950
32.8   Ron Brown: 1985
31.8   Tom Wilson: 1957
30.3   Dick Bass: 1961

LONGEST KICKOFF RETURN
105   Jon Arnett: 1961 vs. Detroit
105   Travis Williams: 1971 vs. New Orleans
103   Tom Wilson: 1956 at Baltimore

COMBINED YARDAGE

(Includes Rushes, Pass Receptions and Runbacks of Pass Interceptions, Punts, Kickoffs and Fumbles)

MOST COMBINED YARDAGE (Career)
9,213   Dick Bass: 1960-69
8,076   Jon Arnett: 1957-1963
7,869   Lawrence McCutcheon: 1973-1979

FIELD GOAL RETURNS

LONGEST FIELD GOAL RETURN
99   Jerry Williams: 1951 vs. Green Bay

LENGTH OF SERVICE

MOST SEASONS
15   Charlie Cowan: 1961-1975
15   Joe Scibelli: 1961-1975
15   Merlin Olsen: 1962-1976
14   Jack Youngblood: 1971-1984
13   Lamar Lundy: 1957-1969
13   Jack Pardee: 1957-1964, 1966-1970
13   Tom Mack: 1966-1978
12   Ed Meador: 1959-1970
12   Rich Saul: 1970-1981

MOST GAMES PLAYED
208   Merlin Olsen: 1962-1976
206   Charlie Cowan: 1961-1975
202   Jack Youngblood: 1971-1984
202   Joe Scibelli: 1961-1975
184   Tom Mack: 1966-1978
176   Rich Saul: 1970-1981
169   Jack Pardee: 1957-1964, 1966-1970
162   Ed Meador: 1959-1970
152   Lamar Lundy: 1957-1969
150   Jack Snow: 1965-1975

MOST CONSECUTIVE GAMES PLAYED
201   Jack Youngblood: 1971-1984
198   Merlin Olsen: 1962-1976
184   Tom Mack: 1966-1978
176   Rich Saul: 1970-1981
159   Ed Meador: 1959-1970
143   David Jones: 1961-1971
142   Jack Snow: 1965-1975
140   Ken Iman: 1965-1974

Glenn Holtzman

Daniel F. Reeves Memorial Award

In memory of the late Rams president, this award is given annually to the club's Most Valuable Player.

1969	Roman Gabriel	**1978**	Jim Youngblood
1970	Merlin Olsen	**1979**	Jack Youngblood
1971	Marlin McKeever	**1980**	Vince Ferragamo
1972	Merlin Olsen	**1981**	Nolan Cromwell
1973	John Hadl	**1982**	Vince Ferragamo
1974	Lawrence McCutcheon	**1983**	Eric Dickerson
1975	Jack Youngblood	**1984**	Eric Dickerson
1976	Jack Youngblood	**1985**	LeRoy Irvin
1977	Lawrence McCutcheon		

Carroll Rosenbloom Memorial Award

In memory of the late Rams president, this award is given annually to the club's Rookie of the Year.

1979	Kent Hill
1980	Johnnie Johnson
1981	Jairo Penaranda
1982	Barry Redden
1983	Eric Dickerson
1984	Ron Brown
1985	Dale Hatcher

Year-By-Year Rams Scores

Cleveland Rams (1937-42, 1944-45),
Los Angeles Rams (1946-85)

Below, Rams' scores are listed first, followed by opponent's scores and opponent name (H-home or A-away).

1937
(1-10-0, Fifth Place) Coach: Hugh Bezdek
0–28	Detroit (H)
21–3	Philadelphia (A)
7–9	Brooklyn (A)
0–6	Chicago Cardinals (H)
2–20	Chicago Bears (H)
10–35	Green Bay (H)
7–13	Green Bay (A)
7–27	Detroit (A)
7–16	Washington (H)
7–15	Chicago Bears (A)
75–207	

1938
(4-7-0, Fourth Place) Coach: Hugo Bezdek
(3 games); Coach: Art Lewis (8 games)
17–26	Green Bay (A)
6–7	Chicago Cardinals (H)
13–37	Washington (A)
21–17	Detroit (H)
14–7	Chicago Bears (H)
23–21	Chicago Bears (A)
7–28	Green Bay (H)
0–6	Detroit (A)
0–28	New York (A)
17–31	Chicago Cardinals (A)
13–7	Pittsburgh (New Orleans)
131–215	

1939
(5-5-1, Fourth Place) Coach: Earl "Dutch" Clark
21–30	Chicago Bears (A)
12–23	Brooklyn (A)
27–24	Green Bay (A)
21–35	Chicago Bears (H)
7–15	Detroit (A)
24–0	Chicago Cardinals (A)
14–14	Pittsburgh (H)

(1939 continued)
14–0	Chicago Cardinals (H)
14–3	Detroit (H)
6–7	Green Bay (H)
35–13	Philadelphia (Colo. Sprgs.)
195–164	

1940
(4-6-1, Fourth Place) Coach: Earl "Dutch" Clark
21–13	Philadelphia (H)
0–6	Detroit (A)
14–21	Chicago Bears (H)
14–31	Green Bay (A)
26–14	Chicago Cardinals (H)
7–17	Chicago Cardinals (A)
14–0	Detroit (H)
13–0	New York (A)
14–29	Brooklyn (A)
25–47	Chicago Bears (A)
13–13	Green Bay (H)
171–191	

1941
(2-9-0, Fifth Place) Coach: Earl "Dutch" Clark
17–14	Pittsburgh (Akron)
10–6	Chicago Cardinals (A)
7–24	Green Bay (A)
21–48	Chicago Bears (A)
7–17	Detroit (A)
14–17	Green Bay (H)
13–17	Washington (A)
0–14	Detroit (H)
13–31	Chicago Bears (H)
14–49	New York (A)
0–7	Chicago Cardinals (A)
116–244	

1942
(5-6-0, Third Place) Coach: Earl "Dutch" Clark
0–7	Chicago Cardinals (Buf.)
24–14	Philadelphia (H)
14–0	Detroit (A)
7–21	Chicago Bears (H)
7–3	Chicago Cardinals (H)
17–0	Brooklyn (A)

(1942 continued)
12–30	Green Bay (H)
14–33	Washington (A)
28–45	Green Bay (A)
27–7	Detroit (H)
0–47	Chicago Bears (A)
150–207	

Rams suspended operations in 1943 due to World War II

1944
(4-6-0, Fourth Place) Coach: Aldo "Buff" Donelli
30–28	Card-Pitt (Pitt.)
19–7	Chicago Bears (H)
20–17	Detroit (A)
21–30	Green Bay (A)
21–28	Chicago Bears (A)
10–14	Washington (A)
7–42	Green Bay (H)
33–6	Card-Pitt (Chicago)
14–26	Detroit (H)
13–26	Philadelphia (A)
188–224	

1945
(9-1-0, First Place) Coach: Adam Walsh
21–0	Chicago Cardinals (H)
17–0	Chicago Bears (H)
27–14	Green Bay (A)
41–21	Chicago Bears (A)
14–28	Philadelphia (A)
21–17	New York (A)
20–7	Green Bay (H)
35–21	Chicago Cardinals (A)
28–21	Detroit (A)
20–7	Boston (H)
244–136	
15–14	*Washington (H)
	*NFL Championship
327–269	

1946
(6-4-1, Second Place) Coach: Adam Walsh
14–25	Philadelphia (H)
21–17	Green Bay (A)
28–28	Chicago Bears (H)
35–14	Detroit (H)
10–34	Chicago Cardinals (A)

(1946 continued)
41–20	Detroit (A)
21–27	Chicago Bears (H)
17–14	Chicago Cardinals (H)
21–40	Boston (A)
31–21	New York (A)
38–27	Green Bay (H)
277–257	

1947
(6-6-0, Fourth Place) Coach: Bob Snyder
48–7	Pittsburgh (A)
14–17	Green Bay (A)
27–13	Detroit (A)
27–7	Chicago Cardinals (H)
7–14	Philadelphia (A)
10–17	Chicago Cardinals (A)
16–27	Boston (H)
21–41	Chicago Bears (H)
28–17	Detroit (H)
10–30	Green Bay (H)
17–14	Chicago Bears (A)
34–10	New York (H)
259–214	

1948
(6-5-1, Third Place) Coach: Clark Shaughnessy
44–7	Detroit (H)
28–28	Philadelphia (H)
21–42	Chicago Bears (A)
0–16	Green Bay (A)
34–27	Detroit (A)
22–27	Chicago Cardinals (H)
6–21	Chicago Bears (H)
52–37	New York (A)
24–27	Chicago Cardinals (A)
24–10	Green Bay (H)
41–13	Washington (A)
31–14	Pittsburgh (H)
327–269	

1949
(8-2-2, First Place) Coach: Clark Shaughnessy
27–24	Detroit (H)
48–7	Green Bay (A)
31–16	Chicago Bears (A)

Year-By-Year Rams Scores

21–10 Detroit (A)
35–7 Green Bay (H)
27–24 Chicago Bears (H)
14–38 Philadelphia (A)
7–7 Pittsburgh (A)
28–28 Chicago Cardinals (A)
42–30 New York Bulldogs (H)
27–31 Chicago Cardinals (H)
53–27 Washington (H)
360–239
0–14 *Philadelphia (H)
  *NFL Championship

1950
(9-3-0, First Place) Coach: Joe Stydahar
20–24 Chicago Bears (H)
45–28 New York Yanks (H)
35–14 San Francisco (A)
20–56 Philadelphia (A)
30–28 Detroit (A)
70–27 Baltimore (H)
65–24 Detroit (H)
28–21 San Francisco (H)
45–14 Green Bay (A)
43–35 New York Yanks (A)
14–24 Chicago Bears (A)
51–14 Green Bay (H)
466–309
24–14 †Chicago Bears (H)
28–30 *Cleveland (A)
  †Conference Playoff
  *NFL Championship

1951
(8-4-0, First Place) Coach: Joe Stydahar
54–14 New York Yanks (H)
23–38 Cleveland (H)
27–21 Detroit (A)
28–0 Green Bay (A)
17–44 San Francisco (A)
23–16 San Francisco (H)
45–21 Chicago Cardinals (H)
48–21 New York Yanks (H)
21–31 Washington (A)
42–17 Chicago Bears (A)
22–24 Detroit (H)
42–14 Green Bay (H)
392–261
24–17 *Cleveland (H)
  *NFL Championship

1952
(9-3-0, Second Place) Coach: Joe Stydahar
(1 game) Coach: Hampton Pool (11
games)
7–37 Cleveland (A)
14–17 Detroit (H)
30–28 Green Bay (A)
16–24 Detroit (A)
31–7 Chicago Bears (H)
42–20 Dallas (H)
27–6 Dallas (A)
40–24 Chicago Bears (A)
35–9 San Francisco (A)
34–21 San Francisco (H)
45–27 Green Bay (H)

28–14 Pittsburgh (H)
349–234
21–31 †Detroit (A)
  †Conference Playoff

1953
(8-3-1, Third Place) Coach: Hampton Pool
21–7 New York (H)
30–31 San Francisco (A)
38–20 Green Bay (A)
31–19 Detroit (A)
38–24 Chicago Bears (H)
37–24 Detroit (H)
27–31 San Francisco (H)
24–24 Chicago Cardinals (A)
21–13 Baltimore (A)
21–24 Chicago Bears (A)
45–2 Baltimore (H)
33–17 Green Bay (H)
366–236

1954
(6-5-1, Fourth Place) Coach: Hampton Pool
48–0 Baltimore (A)
24–24 San Francisco (H)
3–21 Detroit (A)
17–35 Green Bay (A)
42–38 Chicago Bears (H)
24–27 Detroit (H)
42–34 San Francisco (A)
28–17 Chicago Cardinals (H)
17–16 New York (A)
13–24 Chicago Bears (A)
21–22 Baltimore (H)
35–27 Green Bay (H)
314–285

1955
(8-3-1, First Place) Coach: Sid Gillman
23–14 San Francisco (A)
27–26 Pittsburgh (H)
17–10 Detroit (A)
28–30 Green Bay (A)
24–13 Detroit (H)
20–31 Chicago Bears (H)
27–14 San Francisco (H)
3–24 Chicago Bears (A)
17–17 Baltimore (A)
23–21 Philadelphia (A)
20–14 Baltimore (H)
31–17 Green Bay (H)
260–231
14–38 *Cleveland (H)
  *NFL Championship

1956
(4-8-0, Fifth Place) Coach: Sid Gillman
27–7 Philadelphia (H)
30–33 San Francisco (A)
21–24 Detroit (A)
17–42 Green Bay (A)
7–16 Detroit (H)
24–35 Chicago Bears (H)
30–6 San Francisco (H)
21–30 Chicago Bears (A)
21–56 Baltimore (H)

13–30 Pittsburgh (A)
31–7 Baltimore (H)
49–21 Green Bay (H)
291–307

1957
(6-6-0, Fourth Place) Coach: Sid Gillman
17–13 Philadelphia (H)
20–23 San Francisco (A)
7–10 Detroit (A)
26–34 Chicago Bears (A)
35–17 Detroit (H)
10–16 Chicago Bears (H)
37–24 San Francisco (H)
31–27 Green Bay (A)
31–45 Cleveland (A)
14–31 Baltimore (A)
42–17 Green Bay (H)
37–21 Baltimore (H)
307–278

1958
(8-4-0, Second Place) Coach: Sid Gillman
27–30 Cleveland (H)
33–3 San Francisco (A)
42–28 Detroit (A)
10–31 Chicago Bears (A)
24–41 Detroit (H)
41–35 Chicago Bears (A)
56–7 San Francisco (H)
20–7 Green Bay (A)
7–34 Baltimore (A)
20–14 Chicago Cardinals (A)
30–28 Baltimore (H)
34–20 Green Bay (H)
344–278

1959
(2-10-0, Sixth Place) Coach: Sid Gillman
21–23 New York (H)
0–34 San Francisco (A)
28–21 Chicago Bears (A)
45–6 Green Bay (A)
7–17 Detroit (H)
21–26 Chicago Bears (H)
16–24 San Francisco (H)
17–23 Detroit (A)
20–23 Philadelphia (A)
21–35 Baltimore (A)
20–38 Green Bay (H)
26–45 Baltimore (H)
242–315

1960
(4-7-1, Sixth Place) Coach: Bob Waterfield
21–43 St. Louis (H)
9–13 San Francisco (A)
27–34 Chicago (A)
17–31 Baltimore (A)
24–24 Chicago (H)
48–35 Detroit (H)
38–13 Dallas (A)
10–12 Detroit (A)
33–31 Green Bay (A)
7–23 San Francisco (H)
10–3 Baltimore (H)

21–35 Green Bay (H)
265–297

1961
(4-10-0, Sixth Place) Coach: Bob
Waterfield
24–27 Baltimore (A)
17–21 Chicago (H)
24–14 Pittsburgh (H)
0–35 San Francisco (A)
13–14 Detroit (A)
14–24 New York (A)
10–28 Detroit (H)
31–17 Minnesota (H)
17–7 San Francisco (H)
17–35 Green Bay (A)
24–28 Chicago (A)
21–42 Minnesota (A)
34–17 Baltimore (H)
17–24 Green Bay (H)
263–333

1962
(1-12-1, Seventh Place) Coach: Bob
Waterfield (8 games)
Coach: Harland Svare (6 games)
27–30 Baltimore (A)
23–27 Chicago (H)
17–27 Dallas (H)
14–20 Washington (A)
10–13 Detroit (A)
14–38 Minnesota (H)
28–14 San Francisco (A)
3–12 Detroit (H)
2–14 Baltimore (H)
17–24 San Francisco (H)
24–24 Minnesota (A)
10–41 Green Bay (A)
14–30 Chicago (A)
17–20 Green Bay (H)
220–334

1963
(5-9-0, Sixth Place) Coach: Harland Svare
2–23 Detroit (H)
14–37 Washington (H)
6–20 Cleveland (A)
10–42 Green Bay (A)
14–52 Chicago (H)
27–24 Minnesota (H)
28–21 San Francisco (H)
13–21 Minnesota (A)
0–6 Chicago (A)
28–21 Detroit (A)
17–16 Baltimore (H)
21–17 San Francisco (A)
14–31 Green Bay (H)
16–19 Baltimore (A)
210–350

1964
(5-7-2, Fifth Place) Coach: Harland Svare
26–14 Pittsburgh (A)
17–17 Detroit (H)
22–13 Minnesota (H)
20–35 Baltimore (A)

RECORDS

Year-By-Year Rams Scores

17–38 Chicago (A)
42–14 San Francisco (H)
27–17 Green Bay (A)
17–37 Detroit (A)
20–10 Philadelphia (H)
24–34 Chicago (H)
7–24 Baltimore (H)
13–34 Minnesota (A)
7–28 San Francisco (A)
24–24 Green Bay (H)

283–339

1965
(4-10-0, Seventh Place) Coach: Harland Svare
0–20 Detroit (A)
30–28 Chicago (H)
35–38 Minnesota (H)
6–31 Chicago (A)
21–45 San Francisco (H)
20–35 Baltimore (A)
7–31 Detroit (H)
13–24 Minnesota (A)
3–6 Green Bay (A)
27–30 San Francisco (A)
21–10 Green Bay (H)
27–3 St. Louis (A)
42–7 Cleveland (A)
17–20 Baltimore (H)

269–328

1966
(8-6-0, Third Place) Coach: George Allen
19–14 Atlanta (A)
31–17 Chicago (H)
13–24 Green Bay (A)
34–3 San Francisco (H)
14–7 Detroit (A)
7–35 Minnesota (A)
10–17 Chicago (A)
3–17 Baltimore (H)
13–21 San Francisco (A)
55–14 New York (H)
21–6 Minnesota (H)
23–7 Baltimore (A)
23–3 Detroit (H)
23–27 Green Bay (H)

289–212

1967
(11-1-2, First Place) Coach: George Allen
27–13 New Orleans (A)
39–3 Minnesota (H)
35–13 Dallas (A)
24–27 San Francisco (H)
24–24 Baltimore (A)
28–28 Washington (H)
28–17 Chicago (A)
17–7 San Francisco (A)
33–17 Philadelphia (H)
31–3 Atlanta (A)
31–7 Detroit (A)
20–3 Atlanta (H)
27–24 Green Bay (H)
34–10 Baltimore (H)

398–196
7–28 *Green Bay (A)

30–6 †Cleveland (Miami)
*Western Conference Playoff
†Playoff Bowl Game

1968
(10-3-1, Second Place) Coach: George Allen
24–13 St. Louis (A)
45–10 Pittsburgh (H)
24–6 Cleveland (A)
24–10 San Francisco (H)
16–14 Green Bay (A)
27–14 Atlanta (H)
10–27 Baltimore (A)
10–7 Detroit (H)
17–10 Atlanta(A)
20–20 San Francisco (A)
24–21 New York (H)
31–3 Minnesota (A)
16–17 Chicago (H)
24–28 Baltimore (H)

312–200

1969
(11-3-0, First Place) Coach: George Allen
27–20 Baltimore (A)
17–7 Atlanta (H)
36–17 New Orleans (H)
27–21 San Francisco (A)
34–21 Green Bay (H)
9–7 Chicago (A)
38–6 Atlanta (A)
41–30 San Francisco (H)
23–17 Philadelphia (A)
24–23 Dallas (H)
24–13 Washington (A)
13–20 Minnesota (H)
0–28 Detroit (A)
7–13 Baltimore (H)

320–243
20–23 *Minnesota (A)
31–0 †Dallas (Miami)
*Western Conference Playoff
†Playoff Bowl Game

1970
(9-4-1, Second Place) Coach: George Allen
34–13 St. Louis (H)
19–0 Buffalo (A)
37–10 San Diego (H)
6–20 San Francisco (H)
31–21 Green Bay (A)
3–13 Minnesota (A)
30–17 New Orleans (A)
10–10 Atlanta (H)
20–31 New York Jets (A)
17–7 Atlanta (A)
30–13 San Francisco (A)
34–16 New Orleans (H)
23–28 Detroit (H)
31–3 New York Giants (A)

325–202

1972
(6-7-1, Third Place) Coach: Tommy Prothro
34–14 New Orleans (H)

13–13 Chicago (A)
3–31 Atlanta (A)
31–7 San Francisco (H)
34–3 Philadelphia (A)
15–12 Cincinnati (H)
17–45 Oakland (A)
20–7 Atlanta (H)
10–16 Denver (H)
41–45 Minnesota (H)
16–19 New Orleans (A)
26–16 San Francisco (A)
14–24 St. Louis (A)
17–34 Detroit (H)

291–286

1973
(12-2-0, First Place) Coach: Chuck Knox
23–13 Kansas City (A)
31–0 Atlanta (H)
40–20 San Francisco (A)
31–26 Houston (A)
37–31 Dallas (H)
24–7 Green Bay (H)
9–10 Minnesota (A)
13–15 Atlanta (A)
29–7 New Orleans (H)
31–13 San Francisco (H)
24–13 New Orleans (A)
26–0 Chicago (A)
40–6 New York Giants (H)
30–17 Cleveland (H)

388–178
16–27 *Dallas (A)
*NFC Divisional Playoff

1974
(10-4-0, First Place) Coach: Chuck Knox
17–10 Denver (A)
24–0 New Orleans (H)
14–20 New England (A)
16–13 Detroit (H)
6–17 Green Bay (A)
37–14 San Francisco (H)
20–13 New York Jets (A)
15–13 San Francisco (A)
21–0 Atlanta (H)
7–20 New Orleans (A)
20–17 Minnesota (H)
30–7 Atlanta (A)
17–23 Washington (H)
19–14 Buffalo (H)

263–181
19–10 *Washington (H)
10–14 †Minnesota (A)
*NFC Divisional Playoff
†NFC Championship

1975
(12-2-0, First Place) Coach: Chuck Knox
7–18 Dallas (A)
23–14 San Francisco (A)
24–13 Baltimore (H)
13–10 San Diego (A) (OT)
22–7 Atlanta (A)
38–14 New Orleans (H)
42–3 Philadelphia (A)
23–24 San Francisco (H)

16–7 Atlanta (A)
38–10 Chicago (H)
20–0 Detroit (A)
14–7 New Orleans (A)
22–5 Green Bay (H)
10–3 Pittsburgh (H)

312–135
35–23 *St. Louis (H)
7–37 †Dallas (H)
*NFC Divisional Playoff
†NFC Championship

1976
(10-3-1, First Place) Coach: Chuck Knox
30–14 Atlanta (A)
10–10 Minnesota (A) (OT)
24–10 New York Giants (H)
31–28 Miami (A)
0–16 San Francisco (H)
20–12 Chicago (H)
16–10 New Orleans (H)
45–6 Seattle (H)
12–20 Cincinnati (H)
28–30 St. Louis (H)
23–3 San Francisco (A)
33–14 New Orleans (A)
59–0 Atlanta (H)
20–7 Detroit (A)

351–190
14–12 *Dallas (A)
13–24 †Minnesota (A)
*NFC Divisional playoff
†NFC Championship

1977
(10-4, First Place) Coach: Chuck Knox
6–17 Atlanta (A)
20–0 Philadelphia (A)
34–14 San Francisco (H)
23–24 Chicago (A)
14–7 New Orleans (H)
35–3 Minnesota (H)
26–27 New Orleans (A)
31–0 Tampa Bay (A)
24–6 Green Bay (A)
23–10 San Francisco (A)
9–0 Cleveland (A)
20–14 Oakland (H)
23–7 Atlanta (H)
14–17 Washington (A)

302–146
7–14 *Minnesota (H)
*NFC Divisional Playoff

1978
(12-4, First Place) Coach: Ray Malavasi
16–14 Philadelphia (A)
10–0 Atlanta (H)
27–14 Dallas (H)
10–6 Houston (A)
26–20 New Orleans (A)
27–10 San Francisco (H)
34–17 Minnesota (A)
3–10 New Orleans (H)
7–15 Atlanta (A)
26–23 Tampa Bay (H)
10–7 Pittsburgh (H)

194

Year-By-Year Rams Scores

31-28 San Francisco (A)
19-30 Cleveland (A)
20-17 New York Giants (A)
19-20 Cincinnati (H)
31-14 Green Bay (H)
316-245
34-10 *Minnesota (H)
0-28 †Dallas (H)
*NFC Divisional Playoff
†NFC Championship

1979
(9-7, First Place) Coach: Ray Malavasi
17-24 Oakland (H)
13-9 Denver (A)
27-24 San Francisco (H)
6-21 Tampa Bay (A)
21-0 St. Louis (H)
35 17 New Orleans (A)
6-30 Dallas (A)
16-40 San Diego (H)
14-20 New York Giants (H)
24-0 Seattle (A)
23-27 Chicago (A)
20-14 Atlanta (H)
26-20 San Francisco (A)
27-21 Minnesota (H) (OT)
34-13 Atlanta (A)
14-29 New Orleans (H)
323-309
21-19 *Dallas (A)
9-0 †Tampa Bay (A)
19-31 ‡Pittsburgh (Pasadena, Ca.)
*NFC Divisional playoff
†NFC CHampionship
‡Super Bowl XIV

1980
(11-5, Second Place) Coach: Ray Malavasi
20-41 Detroit (H)
9-10 Tampa Bay (A)

51-21 Green Bay (H)
28-7 New York Giants (A)
48-26 San Francisco (H)
21-13 St. Louis (A)
31-17 San Francisco (A)
10-13 Atlanta (A)
45-31 New Orleans (H)
14-35 Miami (H)
17-14 New England (A)
27-7 New Orleans (A)
38-13 New York Jets (H)
7-10 Buffalo (H) (OT)
38-4 Dallas (H)
20-17 Atlanta (H) (OT)
424-289
14-34 #Dallas (A)
#First Round Playoff

1981
(5-10, Third Place) Coach: Ray Malavasi
20-27 Houston (H)
17-23 New Orleans (A)
35-23 Green Bay (H)
24-7 Chicago (A)
27-16 Cleveland (H)
37-35 Atlanta (A)
17-29 Dallas (A)
17-20 San Francisco (A)
20-13 Detroit (H)
13-21 New Orleans (H)
10-24 Cincinnati (H)
31-33 San Francisco (H)
0-24 Pittsburgh (A)
7-10 New York Giants (H)
21-16 Atlanta (H)
7-30 Washington (H)
303-351

1982
(2-7, Fourth Place)* Coach: Ray Malavasi
23-35 Green Bay (A)

14-19 Detroit (H)
17-34 Atlanta (A)
20-14 Kansas City (H)
24-30 San Francisco (H)
24-27 Denver (H)
31-37 Los Angeles Raiders (A)
26-34 Chicago (H)
21-20 San Francisco (A)
200-250
*Strike-shortened season

1983
(9-7, Second Place) Coach: John Robinson
16-6 New York Giants (A)
30-27 New Orleans (H)
24-27 Green Bay (A)
24-27 New York Jets (A)
21-10 Detroit (H)
10-7 San Francisco (A)
27-21 Atlanta (H)
35-45 San Francisco (H)
14-30 Miami (A)
21-14 Chicago (H)
36-13 Atlanta (A)
20-42 Washington (H)
41-17 Buffalo (H)
9-13 Philadelphia (A)
7-21 New England (H)
26-24 New Orleans (A)
361-344
24-17 #Dallas (A)
7-51 *Washington (A)
#First Round Playoff
*NFC Divisional Playoff

1984
(10-6, Second Place) Coach: John Robinson
13-20 Dallas (H)
20-17 Cleveland (H)

14-24 Pittsburgh (A)
24-14 Cincinnati (A)
33-12 New York Giants (H)
28-30 Atlanta (H)
28-10 New Orleans (A)
24-10 Atlanta (A)
0-33 San Francisco (H)
16-13 St. Louis (A)
29-13 Chicago (H)
6-31 Green Bay (A)
34-33 Tampa Bay (A)
34-21 New Orleans (A)
27-16 Houston (H)
16-19 San Francisco (A)
346-316
13-16 #New York Giants (H)
#First Round Playoff

1985
(11-5, First Place) Coach: John Robinson
20-16 Denver (H)
17-6 Philadelphia (A)
35-24 Seattle (A)
17-6 Atlanta (H)
13-10 Minnesota (H)
31-27 Tampa Bay (A)
16-0 Kansas City (A)
14-28 San Francisco (H)
28-10 New Orleans (H)
19-24 New York Giants (A)
14-30 Atlanta (A)
34-17 Green Bay (H)
3-29 New Orleans (A)
27-20 San Francisco (A)
46-14 St. Louis (H)
6-16 Los Angeles Raiders (H)
340-277
20-0 *Dallas (H)
0-24 †Chicago (A)
*NFC Divisional Playoff
†NFC Championship

Rams Preseason Game Results

The following preseason game results are listed by Rams' score first, then opponent's score, opponent name (site of game).

1946
0-16 College All-Stars (Chicago)
16-14 Washington (Los Angeles)

1947
20-7 Washington (Los Angeles)
24-0 Boston Yanks (Des Moines)
21-0 Detroit (Indianapolis)
3-30 N.Y. Giants (New York)

1948
10-21 Washington (Los Angeles)
41-20 Hawaiian Warriors (Honolulu)

42-7 Hawaiian Warriors (Honolulu)
7-21 Philadelphia (Dallas)

1949
28-34 Washington (Los Angeles)
21-14 N.Y. Bulldogs (San Antonio)
24-24 Philadelphia (Little Rock)
14-7 N.Y. Giants (Omaha)

1950
14-17 Washington (Los Angeles)
34-31 Chi. Cardinals (Los Angeles)
14-49 Philadelphia (Los Angeles)
70-21 Baltimore (San Antonio)
14-24 N.Y. Giants (New York)

1951
55-2 11th Naval Dist. (San Diego)
58-14 Washington (Los Angeles)

42-14 Chicago Bears (Los Angeles)
31-26 Philadelphia (Little Rock)
21-36 Chi. Cardinals (Salt Lake City)
6-7 Cleveland (Cleveland)
23-21 N.Y. Giants (New York)

1952
45-6 11th Naval Dist. (San Diego)
10-7 College All-Stars (Chicago)
45-23 Washington (Los Angeles)
24-14 Chi. Cardinals (Portland)
7-17 San Francisco (Los Angeles)
14-35 Philadelphia (Philadelphia)
17-30 N.Y. Giants (New York)

1953
24-0 Fort Ord (Long Beach)
72-19 11th Naval Dist. (San Diego)
20-7 Washington (Los Angeles)

27-9 Cleveland (Los Angeles)
35-10 San Francisco (Los Angeles)
10-23 Chi. Cardinals (Portland)
17-28 Philadelphia (Little Rock)
49-6 Pittsburgh (Pittsburgh)

1954
34-13 Fort Ord (Long Beach)
30-7 N.Y. Giants (Portland)
27-7 Washington (Los Angeles)
38-10 Cleveland (Los Angeles)
51-17 Chi. Cardinals (Portland)
27-28 San Francisco (Los Angeles)
21-24 Philadelphia (San Antonio)

1955
44-17 Fort Ord (Long Beach)
35-24 Pittsburgh (Portland)
28-31 Washington (Los Angeles)

Rams Preseason Game Results

23–17 N.Y. Giants (Portland) (OT)
38–21 Cleveland (Los Angeles)
10–31 San Francisco (Los Angeles)
21–35 Philadelphia (Denver)

1956
62–7 Armed Forces (Long Beach)
21–39 Washington (Los Angeles
17–6 Cleveland (Los Angeles)
10–20 N.Y. Giants (Seattle)
69–21 Chi. Cardinals (Los Angeles)
33–24 San Francisco (Los Angeles)
17–20 Pittsburgh (Portland)

1957
84–0 Calif. All-Stars (Long Beach)
45–14 Washington (Los Angeles)
7–24 N.Y. Giants (Los Angeles)
63–21 Chi. Cardinals (Portland)
20–14 Cleveland (Los Angeles)
58–27 San Francisco (Los Angeles)
14–3 Washington (Mobile)

1958
73–0 Calif. All-Stars (Pasadena)
31–10 Washington (Los Angeles)
38–10 N.Y. Giants (Los Angeles)
10–13 Cleveland (Los Angeles)
26–27 Chi. Cardinals (Seattle)
40–38 San Francisco (Los Angeles)
31–6 Pittsburgh (Los Angeles)

1959
20–20 Detroit (Boulder)
21–23 Washington (Los Angeles)
34–21 Chi. Cardinals (Los Angeles)
24–27 Cleveland (Los Angeles)
4–14 San Francisco (Los Angeles)
31–28 Philadelphia (Los Angeles)

1960
7–20 Philadelphia (Los Angeles)
26–21 Washington (Los Angeles)
22–17 Cleveland (Los Angeles)

49–14 Dallas (Pendleton)
28–17 San Francisco (Los Angeles)
6–20 N.Y. Giants (Los Angeles)

1961
26–7 Washington (Los Angeles)
17–17 N.Y. Giants (Los Angeles)
17–34 Cleveland (Los Angeles)
20–38 San Francisco (Los Angeles)
21–17 Minnesota (Minnesota)

1962
37–7 Washington (Los Angeles)
33–24 Minnesota (Portland)
24–31 N.Y. Giants (Los Angeles)
24–26 Cleveland (Los Angeles)
3–19 San Francisco (Los Angeles)

1963
14–17 Dallas (Los Angeles)
3–27 Minnesota (Los Angeles)
20–17 Dallas (Portland)
14–23 Cleveland (Los Angeles)
17–0 San Francisco (Los Angeles)

1964
17–6 Dallas (Los Angeles)
31–56 Cleveland (Los Angeles)
25–16 Dallas (Portland)
23–34 Minnesota (Los Angeles)
21–17 San Francisco (Los Angeles)

1965
9–0 Dallas (Los Angeles)
19–21 Cleveland (Los Angeles)
14–28 Chicago (Nashville)
10–0 Philadelphia (Los Angeles)
34–14 San Francisco (Los Angeles)

1966
16–6 Cleveland (Los Angeles)
10–20 Dallas (Los Angeles)
10–24 St. Louis (Los Angeles)

32–14 St. Louis (Los Angeles)
29–0 San Francisco (Los Angeles)

1967
16–7 New Orleans (Anaheim)
20–6 Dallas (Los Angeles)
24–17 Cleveland (Los Angeles)
50–7 San Diego (San Diego)
44–24 Kansas City (Los Angeles)
34–7 San Francisco (Los Angeles)

1968
21–17 New Orleans (Anaheim)
23–21 Cleveland (Los Angeles)
10–42 Dallas (Los Angeles)
13–35 San Diego (San Diego)
36–16 Kansas City (Los Angeles)
21–20 San Francisco (Los Angeles)

1969
24–17 Dallas (Los Angeles)
3–10 Cleveland (Los Angeles)
14–42 Kansas City (Los Angeles)
24–14 San Diego (San Diego)
50–20 Buffalo (Los Angeles)
31–28 San Francisco (Anaheim)

1970
30–17 Cleveland (Los Angeles)
17–10 Dallas (Los Angeles)
34–23 Oakland (Los Angeles)
16–14 San Diego (San Diego)
20–3 Houston (Pasadena)
17–14 San Francisco (Los Angeles)

1971
17–6 Houston (Canton)
21–45 Dallas (Los Angeles)
17–5 Cleveland (Los Angeles)
7–20 Oakland (Berkeley)
31–21 New England (Foxboro)
14–20 San Diego (Los Angeles)
23–20 San Francisco (Los Angeles)

1972
13–3 Cleveland (Los Angeles)
13–27 Dallas (Los Angeles)
9–34 Oakland (Los Angeles)
13–19 Kansas City (Kansas City)
13–14 San Diego (San Diego)
14–17 San Francisco (Los Angeles)

1973
7–24 Dallas (Los Angeles)
21–21 Cleveland (Los Angeles)
3–16 Oakland (Berkeley)
14–17 Miami (Miami)
30–17 San Diego (Los Angeles)
38–10 San Francisco (Los Angeles)

1974
24–21 Cleveland (Los Angeles)
6–13 Dallas (Los Angeles)
58–16 Kansas City (Los Angeles)
31–13 Miami (Los Angeles)
30–16 San Diego (San Diego)
17–7 San Francisco (San Francisco)

1975
35–7 Dallas (Los Angeles)

10–6 San Francisco (Los Angeles)
24–31 Buffalo (Buffalo)
14–6 Kansas City (Kansas City)
35–0 Philadelphia (Los Angeles)
6–0 Oakland (Los Angeles)

1976
26–3 Tampa Bay (Los Angeles)
26–14 Dallas (Los Angeles)
16–13 Seattle (Seattle)
23–14 Oakland (Oakland)
31–17 Buffalo (Los Angeles)
10–3 San Francisco (Los Angeles)

1977
17–22 Minnesota (Los Angeles)
20–3 Philadelphia (Los Angeles)
14–23 San Francisco (San Francisco)
19–27 Kansas City (Kansas City)
25–26 San Diego (Los Angeles)
0–21 Oakland (Los Angeles)

1978
7–14 New England (Los Angeles)
0–17 San Diego (Los Angeles)
26–7 Seattle (Seattle)
28–3 Oakland (Oakland)

1979
20–14 Oakland (Los Angeles) (OT)
15–3 New England (Foxboro)
21–17 Seattle (Los Angeles)
23–7 San Diego (Los Angeles)

1980
31–35 New England (Anaheim)
16–19 Dallas (Anaheim)
26–13 Denver (Denver)
34–17 San Diego (Anaheim)

1981
21–34 New England (Anaheim)
33–21 Dallas (Anaheim)
29–33 San Diego (San Diego)
34–31 Minnesota (Anaheim)

1982
20–33 Denver (Anaheim)
23–26 Cleveland (Cleveland)
23–13 Seattle (Anaheim)
20–14 San Diego (Anaheim)

1983
34–20 San Diego (Anaheim)
7–30 Dallas (Anaheim)
13–7 New England (Anaheim)
17–27 San Diego (San Diego)

1984
10–17 San Diego (San Diego)
10–21 Cleveland (Anaheim)
27–27 Green Bay (Anaheim)
47–14 San Diego (Anaheim)

1985
7–3 Houston (Anaheim)
39–7 St. Louis (Anaheim)
12–14 Philadelphia (Columbus)
14–13 New England (Anaheim)

Above: Ron Waller. **Page 197:** Running back Willie Ellison (33) breaks through the Buffalo line for a long gain. Ellison gained 2,901 yards in six seasons with the Rams from 1967-1972. **Page 198:** Charlie Cowan, Bob Klein, and the Ram bench.

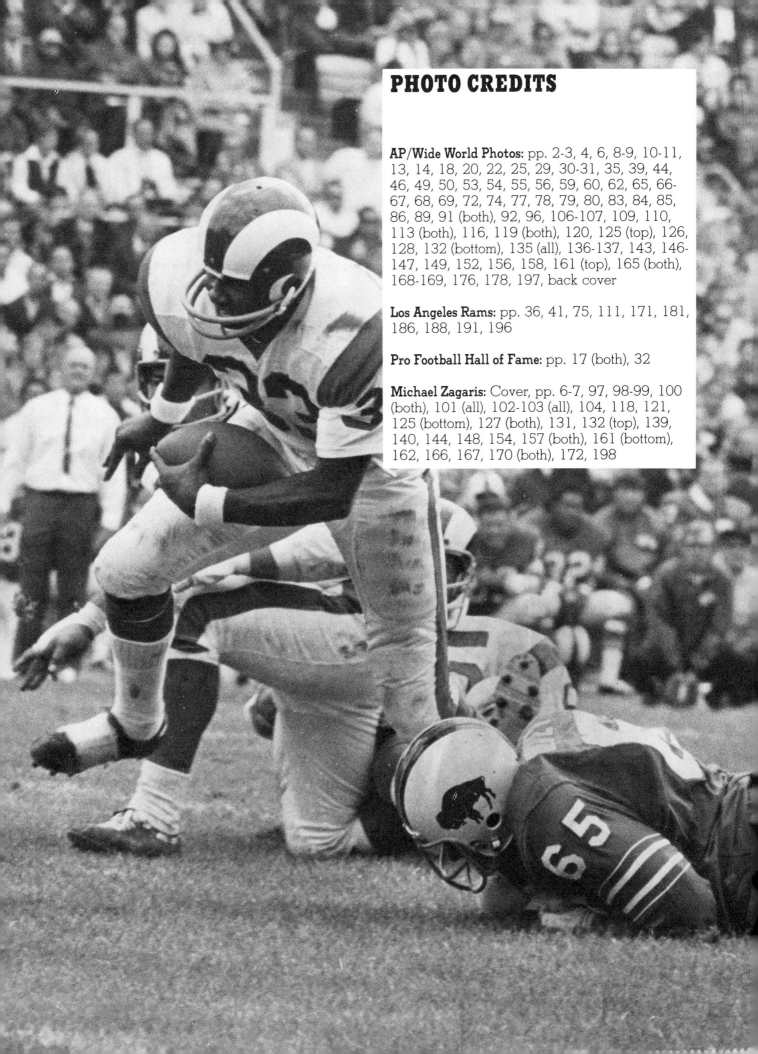

Abramowicz, Danny 120
Adderly, Herb 64
Alcindor, Lew 117
Alexander, Kermit 117
Allen, George 75,80, 82, 91, 94, 95, 96, 105, 108, 111, 112, 119,123, 124, 142, 143
Allen, Marcus 172
Anderson, Donny 105
Andrews, George 145
Andrews, William 160
Arnett, Jon 69, 70, 75, 79, 80, 85
Autrey, Gene 83

Bacon, Coy 122, 174
Bahr, Matt 150
Baker, Terry 33, 82, 83, 84, 86, 90, 91
Baker, Tony 122, 127, 130
Ball, Lucille 23, 42
Banta, Jack 26, 33
Barber, Mike 158, 161
Barnes, William 119
Barry, Paul 49
Bass, Dick 70, 75, 76, 79, 80, 82, 83, 85, 90, 94, 95, 96, 105, 108, 125, 164
Baugh, Sammy 13, 17, 21, 22, 23, 24, 39, 40, 61, 63, 69
Baughn, Maxie 105, 111, 114, 119
Baumgardner, Rex 53
Beban, Gary 33, 82, 105
Bednarik, Chuck 28, 38
Bedzek, Hugh 13, 15, 21
Bell, Bert 13, 70
Benton, Jim 15, 16,22,24, 25, 26, 32
Bergey, Bill 82
Berry, Raymond 79, 80, 93, 94
Bertelsen, Jim 122, 130
Bingaman, Les 42
Blaik, Red 48
Blair, Matt 138
Blanchard, Doc 45, 47, 48
Bleeker, Mel 29
Borg, Bjorn 153
Bosley, Bruce 112
Bouley, Gil 16, 22, 23, 24, 34, 40
Box, Cloyce 52, 56
Boyd, Bob 28, 49, 58
Bradshaw, Terry 150
Bratkowski, Zeke 74, 79, 80, 81, 84, 95
Brink, Larry 53, 55
Brock, Dieter 167, 170, 175
Brodie, John 90, 96, 105
Brooks, Larry 153
Brown, Bob 113, 114
Brown, Don 70
Brown, Ed 86
Brown, Jim 42, 87, 91, 94, 112, 124, 164
Brown, Paul 16, 18
Brown, Roger 76, 85, 96, 105, 123
Brown, Ron 171
Brudzinski, Bob 139, 153, 155
Brunch, Ed 12
Bryant, Bear 142
Bryant, Bobby 138
Bryant, Cullen 122, 129, 149, 157
Buferd, Marilyn 21

Bukich, Rudy 61, 63
Burroughs, Don 93
Butkus, Dick 64, 76, 82, 130
Butler, Kevin 175

Cannon, Billy 33, 73
Cappelletti, John 33, 138, 145
Carbo, Tom 15, 16, 42
Carollo, Joe 80
Carr, Joe 12, 21
Carter, Jimmy 153
Casey, Bernie 105
Charles, Ray 73
Christman, Paul 42
Ciefers, Ed 29
Clark, Dutch 15, 21
Clark, Ken 145
Clarke, Leon 70
Cobbledick, Gordon 13
Colella, Tom 16, 21
Coleman, J.D. Stetson 83
Collins, Jim 155
Corral, Frank 143, 145, 150, 157
Coryell, Don 64
Cothren, Paige 70, 90
Cowan, Charles 74, 79, 108, 113, 114, 173
Cox, Fred 142
Crabb, Claude 95
Cromwell, Nolan 139, 145, 159, 160
Cross, Irv 95, 105
Crow, Lindon 84
Curran, Pat 108

Dale, Carroll 84, 85, 95
Darin, Bobby 73
David, Jim 52
Davis, Glenn 21, 24, 33, 38, 42, 45, 46, 47, 48, 49, 50, 53
Dempsey, Tom 138
Dennard, Preston 155, 165
Derek, John 24
Dickerson, Eric 58, 75, 76, 130, 161, 163, 164, 166, 170, 174
Dickey, Lynn 158
Dietrich, John 13
Disney, Diane 64
Donelli, Aldo 15, 21
Dorsett, Tony 144, 149, 155, 175
Doss, Reggie 143
Drake, Johnny 13, 21
Dryer, Fred 122, 127, 132, 155
Dyer, Henry 108

Eason, Roger 32, 34
Eckern, Carl 138
Eischeid, Mike 125
Ellard, Henry 161, 167, 171
Eller, Carl 112, 114
Ellis, Jimmy 117
Ellison, Willie 96, 113, 117, 122
Elmendorf, Dave 119, 159
Elway, John 164, 170
Evans, Billy 15
Fanning, Mike 131
Farmer, George 165
Faumina, Wilson 157
Fears, Tom 24, 27, 28, 36, 37, 38, 39, 40, 48, 49, 50, 52, 53, 55, 56, 58, 61, 63, 65, 96

Ferguson, Larry 84
Ferragamo, Vince 139, 144, 145, 149, 150, 153, 155, 159, 165, 166
Firestone, Frank 83
Flutie, Doug 33, 167
Foreman, Chuck 138
France, Doug 131
Francis, Dean 12
Frazier, Joe 117
Fry, Bob 61
Fuller, Frank 70

Gabriel, Roman 75, 80, 81, 82, 83, 84, 85, 86, 90, 91, 95, 96, 105, 108, 112, 114, 122, 142
Galimore, Willie 76
Gallarneau, Hugh 26
Garrett, Mike 33, 95
Geddes, Ken 132
Gehrig, Lou 173
Gehrke, Fred 16, 21, 24, 25, 32, 33, 34, 36, 40
George, Bill 74, 82, 85, 88, 111
Gifford, Frank 63
Gillette, Jim 16
Gilliam, John 96
Gillingham, Gale 105
Gillman, Sid 52, 62, 70, 74, 79
Gossett, Bruce 86, 90, 108, 113, 141
Goux, Marv 161
Graham, Otto 41, 51, 53, 62, 65, 70
Grant, Bud 81
Gray, Jerry 160, 167
Green, Gary 160, 166
Greenwood, Don 16
Gregg, Forrest 105
Grier, Roosevelt 84, 94, 96, 111, 123
Gries, Bob 12
Groza, Lou 24, 41, 48, 51, 53, 62, 69
Guman, Mike 153, 157

Hadden, John 12
Haden, Pat 135, 138, 143,145, 153, 155, 159
Hadl, John 122, 125, 127, 128, 130, 131, 142, 144
Halas, George 28, 29, 32, 34, 42, 64, 73, 74, 91
Hall, Parker 15
Hamilton, Ray 16
Hanna, Don 12, 13, 15
Harder, Pat 26, 40, 42, 56
Hardy, Jim 22, 25, 33, 34, 36, 39
Harmon, Tom 22, 25, 26, 32, 33, 34
Harrah, Dennis 131
Harris, James 128, 131, 135, 139
Hart, Jim 105
Hart, Leon 52, 56
Haskell, Gil 161, 175
Hatcher, Dale 167
Hauser, Art 70
Hayes, Bob 94
Heckard, Steve 95
Hegman, Mike 149
Henry, Urban 79
Hickey, Red 16, 36, 58

Hickman, Larry 70
Hilgenberg, Wally 131
Hill, David 165
Hill, Drew 145
Hill, Kent 145
Hirsch, Elroy 24, 28, 37, 38, 39, 40, 42, 48, 49, 52, 55, 56, 58, 61, 62, 63, 125
Hoerner, Dick 24, 38, 42, 49, 50, 53, 55, 58
Hoffman, Bob 36
Hogan, Ben 21
Holtzman, Glenn 70
Hoover, J. Edgar 42
Hope, Bob 58, 63, 83, 88
Horvath, Les 33
Houk, Hudson 161
Houston, Kenny 130
Howard, Frank 73
Howton, Bill 52
Huff, Sam 76, 130
Huffman, Dick 53
Hughes, Howard 16, 40
Humphrey, Buddy 73
Hutson, Don 34, 38, 40

Iman, Ken 82, 113
Inglis, Dave 12
Irsay, Robert 122
Irvin, LeRoy 153, 157, 160

Jabbar, Kareem Abdul 153
Jackson, Harold 105, 122
Jackson, Monte 131, 132, 160
Jackson, Rusty 138
Jaworski, Ron 122, 131, 135, 139
Jessie, Ron 138, 145
Jeter, Bob 95
Jobko, Bill 79
Johns, Bill 17, 18
Johnson, John Henry 79
Johnson, Johnnie 153, 160
Johnson, Magic 153
Johnson, Rafer 70
Jones, Bert 158
Jones, Cody 122, 132, 161
Jones, Deacon 74, 79, 83, 84, 90, 94, 105, 111, 114, 122, 123, 174
Jones, Dub 51, 53, 62
Jones, K.C. 62
Jordan, Michael 82
Josephson, Les 86, 90, 96, 113, 117, 122
Jurgensen, Sonny 128

Kalmanir, Tom 40
Kapp, Joe 114
Karras, Alex 76
Kavanaugh, Ken 26
Keane, Tom 49
Kemp, Jack 74, 79
Kemp, Jeff 166, 167, 170
Kennedy, John 73, 85
Kilgore, Jon 95
Kilmer, Billy 79, 128
Klein, Bob 108, 113, 128
Knox, Chuck 122, 125, 127, 128, 130, 138, 142, 143, 155
Konetsky, Floyd 16, 17
Kramer, Jerry 105, 145
Kuharich, Joe 70, 88

Lambert, Jack 150